Real-Life South African Adventures Gone By, A Memoir

Marge and Howard Trumbull, Valentine's Day 2008

Real-Life
South African Adventures
Gone By, A Memoir

by

Marge Trumbull

Greencroft Friends

Marge & Howard

Trumbull

Alumni Association of the Bronson Methodist Hospital
School of Nursing
2008

Trumbull, Marjorie Fletcher, 1923–

Real-life South African adventures gone by, a memoir. Kalamazoo, Mich.: Alumni Association of the Bronson Methodist Hospital School of Nursing, 2008.

x,312p. Includes index.

1. Trumbull, Marjorie Fletcher, 1923– 2. Missionaries—South Africa—Biography 3. Married people in missionary work 4. Family—Religious aspects—Christianity 5. Christmas—South Africa 6. Bronson Methodist Hospital (Kalamazoo, Mich.) School of Nursing—Alumni and alumnae 7. McCord Zulu Hospital (Durban, Natal) 8. Game preserves—South Africa 9. South Africa—Race relations 10. Deportation—South Africa 11. Natal—Mission stations 12. Botswana—Social conditions I. Title

921 T86

ISBN 978-0-9763413-6-9

Layout and design by LanWord, Kalamazoo, Michigan.
Printed by Fidlar-Doubleday, Davenport, Iowa.

CONTENTS

PREFACE

I was challenged to write my life story when a college professor gave a talk that I went to. He said to make a Time Line of important events and milestones in my life, and use that as a guide to writing my life story. I had four full pages that I taped up on the door to my clothes closet to use as my guide.

I was 68 years old when I started writing my story, and I am 85 now. Many of the details which I might have forgotten were resurrected after my mom died in 1998. During the time when the five of us kids were cleaning out her house, we found a big, old-fashioned trunk in the basement that contained a large pack of dated letters I had sent home while doing mission work in South Africa. Of course, the Time Line I made began with much earlier events and also included events after we all came back to the States, right up to the present.

My story became this book through the efforts of many people: my granddaughters Sara Harrison, Elizabeth Michael-Trumbull and Laura Michael-Trumbull teamed up to keyboard my story that started the process; then people from my church, Diana Artz-Iffland, Carol Beveridge and Pat Pratt, made electronic versions of all the included handwritten letters; finally, Holley Lantz and Diane Worden put everything together and acted as my agent with the printer.

Marge Trumbull
May 2008

CHAPTER 1. Growing Up

The First Home I Remember

We moved from Keeler, Michigan, to Dowagiac in 1925, when I was 2 years old. I think the address was 208 Oak Street. It was a small house for five children and mom and dad. There were two bedrooms fortunately large enough so that two double beds fit all right. My brother, Marion, slept in one bed with my dad. I slept in the other bed with my mom. Now I wonder how they ever made love. I don't ever remember being awakened by them. My poor mom had to put up with my bed wetting until I was past 4 years old. She should have put diapers on me! I guess I didn't wet the bed consistently. I think she was trying to trust me to wake up.

Caryl, Fern, and Dottie slept in the other bedroom. Our dining room had a potbellied stove. I believe that was the only source of heat in the house. A day bed was in the dining room. If any of us were sick we would be in that bed by the warm stove. We didn't do any entertaining. I don't even think we had a dining room table in the dining room.

The kitchen was a fairly good size. We had table and chairs in the kitchen where we ate our meals. We had no running water, only a sink and a pump. There was a trap door to pull up to go into the basement which was called a Michigan basement. It was crude with dirt floors and a foot and a half-wide ledge around the outside walls to put jars of fruit and vegetables on. It was a spooky place. I never would go down there by myself.

We didn't even have an indoor bathroom. Before going to bed and during the night, we used a slop jar which had a

1

lid to keep the smell from permeating the house. Our outhouse could get very cold in the winter.

Saturday was bath day. Water was heated up on the stove in the kitchen. We used a round, one sink tub which was put in the kitchen for a bath. At least two of us had to use the same water and sometimes more if we weren't very dirty. It must have been hard on the older children not to have much privacy. We lived in that house for seven years until I was 9 years old.

Illnesses as a Child

When I was 3 years old is the first remembrance I have of anything about my life. Just getting over the measles (the hard kind), I then picked up the whooping cough bug from somewhere. I coughed, coughed, and coughed. Now, wouldn't you think that was enough to be inflicted with? Before completely getting over the whopping cough, I came down with pneumonia. No antibiotics to take then for a quick recovery. I was in bed for three weeks, too weak to stand up. Mom pulled me through with her vigilant care. I don't think she got into her pajamas the whole time.

When I was in the second grade, the Public Health Department came to the school and tested all the students for T.B. My test was positive, so I had to have a chest x-ray taken. It showed that I had had T.B. at one time, but it had been arrested and just showed up as some scar tissue areas. I don't remember having typical T.B. symptoms. I must have picked up the T.B. bacteria after I was run down from the triple illness when I was 3 years old.

Another time I remember being ill was when I had the stomach flu when I was 7 years old. I was lying on the day cot in the dining room by that warm potbellied stove. I called by mom to tell her I felt a bit squeamish in my tummy. She said, "I'll bring you the slop jar. It hasn't been emptied yet though." I said, "That's O.K. I just want to have something near by." I would get waves on nausea and then the feeling would go away. I thought if I could just vomit I'd probably feel a lot better. So the next time I felt that nausea feeling coming on, I took the lid off the slop jar and put my face near—and that did it! The aroma was enough to make anyone heave their insides out. You know, I did feel better after that good cleaning out.

The doctor had diagnosed me as having pinworms. I was probably about 6 years old at that time. I just couldn't get the hang of swallowing pills, so mom had to crush the pills in a teaspoon. The previous year, I had to take that same medicine for the same condition. It was absolutely horrible tasting. I told mom that I was going to stand on the back steps to take it because I knew I wouldn't be able to keep it down. Sure enough, I started gagging and up it came. I heard the grinding of the teaspoon and knew another dose was coming. I knew there was no getting out of it. So I closed my eyes, put that teaspoonful of yuk in my mouth, and downed it very quickly, followed by some juice. I didn't give myself a chance to even taste it. When you know you gotta, you do.

My Sister and Long Finger Curls—Ugh!

My mom bought a taxi business in our small town, Dowagiac, which had about 3,000 people. I was 3 years old at the time and the youngest of five children. My sister Caryl was the oldest. She was ten years older than I was. Apparently, when my mom went to work, she appointed Caryl to be in charge of me. It didn't take me long to realize how much I didn't like this arrangement.

I had naturally curly auburn hair. Caryl delighted herself in brushing and combing my hair. I hated it. She didn't pay any attention to my utterances of pain and tears. Her main goal was to form those long finger curls. Caryl was a perfectionist and practiced her obsession at my expense! I couldn't care less what I looked like at that time in my life. I was so happy to have my hair cut short when I was 9 years old. What a relief to be able to comb it easily and no more standing still to have those long finger curls made. Another thing, I had to be careful about was choosing the right color of clothes that would go together, and the anklets had better not clash either. Caryl was a good seamstress and she made most of my clothes. She took great pride in making clothes and I guess I became her show piece . . . so I had better not shame her!

When she was in her later teens, she worked in a dime store. When I walked downtown to go see my mom at the taxi office, I deliberately walked on the opposite side of the street of the dime store. I was fearful that she might be looking out the window and see me. She would send me back home if she didn't approve of how I looked.

One time we were going to a lake for a swim. As we were walking to the beach, I was happily twirling my bathing cap in my hand. The strap buckle hit Caryl in the face, very near her eye. She made me sit on the blanket the whole time and wouldn't let me go swimming. I was so resentful and bitter over this unfair treatment.

In my opinion, it's not easy being raised by an immature sibling. I didn't like her perfectionism and making my young life miserable with her standards. Now I want to tell you about the good things Caryl did for me as I was growing up.

When I was 9 years old, Caryl took me to a dance studio and signed me up for tap and aerobic lessons for at least two years. She bought me my tap shoes, and she made all my dancing costumes for our recitals. I loved dancing. I began taking ballroom dancing lessons when I was 11 years old, paid for by Caryl. My partner was Don Feathers who was 12 years old. His mother was the instructor, and she gave us private lessons. Don and I eventually performed our ballroom dancing skills for our school assembly program one day. I was scared and nervous, but once we got into our special dance routine his mom had been teaching us, I forgot all about the kids watching us.

Much to my disappointment, my husband Howard has never cared much about dancing. He says he feels like he's got two left feet. After we retired and moved to Arkansas in 1985, we did take a series of eight dancing lessons. He didn't want to practice so he never felt very confident in what we were learning. Then I tried to get him to go square dancing with me. Howard flatly refused even that kind of dancing, so I guess I might as well accept that my dancing days are over. Anyone need a partner?

Smoking Behind the Barn

Being the youngest of five children, I always wanted to be involved in whatever the older ones were up to. One beautiful sunny fall day, we children were out behind the barn gathering some old dried corn silk from the corn field. We had some cigarette papers that we rolled the corn silk in. I was about 8 years old, and this was my first experience of trying to inhale some of that corn silk cigarette smoke. Something went terribly wrong. I don't know what I did, but I thought I was going to choke to death. I couldn't breathe or talk. I kept coughing until I was blue in the face. At last I got a breath of fresh air. I hadn't realized that fresh air was so precious. What a relief to be able to breathe again! Believe it or not . . . that little experience has given me a psychological block from ever inhaling whenever trying to smoke a cigarette.

When Howard and I were married, he smoked and I didn't. I drank coffee and he didn't. We both thought we'd get each other sharing our bad habits. Neither one has happened. Howard stopped smoking in 1982. I still drink coffee, but now limit myself to one or two cups a day.

Grandma Evans

My mom's dad, Robert James Evans, was born in 1856. He was a farmer. I wish I could have known my grandpa. He died on October. 26, 1911, of a massive heart attack. He was only 55 when he died. There were six children, three boys and three girls. Rosina Fredricka Haerle, my grandmother was nine years younger than my Grandpa Robert. Grandma was only 46 when Robert died. There were three children still at home to care for.

5

Grandma came to U.S.A. from Stuttgart, Germany when she was 16 years old and didn't know a word of English. She was hired as a nanny and a housekeeper, and began to learn English before she was married to Robert. I don't know how my grandmother supported her three children still living at home. Uncle Dick Evans, the youngest child was only 2 years old when grandpa died. They were living on a farm in Keeler and eventually moved to Dowagiac. My mom, Laura, the oldest child still living at home was always resentful that she only had had an eighth grade education, but she was needed for helping on the farm.

Grandma was about 60 when my Uncle Dick left home to teach school. Grandma didn't like living by herself. My family lived only three blocks from grandma so my 8 year-old sister, Dottie, began to stay with her. She lived with grandma for five years. By that time I was 8 years old, so I was elected to be grandma's companion. We shared a double bed at night.

Grandma taught me to say the prayer:
Now I lay me down to sleep.
I pray the Lord my soul to keep.
If I should die before I wake,
I pray the Lord my soul to take.

This is the first remembrance I have of saying a prayer. Those last two lines scared me a bit. I marvel that she could tolerate sleeping with a wiggle worm like me. I'm glad though, because it was nice being close to her.

The Oak Street School I went to was only two blocks away. In the summer I would often go to the playground to swing, slide down the giant slide, climb the monkey bars, and swim in the pool which was only two and a half feet deep in the deepest end.

A year after I started living with Grandma, my family moved from a two-bedroom home to a five- bedroom home in another school district. So after that I had to walk about two miles to school. My mom finally bought a bike for me. I could ride it in the fall or spring, but when it was snowy and icy, I had to walk. I don't remember grumbling or being unhappy about this situation. I realized it was pretty special having my grandmother all to myself. She gave me lots of freedom to play with the neighborhood kids. I don't remember her ever getting cross or angry at me.

Grandma didn't have much money, but occasionally she would give me money to go to the neighborhood store a block away to buy a pint of ice cream to bring home to share together—what a treat! She didn't have an ice box, so my mom would come each day to bring groceries that we would need for that day. In the summer we kept some things in the basement where it was cooler, especially butter; otherwise it would melt to a liquid. Sometimes we would be invaded with these tiny red ants. We would put water in a round tin tub and put a brick in the middle to set the butter dish on so the ants couldn't get to it.

Periodically, I had tummy aches and Grandma was sure it was worms. Guess what her remedy was? She made a paste of lard and turpentine and spread it thick on my tummy and then put warm moist clothes on top of that. I guess it must of been soothing 'cause I always went to sleep and woke up feeling fine.

In the summer when it was too hot in the bedroom to sleep, I would fold up a blanket and lie on the floor in front of the locked screen door. That was the only air conditioning we had. It would have been nice to have had a fan. Sometimes the air was so still on those hot summer nights.

When Uncle Dick came home for a visit, he taught me how the play chess. I was 9 years old, and I felt so proud to be playing chess with my Uncle Dick. I beat him sometimes. Now I wonder if he deliberately made mistakes so I could win.

I was about 10 years old when Grandma let my 16-year old sister, Dottie, have a Halloween party at her house. I remember that house being full of costumed young people. Bobbing for apples in a tub of water was difficult. The only way you could bite into an apple would be to try to get an apple down to the bottom of the tub, so you could have something firm to push against to sink your teeth into. There were many wet heads and cheering onlookers. We had to wind up the Victrola to play records on. Grandma let us push the dining room table back so we could dance. Grandma was such a special lady. I don't ever remember telling her, "I love you." That's one of my regrets. I wish she was still here with us. I miss her.

One evening I arrived at my grandmother's place after dark. It was a summer time. I thought that it was odd that the house was all dark, not a light on anywhere. I went up to the front door. The door was open but the screen was locked. I called, "Grandma, come open the door for me." I heard a shuffling noise and she finally came to the door and unlocked the screen. I could tell by the street light that only one side of her mouth was drawn up, and she couldn't talk and her right leg was dragging. I managed to get her seated in a chair. I told her to sit right there and don't get up. Grandma didn't have a phone so I raced up to the neighborhood store and used their phone to call my mom. She came right away and called the doctor. He said that her blood pressure was 250/130, and she had had a stroke. He said to keep her in bed and keep it quiet.

In two weeks time, there was no change. She was paralyzed on the right side and couldn't talk. My mom got a hospital bed and put it in our dining room, and we moved my grandma to our house on Center Street. She was 71 years old, and I was 13. My mom and all of us five children had a part in her care. We got her up in a chair for every meal. The only word she could say was, "Adoe." We would tease her sometimes and she would respond with a continuous string of "Adoe's" each with a different inflection and tone. We would laugh and laugh, and get her laughing too. She lived with us in the dining room for five years. She died on February 10, 1941, at 76 years old when I was a senior in high school. That was a sad day. We missed her so much, not being in our dining room.

Moving to Center Street

I was living with Grandma when my family moved to a big home on Center Street. It seemed like a palace to me compared to our home on Oak Street. It had five bedrooms, but we couldn't use one of the bedrooms in the winter because it had no heat. It was called a sun room on the second floor, up over the downstairs back entrance. We loved to sleep there in the summer because it was so cool. Three sides were outside walls and there were about five windows on each side which opened. It was like sleeping outside.

There was a half-bath downstairs and a complete bath with a tub upstairs. We didn't have a shower. I don't think showers were as common as they are now. My poor brother had to compete with four sisters.

We redid the living room and dining room floors with parquet blocks. It was a beautiful floor. We had a nice basement. At least I thought it was nice and far better than the basement on Oak Street. It had cement floors and walls. There was one of those monstrous, big, forced-air furnaces. It had originally burned coal, but had been converted to gas before we bought the home. We had a fireplace in the living room. It was painted red by the previous owner. I didn't like it. I guess we got used to it because we didn't paint it a different color. We had a heat register on the floor of the dining room. It was super cozy on the register while the house was heating up. On Sunday evenings we had popcorn and apples, and listened to a radio program called "The Shadow."

This house was only about four blocks away from the school we went to, so we could come home for lunch. In the morning and late afternoon I had a two-mile walk or riding my bike from Grandma's house where I lived so she wouldn't have to live by herself.

In the fall we would get the kids from the neighborhood raking leaves with us. After we got the leaves in a big pile, mom bought marshmallows for a treat for us. When we had enough running and jumping on the leaves, we raked the leaves up in a big mound and mom put a match to the pile, and we all roasted marshmallows. Usually the marshmallows got a black crisp outer coating that we would slip off and eat, only then would we burn the next layer and eat it, until the marshmallow was completely eaten— layer by layer. That was so-o-o good.

First Visit to the Dentist

Money was scarce so my parents couldn't afford to send us to the dentist. When I was 12 years old, I began to baby-sit for the neighbors children. After earning some money I made an appointment with the dentist. I had lots of cavities and especially big ones in the lower back molar teeth. I suffered through all the drilling without local injections for deadening the discomfort. After the dentist completed all the necessary fillings, he gave me a pretty thorough lecture about taking care of my teeth.

He said, "Drink coffee or tea without sugar so that you can swish the liquid around in your mouth after eating something sweet and eat raw carrots or celery sticks after eating crackers or sweets." I listened carefully to him. I did the things he suggested and I haven't had many cavities since my first visit to the dentist when I was 12 years old.

Now when I have a needed filling done, I refuse the deadening injection because these new dental drills are so far superior to those old drills, when I first went to the dentist.

Dating

I had always liked boys—way before that feeling of warmth when your eyes would meet in the school hallway, your heart skipped a beat, being tongue-tied, and not being able to fall asleep at night because of thinking of "him". I was a tomboy, always wanting to do what the boys were doing—touch football, softball, marbles, fishing, and swimming in that dangerous river. Boys were more adventurous and daring, and I liked that.

I was a freshman in high school when that special guy, Kurt Hasper, caught my fancy. We were in several classes together, and it was always special when our eyes would meet in the hallway between classes. My mom wouldn't let me have a real date with him when I was a freshman, so we just saw each other at school and sometimes he would carry my books and walk me home after school. He was on the football team, and the coach saw his potential and worked him hard. I loved the games on Friday nights. There were four of us gals that usually did things together. They also couldn't date yet.

In my sophomore year I was allowed to go to the dances in the school gym after the games, and Kurt could bring me home. Sometimes we dated on Saturday evening too, but had to be in by 10 p.m. No dating on Sunday evening or school nights. Kurt and I dated all through high school. He was captain of the football team in our junior and senior years. Many gals tried to take him away from me. They were so jealous of me.

Kurt worked at a gas station after school and weekends. He had bought a big secondhand Chrysler, and taught me how to drive in the rural area where there wasn't much traffic. I practiced and practiced on using that stick shift— backwards and forwards, stopping on a hill and starting up. I thought I would never get the skill of a smooth shift, especially on a hill. We didn't have school driving classes like nowadays. Eventually I got pretty good with smooth shifting and no longer had beads of perspiration on my upper lip.

Kurt wanted to get married before I entered nurses training and keep it a secret, but I said no. We couldn't stay in nurses' training if we got married. I had wanted to go into nurses' training ever since I was 3 years old when I was always playing doctor and nurse. So I was determined to get my nursing degree. Kurt and I dated for another year while I was in training, and then I wanted to date other guys. We did a lot of heavy petting, but never to actual intercourse. Guess I about broke his heart. Love can hurt so bad sometimes.

11

I especially remember with fondness two fellows whom I dated. One was Bob Morris. I can't remember how we met. He worked at the YMCA in Kalamazoo, which wasn't too far from my nursing school. He had very high morals and principles, and always seemed to keep us with other people when we dated. He was soon called to the armed service and was killed in the Second World War. The other guy was Chic Cicero, an Italian. I met him at the U.S.O. Some of us students would go sometimes and play ping-pong and dance with the soldiers. He too was sent away, to California. He wanted me to come to California by train during my three-week vacation in my senior year, but somehow it just didn't seem to work out.

During that three-week vacation in my senior year of nurses' training, mom rented a cottage at Twin Lakes for all of our family. That was where I met Howard Trumbull, which I'll tell you about in another story.

12

CHAPTER 2. Young Adulthood

My Substitute Mom

During my first year of nurses' training at Bronson Methodist Hospital's School of Nursing in 1941, we had a three-month probationary period. During that three-month period of time, we student nurses did not wear a nurse's cap. At the end of the three months, there was a capping ceremony. Some of the students never received caps and were told to think of some other career to pursue.

Capping was a very special milestone ceremony. It was a big event. Parents, relatives, and friends were invited to share in the joy of the students. My family couldn't come because they were too far away. I was heartbroken to see other students surrounded by family and friends after the ceremony when I didn't have anyone to share this experiment with.

During that first three months, we did simple nursing bedside tasks. I became very fond of a patient about my mom's age. Her name was Marty Lind. She was a very warm friendly person, and always had a bright word for us. She wrote a beautiful poem about me as a nurse, which I have in my nursing scrapbook. I told her we were having a capping ceremony in a few weeks. She said, "Maybe I'll be there."

After receiving my cap, I was milling around in the crowd of people getting some yum-yum cookies when I saw Mrs. Lind. She wanted to meet my mom. I said, "She couldn't come because of living too far away." Mrs. Lind said, "How about me being your mom for this evening?" She noticed I was sad, not having any of my family present. My spirit and countenance brightened immediately. We had

13

such a fun time together visiting with my other classmates and telling them about my substitute mom. Many knew her when she was a patient in the hospital and were so happy to see her again.

That evening has been a fond memory of a very special lady in my life.

My First Date with Howard Trumbull

Howard's folks lived on the other side of Twin Lakes from where my mom had rented a cottage for our family. Howard was a sergeant of the six-person machine shop inside the hangar of an Army Air Force base at Stout Field in Indianapolis, Indiana. He would get a three-day leave once a month and hitchhike to his folks' home for a weekend visit. Bob and Ruth Dowsett were friends of his family, and they got him dates with local gals a few times when he was home. Howard said he wasn't much impressed with them and wished they would quit getting him dates.

I was in town one day and saw Ruth Dowsett. We had a nice chat. During high school I had worked at Harvey's gift shop and soda fountain store after school and weekends. Bob often came in for a cup of coffee, and we had time to chat if I wasn't too busy. He used to call me Pinky because of my auburn hair.

Bob knew that Howard was in town one weekend and finally persuaded him to have a date with me. That Friday evening, our first date, we decided to go dancing at Sister Lakes—a place called Ramona Park. Bob and Ruth invited us to stop at their house for a visit before we went dancing. Bob asked us what we would like to have to drink. They all rattled off some hard liquor drink. I had never had a drink of that kind before and had no idea what to order so I just said, "I'll have what you are having, Bob."

Howard went out to the kitchen to help Bob. Bob asked Howard if I was used to drinking and of course Howard didn't know. Bob decided he'd better make mine weaker than his drink. I can't say that I liked the taste of that drink, but I did like the warmth and it helped me be not so shy. When it was time for us to leave, I got up and almost fell down. What a surprise! I had no idea that drink would do that to me. It's a good thing Bob made my drink half the strength of his.

We had a very good time at that dance, and Coca-Cola was the drink of the evening. There were some very special vibes between us. It was about 12 midnight when we got home. It was such a nice warm evening. I suggested we get our swim suits and go over to the public beach for a swim. Years later he told me that he thought I was going to be an easy "Make" because of that suggestion. He soon found out differently.

On Saturday, the next day, Howard's folks invited me over for dinner. His dad was rather quiet and reserved. His stepmom, Dora, was an extrovert and fun to be with. Throughout the years, whenever we are together, Dora and I have some laughing good times.

When Howard went back to Stout Field on Sunday, he made plans to see me in a month at Bronson Hospital in Kalamazoo, Michigan. I dated Howard in July and again on his three-day pass in August. When we were together in August, he asked me to marry him. A few weeks later I was surprised to receive a parcel in the mail.

We senior nursing students (19 of us) lived in a big home in the same block where the hospital was. We were like family, sharing joys and sorrows. There were at least six other nurses who were not on duty surrounding me when I opened the package. Guess what? It was my engagement ring. What a surprise! Howard didn't tell me he was going to send it. There were lots of hugging and crying. It was special to be sharing this tremendous joy with my friends.

Wedding

I finished my three years of nurses' training in September 1944. I moved back home to Dowagiac until we were married. We set our wedding date for December 8, 1944, after knowing each other for only six months. We only saw each other once a month for five months. It sounds a bit risky to take that big step of marriage before knowing each other better. However, it was not normal times; the Second World War was in full force.

As of this writing [January 1991], we have been married for 47 years. We've weathered plenty of ups and downs in our years together. We are glad now that it wasn't fashionable or common to split when there are problems to be faced. Priorities and needs were so different than they are now. We've both mellowed and have discovered those big problems were mostly from immaturity and me-ism and also thinking we would change each other—not a chance!

Acceptance is where it's at in a relationship. It took us many years to discover for ourselves the importance of acceptance. We are enjoying our retirement together, and we love each other. What a super gift!

Now back to the wedding day . . . money was scarce. Shopping for a wedding dress was disheartening. I finally found one for $25. I made a half-slip out of an old sheet, put layers on it, then starched it to make the dress flair out. That made it look very nice on me.

We had one counseling session with the minister, mainly warning us of the three areas that trouble marriages the most in this order: money, in-laws, and sex. I don't think his counsel was very meaningful because we lacked experience to understand what he was saying. Besides we felt that "LOVE" would conquer all. It probably would have if it had been "MATURE LOVE", but that took years to unfold.

We were married on a Friday evening, Dec. 8, 1944, at the Federated Church in Dowagiac, Michigan. My sister, Dorothy Ames, was my bridesmaid and Howard's best man was Jack Waters, a friend from the Air Force. Most of my nursing classmates were there. The wedding seems such a blur to me. I guess I was just too excited and on Cloud Nine. We had the reception in the basement of the church, and served cake, punch, nuts, and candies. Wish we could have had videos taken back then like they do now. The only pictures we had taken were done at a professional studio before the reception.

Honeymoon

When Howard was visiting me in Dowagiac during October before our wedding, we scouted around for a place to go for our honeymoon. We were driving one afternoon towards South Bend, Indiana, and just a short way past Niles, we saw four little log cabins that were overnight rentals. We went in to inquire about renting one.

The owner said, "We close at the end of October and don't open again until May." We told them why we wanted to rent one in December and he agreed to rent one to us for our honeymoon. When we got there that Friday night, there were flowers on the table plus a toaster and breakfast food for us. They were so nice to us. You probably think that's not much for a honeymoon, but when you have only $75, you plan accordingly.

Starting Life Together

Howard had to get back to Army Air Force duty in a week's time. Before our wedding, he had found an apartment for us to rent in Indianapolis near to Stout Field.

I got a job right away in one of the big hospitals, working in the nursery. There were 90 babies most of the time. To bathe them, we had sinks with an attached drain board and a pipe hanging over the sink. We would put the baby on the drain board, put water and soap on our hands, and soap them all over with our hands. Then we turned the water on from that pipe over the sink and held the baby under the flowing water to rinse off. It was a quick way to bathe them and, with that many babies, you had to have a fast method to get them all bathed.

Every three hours at feeding time, the babies were in attached cribs on rollers, with a basin of disinfectant on each 10-crib roller cart. We rolled the cribs down the hallway. We had to put our hands in the disinfectant before picking up another baby to take to its mother. We were proud of our

17

nursing record of low infection rate. We stayed in Indianapolis about four or five months.

Living in Neosho, MO

Howard was temporally transferred to the Army Signal Corps' Camp Crowder near Neosho, Missouri, where we had a hard time finding a place to rent. Neosho was such a small town and many soldiers wanting to live off base. Someone mentioned to us that the hospital was looking for nurses and maybe it could find us a place to rent. Sure enough, they wanted me to start working right away and found a place for us to rent that evening. The apartment was above a garage; it was just one room, but a nice size. We weren't supposed to do any cooking, but we had simple things like cold cereal and sandwiches and fruit, and we ate out for main meals.

The hospital had only 35 beds. I worked the 3:00–11:00 second shift all by myself. When Howard came off the base, he came and helped me answer lights. I had a 3-pound preemie to care for too, and Howard was good at that.

Howard saw two births while I worked there. The first lady was in her mid-thirties, and this was her first baby. I called the doctor when I thought she was near to birthing. He had a social function he wanted to attend so he decided to give her anesthesia and use forceps to speed the process along. That was when you dripped ether over a gauze-covered cone that would be over the patient's nose and mouth. I was administering that when the doctor put in the forceps and began to pull and tug. The table was on rollers without locks so I was also trying to hold the table back. Howard was dressed up in a gown and mask, and I could tell he was getting white—not only from the ether smell, but the terribleness of this kind of birth. I told him to go out and sit, and hang his head down.

The doctor finally got the baby out, took off his gown and mask, and left. The baby was O.K., with just some bruises on his cheeks from the forceps. I gave the mom an injection of Pitocin to prevent bleeding and waited for her to wake up. In the meantime, Howard revived and came in to help me. He still had his gown and mask on when mom woke up and, of course, she thought he was the doctor. She was too groggy to be convinced otherwise. I bet that was the quickest doctor's degree that was ever handed out!

Howard was really worried about me having a baby, if that was the way babies came into the world. Fortunately, the other birthing he saw was a lady who had four previous births. So that birth was normal, and Howard felt better.

While I worked in the Neosho hospital, penicillin was recently put on the market to be given by injection every three hours at a time. I began having nightmares of needles, needles, needles. I guess I was getting that burned-out syndrome of being overworked and having too many responsibilities. Howard finally convinced me to quit, and I got a job working on the Army airbase working with an oral surgeon. That was a breeze. My nightmares became a thing of the past.

We enjoyed Missouri. We didn't have a car so we hitchhiked to various places. I remember going to Eureka Springs, Arkansas, that had a quaint little Swiss-looking village which attracted many tourists. We were in Neosho about three months.

Greenville, SC

Howard was again transferred, this time to Greenville, South Carolina, and again it wasn't easy to find something to rent. We finally answered an ad for a room to rent. The lady was a widow. She had been used to slave-like help from the black community, but by now this was the thing of the past. We decided to rent the room out of desperation. We had to clean and scrub the room and, especially, the bathroom before we felt comfortable using them. No servants for a number of years really left a pile of grime and dust. The bed had an old-fashioned, feather tick mattress where we either sunk in the middle or into our own individual areas.

I worked days in the local hospital as staff nurse on the medical wing. I think it was late 1945 that Germany surrendered and the war ended. Since we knew we were going to get out of the service soon, we decided to have a baby. If I got pregnant before Howard would be discharged, then U.S.A. would pay the cost of delivery (that was important to us since we didn't have insurance). Howard was discharged on February 15, 1946. Yes, I did get pregnant, and I'll tell you about that shortly.

Living in Detroit

We decided to settle in Detroit because Howard had left a job as tool-and-die maker at Vickers Corporation there when he went in the service. Vickers said they would have a job for him when he got out of the service, so that was the most logical place to go. It was hard to find accommodations again. We finally found an apartment on Seward Avenue in a predominantly Jewish neighborhood. We had to buy the furniture ($600) in order to rent the apartment; the furniture wasn't very good. It took all our savings, but we did need a place to live.

I started cleaning the apartment, even washing the walls. Maybe all that stretching caused me to cramp and bleed. I went to the hospital, and lost the baby when I was two and a half months pregnant—what a sad time for us!

I got a job in a hospital as staff nurse on the 3:00–11:00 shift, and Howard worked at Vickers on the same shift. He decided to take a couple of courses towards a degree during the daytime. He had the equivalent of one year premed in college before he went into the service, but he changed his mind by the time he got out of the service.

After a few months working in the hospital, I was offered a full-time job in Dr. Cowen's urology office. That was a lot less stressful and tiring, and much closer to where we lived. We used public transportation; it was nice not having to go so far. Meanwhile, Howard was getting dissatisfied with his job. The main conversation with the other workers was cars, drinking, women, and sex. That was boring to him, so he decided to go to college full time and quit working.

We lived on my salary and Howard's GI bill allowance for his college and living expenses only with careful budgeting. Howard got his degree in two years by going all summer and all year. During that time, he switched his major to business. I was beginning to think he didn't know what he wanted to be. That was foreign to me because I knew I wanted to be a nurse ever since I was a wee tot playing doctor and nurse. After graduation he started working for a CPA firm to get certified. His salary was pretty low, but with mine we were doing fine.

Then I got pregnant. I planned to work until the eighth month, but I started spotting after a couple months. With my previous history of losing one pregnancy after two and a half months, the doctor thought I should quit my job and be in bed for a month or so. We tried to get along on Howard's salary. He finally had to quit and find another job. He started working for the Internal Revenue Service, while I was a lady of leisure, soon making friends with a number of gals in the apartment building. There was a lot of going back and forth. In fact, I was having a hard time getting any of my own housework done. Sometimes I ironed in the evening, and I got a bit of flak from Howard over that. Anyway, that nine months of pregnancy went pretty fast.

I wanted to have a natural birth—no drugs, no forceps, etc., which were used regularly at that time. I read Dr. Grantly Dick Reed's book from the library on natural childbirth so I was well prepared to go that route. I did some scouting around to find a hospital that would let me keep my baby in my room—another rare thing for hospitals. Women's Hospital agreed to let me have my way. My due date was at the end of December, but on December 14th my water broke with no contractions.

My doctor said I should go to the hospital because of the infection danger after the water breaks. I went in mid-morning. He gave me Pitocin to try to start labor. I had contractions, but more like Braxton Hicks contractions that you have during pregnancy. By 10 p.m. the doctor thought I should get a good night's sleep, and he would try the Pitocin

21

again in the morning. He ordered a sleeping pill so I did have a good sleep. At 6 a.m., with another injection of Pitocin, I took off with the real thing. I walked the whole time of labor and was doing O.K., and then about 2 p.m. the second stage began. What a surprise! I could hardly get up on the bed and, before I knew it, the doctor stuck a needle in my vein and told me to count. I only got to ten, and I was out completely until after the birth. He had given me Pentothal.

Afterwards I was furious about not being able to carry out my carefully laid plans for the birth. The doctor knew all along that he was going to do what he did. He said my coccyx bone was bent in a fixed position, and he knew he would have to break it in order for me to give birth. He didn't tell me because he didn't want me to worry. So I had a drug, and forceps were used. Sometimes I wonder if he didn't break my coccyx by using forceps.

We named our first son David Allan. It was a good thing I had him in a crib beside me because, as I was watching him, he turned blue and purple. I grabbed him and yelled for the nurse. He had to go back to the nursery and was given oxygen for 24 hours. I guess the forceps caused a bit of edema in the brain. After the second day, I had him with me for the rest of the week. We stayed in the hospital for a week at that time. You have no idea how excruciating painful that broken coccyx was, especially right during a bowel movement. I sat on an air-filled donut for a month.

Breastfeeding went well, except for sore nipples for awhile. I remember stamping my feet when he would first latch on—ouch, ouch, ouch! A few days after I got home, my temperature started to go up. What now!? I didn't think I had phlebitis which sometimes happens after delivery. The doctor came to the house. He put one fist on a kidney area and hit his fist with the other hand; no problem with the left side, but another story on the right side—a really big ouch! I had a kidney infection that cleared up quickly with antibiotic medication.

The doctor had advised not gaining more than 18–20 pounds during pregnancy. Today, it's 25–30 pounds. I was back to my pre-pregnancy weight within a couple weeks. In fact, it was hard to keep my weight up with breastfeeding. The 25–30 pounds is better to get breastfeeding going well. My mom came to be with me for a week.

David had colic for three months. He usually cried constantly from 6:00–10:30 p.m., and filled his pants royally. I'm glad it was the evening hours because Howard was home to help. I can see him so clearly, walking the floor with David and singing. By the time David was 9 months old, we decided we didn't want to be living in Detroit to raise a family. So Howard asked for the first transfer that came up, which happened to be St. Joseph, Michigan, and once more we couldn't find anything to rent in St. Joe.

Living at Indian Lake

While we were visiting my mom in Dowagiac, we heard about a winterized cottage at Indian Lake which we rented. It was a 15–20 mile trip for Howard to go to and from work. There was a lot a anxiety for winter-time driving. Soon after we moved into the cottage, I got pregnant again. I decided to go to St. Joseph's Hospital in South Bend, Indiana, for the birth. My OB doctor assured me that my coccyx bone was fine and I would have no trouble giving birth. So I would try again to have a natural birth.

On the 25th of April 1950, I woke up with contractions. I was so glad Howard still hadn't taken off for work. My contractions were pretty hard so, as soon as we contacted my neighbor to take David, we left for South Bend. I was doing great with the type of relaxation breathing that Dr. Reed's book taught. In fact, labor was progressing a bit too fast so I had to tighten up some to slow the progress down.

We got to the hospital where I was examined and taken into the delivery room. There wasn't even time for an enema, the usual system after being shaved. The doctor wasn't there yet so they made me cross my legs. After 15 minutes, I said, "I'll catch this baby, doctor or no doctor."

They finally called in an intern, and Pamela Beth was born with no episiotomy and no tearing. I had my natural childbirth, but the hospital wouldn't let me have her in my room. You win some and lose some. Poor little Pam—her face was scratched by her finger nails and crying so much. They often brought her to me with her arms strapped down close to her body so her hands couldn't reach her face. What a cruel system!

David was 16 months old when we brought Pam home. Pam's colic was more severe than David's was and lasted for five months. I was breastfeeding Pam and, after about two months, I thought it must be me giving her the colic so I put her on formula for a week. Her colic was worse. In the meantime I had been pumping my breasts so I put her back on the breast.

It seemed there was no let up to her discomfort. When Howard came home from work, and as quick as we had finished dinner, I escaped into the bedroom and let him take over. Thank goodness for a good daddy. I wonder how these single gals with babies do it without any help from a spouse.

After Pam got a few months older, we started thinking about building a home in St. Joseph. We bought a lot on Coles Avenue across from a grade school. As Internal Revenue Officer, Howard was checking a lumber company that gave us a lot of magazines with home-building ideas. We chose a modest, one and a half-story brick home that cost us $10,000 which sounded like an absolute fortune to us. We continued to live at Indian Lake while our home was being built. In 1957 Howard quit the Internal Revenue Service job because there was not much chance of advancement.

Birth of Our Third Child: Michael Jay

Dave was 3-1/2 and Pam 2 years old when we moved to our new home on Coles Avenue early in 1952, and I was pregnant again. Actually our own desires were to have two children fairly close together, wait until they started school, and then have two more. Well, the best laid out plans don't always materialize, which is fine. Now and then we need to be assured that "WE" aren't always in control of our lives or destiny.

Michael Jay was born on August 4, 1952, after another short labor of about three hours. The hospital in St. Joseph, Michigan, did agree to let me keep Mike in my room, but the obstetrician said, "If you have another baby, you better let me know as soon as you feel a cramp." He almost didn't make it to Mike's birth. Mike also had colic, but it was not as severe as the others' and only lasted two and a half months. That was much easier to handle. When David was born, we had him circumcised. I wasn't very impressed with how it was done, so we opted not to have Mike circumcised which was quite out of the ordinary at that time. Now many parents do not have their boy babies circumcised. I didn't realize what a paranoid woman I was way back then. Everything I wanted is practical now.

Having three children in three and a half years took a toll on my energy level. Getting up at nights for feeding and Howard's amorous needs kept me exhausted.

Divorce: A Big Trauma

When Howard told me in 1953 and after nine years of marriage that he wanted a divorce, I thought it was the end of the world for me.

He thought I could go back and live with my mom. In much tribulation and many tears, I called my mom. She was very sympathetic to my pain but also firm in her reply. She said, "You are both intelligent and good people. Get counseling and work out your problems. You have a great responsibility to those children." Bless her. She was part of keeping us together as we lived through our me-ism stages and gradually grew more mature.

We settled in to getting on with life to the best of our ability with plenty of ups and downs, joys and pains.

Braces

I was 32 years old when I went to an orthodontist about my teeth. On the left side, next to my big front teeth, my tooth stuck out. I was so self conscious about that tooth. It affected my personality. I felt shy and tried to stay in the background. I didn't want to smile or show that tooth sticking out. The orthodontist said it could be straightened easily. He removed a couple of teeth and then put braces on. What a hallelujah time that was when my braces came off, and my tooth was in the right place. I wish I could have had it done in my early teens, but there had been no money. All the children inherited my teeth's overcrowded tendency.

Our First Boat

In the summer of 1955, we purchased a 22-foot aluminum cabin cruiser. Most every evening I would have a picnic meal prepared and we'd go down to our boat when Howard got home from work. We had many wonderful family hours on that boat. Many weekends we would pack food and take off on Friday evening for the nearest port up Lake Michigan about 20 miles away. It was fun and interesting, getting acquainted with other boaters. It didn't matter if our boat was a little midget docked up beside a bigger boat. We were all friendly with each other, and there were always other kids for the children to play with.

The children slept in the cabin. I made a large mosquito net that fit over the cockpit where Howard and I slept. We had a blow-up mattress to sleep on. Ginger was conceived that summer, having waited three and a half years gave my body time to get back to normal.

Our Fourth Child: Ginger Kay

I felt stronger and more rested during this pregnancy. Our other children were old enough to observe that my tummy was beginning to protrude. They were curious and full of questions. They wanted to put their hands on my tummy and feel if the baby was moving. They would put their ears on my tummy to try to hear the heartbeat. It was an exciting time waiting for this baby to arrive.

Ginger arrived on April 20, 1956, three weeks ahead of my due date. She was so tiny, just over 6 pounds. The hospital in St. Joseph, Michigan, again agreed to let me keep her in my room, although they wouldn't allow Dave, Pam, and Mike into the hospital to see Ginger so I would hold her up to the window for them to see her. Howard always took a week off work so he could be with the children whenever I had a baby. Howard and I had the name, Peggy, picked out for a girl, but Dave, Pam, and Mike wanted to call her Ginger because of her auburn hair. They won!

We didn't have a name for our cabin cruiser yet, so "Ginger" was unanimously chosen. Ginger was only two weeks old when we took a weekend trip up the coast of Lake Michigan. She slept in a cardboard box up on the counter in the cabin. She was such a good baby, hardly ever crying. She was the only one of our children that did not have colic. What a blessing that was!

CHAPTER 3. Early Middle Age

Slipped Disc, 1956

I wanted to make a vegetable garden in back of our garage. We took off the top layer of sod with grass and put it in area in our lawn where the grass seed did not grow. Then we took about 6 to 8 inches of dirt out of the garden area and had good black soil brought in. Our soil had a lot of clay in it. Apparently I carried too many heavy clumps of sod. By evening I had a very painful back. It was excruciating to walk, sneeze or cough. I went to the chiropractor who didn't help much. I couldn't drive the car because I couldn't use my legs and feet to press on the clutch or brake. It was very painful to put my legs out straight in a sitting position. No doubt that made the nerve in my spine more taunt and the nerve rubbed against the protruding disc which caused severe pain.

It was a month before I felt any improvement. I was supposed to be in bed as much as possible and I was not to lift. I don't really remember how we managed. I think Howard took off a bit from work and David was 8 years old so he helped me a lot, especially with Ginger. She was only a few months old. My back improved gradually. It was wonderful to be free of pain and feeling my normal self again. I had a little bit understanding of what it would be like to have a chronic illness, like crippling arthritis, but how awful to know that there wouldn't be any improvement for the better. I view these people with much respect and compassion.

Our First Puppy, 1956

Up to now our pets consisted of a hamster and a big fish tank with many different kinds of fish. The hamster got away from us one time when we had it outside the cage to play with. We couldn't find it anywhere. Finally we discovered it had gotten into the front closet where our coats were. I had just made a very nice coat out of a pretty, blue, heavy wool blanket. The hamster ruined it by tearing at it to get wool fibers to made a nest. That hamster went back to the pet shop, pronto!

Grandpa Trumbull brought the children a hound puppy for Christmas. It was so cute and so much fun. When the puppy was just a few months old, it became very ill with diarrhea and vomiting. I finally took it to the vet and he asked us if we used Dial soap. Sure enough we did. He said that he has had several cases of puppies licking Dial soap and becoming extremely ill. Our puppy died. What a sad family we were.

Speed Reading Course

I didn't read books very much as I was growing up. I was a slow plodder when it came to reading. Howard told me his family went to the library every week, brought sacks of books home, and the kids had competitions by writing down every book and author that they read. We took our children to the library weekly too. Dave and Ginger were our readers, and Pam and Mike were our activists who liked to be doing something rather then settling down to read.

I enrolled in the "Speed Reading Course" at the community college in Benton Harbor. That was a great boon to my reading ability. They taught us how to scan down the middle of the page and not read every word. Skim briefly what you were familiar with. It also taught us to read the beginning and ending paragraph, then skim the middle to get the gist of the article. The course changed me from a plodder, who thought I had to read every word, to a much faster reader. I'm so thankful that I took that Speed Reading Course.

Moving to a Five-Bedroom Home

In the summer of 1957 we sold the home that we had built and moved to a lovely, big, family home on Niles Avenue in St. Joseph, Michigan. It was about a mile and a half outside of town and next to a cemetery. Quietest neighbors we ever had!

There were five bedrooms upstairs, and all the children had their own room. That was a special bonus for keeping the squabbling low. On the main floor was a nice kitchen with a dishwasher which we all loved. A family dining room had wall-to-wall windows on two sides so we could see the beautiful changing seasons. The dining room and living room together measured 44 ft. and went the length of the front of the house.

We all enjoyed our family room—the most lived in room of our home. That family room was a big boon in keeping our living room looking decent. It was like having an old fashioned parlor that was only used when we had company.

We had many family gatherings and social events. One time we had 11 tables of bridge. The church had given each of us $2.00, and we were to use our talents and increase the money. So we had a fun evening of playing bridge with each person paying $2.00 to play bridge.

The basement had tiles on the floor and one area had paneled walls. The children played down there a lot with each other and with other friends. They especially liked to roller skate. We didn't have sidewalks so the basement was their roller skating rink. When we moved out there, Dave was 9-1/2, Pam 8, Mike 5, and Ginger 1-1/2.

We had a large lot which went back to a river. Fortunately, a riding lawnmower came with the house when we bought it. There were lots of big trees so the grass didn't grow too fast. Even so, Howard spent many hours keeping our lawn looking groomed.

We were given another puppy by a neighbor. This one was a mixture of breeds. We heard that mixed breeds were healthier than purebreds. She had a white tip at the end of its tail, so we called her, "Tippy". We trained Tippy to be only in the kitchen, breakfast room, and basement where there was tile or linoleum flooring. The kids would tease her sometimes by running into a room where there was a rug, and then watch her skid on all four trying to stop at the rug line. She grew to be about the size of a cocker spaniel. She was a great companion to the children, especially Mike.

Mike did not go to kindergarten that fall. He was small in stature and we thought it would be better for him to start the next year when he was 6 years old. Mike and Tippy went outside together many days. Often they would go over to the cemetery and follow the caretaker around. Sometimes if the caretaker hadn't seen Mike for a few days, he would come over to see if he was O.K. I think they really enjoyed each other.

Mike loved to go fishing. I would put a lifesaver vest on him and give him fishing pole and bait, and tell him to go to the river and fish if there was someone else fishing too. Sometimes he would come back, but more often he would find someone else fishing and he would stay. I fretted a bit over this freedom for Mike, but he was always trustworthy about coming back if there was no one there.

Cutting Our Own Christmas Tree

For a number of years, we had family fun in choosing and cutting our own Christmas tree. We usually went on a snowy Sunday afternoon to a pine tree farm. Choosing just the right one was the fun part, and we all had to agree. We would scrutinize the trees on every side and finally there it was—the perfect one. Howard cut it down with his saw. We brought a sled to bring it back to the car. The first Christmas that we were in our big family home, we decided to invite a number of our friends who had children to go along with us. The kids loved it. After each family got their tree, we went back to our house and had hot chocolate and sandwiches.

31

We had a full house of people that day. It was nice to have a big home and be able to do things like that.

Frail Little Ginger

Ginger was not very well the first three years of her life. She began having ear infections when she was 6 months old. She had a problem with allergies. Her little nose was constantly running. It seems like her ears would flair up every few months. Apparently her tonsils were enlarged and often inflamed. Finally, when she was 3 years old, the doctor decided to take her tonsils out. It was touch and go to keep her free of flair ups in order to have them removed. The doctor put her on antibiotics for a week before the scheduled operation. We noticed a big change in her in a year's time. She was putting on weight and no longer was plagued with ear infections every few months.

Dave and Pam's Spiritual Birthdays

Pam had a friend from school who invited Pam to go with her to a lady's house one afternoon every week after school. She didn't live very far from us. Her name was Mrs. Peete. I hadn't met her yet. Quite a few kids went to this lady's house every Wednesday afternoon. They seemed to love it. Pam soon had David going with her. They really looked forward to those afternoons One day they both came home with sparkling eyes and said today was their "Spiritual Birthday". They had accepted Christ as their personal Savior.

I decided I had better go over and talk with Mrs. Peete to make sure it wasn't some kind of way out religious group. Howard and I hadn't gotten involved much in the church yet. When we lived in town I took the children to an Anglican Sunday school which was close by. Mrs. Peete was a very nice, gracious lady, and her only aim was to help the children understand God's great love for them.

My Spiritual Awakening

Mrs. Peete said, "What about you? Do you have a Living Faith?" I didn't even know what she meant. She asked me if I read the Bible. I said, "I've tried reading it, but I didn't understand it much." She offered to study with me two afternoons every week. What questions she couldn't answer she would call her pastor. Mrs. Peete attended a Baptist church. We studied for six months together, and I helped her with the children's class on Wednesday afternoons.

That was an exciting time for me. My heart and eyes were opened to God's word and love for me. I felt as if I was on Cloud Nine. My increased energy level amazed me. Howard was wondering what was going on with me. I would sit up reading Christian literature until 12:00 or 1:00 a.m. many evenings. Always before, I couldn't stay awake much past 10:00 p.m.

I started attending the First Congregational Church in town and taking the children there to Sunday school. Howard didn't go yet and, once in awhile, Dave would say he would stay home with dad. It was about this time that Howard's boss at Whirlpool Corporation asked Howard if he would be treasurer at that Congregational church. So that was actually how Howard started going there with us. Isn't God wonderful in working things out for the good? Howard told his boss that he would be treasurer there, hoping that would increase his chances for climbing the corporate ladder at Whirlpool. God had other plans for us though.

At the same time all this was going on, I was invited by a friend to join four another women who were meeting once a week. We were very different spiritually. One was an agnostic, one was into spiritual frontiers, one was a normal Catholic, and two of us were growing in our Christian walk. This group was a great help to me. We were all seeking to try to understand ourselves. The first book we explored together was *The Mature Mind* by H.A. Overstreet (1949). This book really set me on fire. I hadn't realized that life was a matter of loving or you literally die. The forces within and without that keep us from truly loving destroy us and others, and perpetuate a state of disharmony. Love is the power that is creative, constructive, and everlasting—this never dies—so it's as plain as that, we either love or perish.

Next we read *Love or Perish* by Dr. Smiley Blanton (1957). This book propelled me onto my search of life everlasting and how to love my neighbor. It was through this book that I became aware that everything has its opposites and we, in our humanness, have to live with these forces around us and within us. Love and hate, aggressiveness and shyness, anger and tranquility, sorrow and joy, affection and aloofness. My life had been a jumble of these forces, and I knew that this author was meeting my experiences. Now I realized I was linked with the vast multitude that had to cope with opposing forces at work within and the opposing forces to others. But how? Love or perish. This book was the one that motivated me into accelerating my understanding of God's love for us through his people. Love the not so loveable and love the enemy!! What a huge order! I'm still working at it.

Howard and I also were attending a Bible study at our church. There were only eight of us out of a membership of 500 that were interested in studying together. This too was a good step in my growth. The librarian of our church said I was her most frequent customer. There had been a void in my life. I was like a thirsty, dry sponge trying to fill that void, and it was so exhilarating and exciting.

Once I truly became aware through my vast reading of Christian books that God is and God loves and He loves me, then I was drawn to reading the Bible. There was much I didn't understand because a lot of history and culture was in the writings. I soon found out that I could get help by reading interpretations of scripture. This has been a great help to me and I keep reading more and more as the years roll by. New meaning and new revelation keeps opening up to me as I continue to discover God's promises to me and really believe them.

A Change in Boats

As the children got a bit older the cabin cruiser was too limiting and confining. So in the spring of 1958, we sold our cruiser and bought a speed boat. One weekend that summer we rented a tent, loaded all the paraphernalia in the boat, went to a lake, and set up our tent. By the end of the weekend, all knew we were addicted to this wonderful, family fun. So we bought a family size tent and all kinds of camping gear, and spent many happy weekends and vacations camping.

We all learned to water ski—even with only one ski. Ginger was too little, so we bought a water board for her to ride on. We made some lasting friendships during those camping years. We still keep in touch with a few at Christmas time.

Going to Family Church Camp

I was determined to get us to family church camp that summer of 1960. Howard was not too keen on going, so I chose to attend the last camp in August. All summer I kept saving money out of my grocery allowance and finally had enough to send in our family reservations for August. Can you believe it? I sent in cash because I couldn't write a check since Howard was dragging his feet about church camp. Howard would think I was not listening to his not wanting to go if he saw that I had a written check. I was going on faith that somehow he would agree to go. Several families in our church went to the family camps in June and July, and they came back with much enthusiasm, especially the men. That was the turn around. Howard decided he could give a week to go to family camp out of his hard-earned three weeks of vacation.

We had a wonderful time, and it was because of attending that family camp that the seed was planted for mission service overseas.

The camp minister was Miles Shishito. He was in the States from Hawaii, getting his doctorate in theology. He and Howard really enjoyed each other. They stayed up late

35

many evenings playing chess and talking. Howard shared with him his disenchantment with his work at Whirlpool and that he was looking around for another job, but knew it probably wouldn't be much better. He disliked the insensitivity and politics of the business world with its new instructions of making the product wear out in seven years time so people would be forced into buying new appliances. The old work ethic of making the best possible product was becoming obsolete.

Miles Shishito pulled a brochure out of his pocket about the need for skilled people overseas. He said there was a big need for skilled accountants and business majors in the mission fields. All this sharing and talking put a spark and hope in Howard's heart about the future, but he was sure I wouldn't go along with this spark of his. All this was going on without my knowledge. I thought they were just playing chess. Miles finally encouraged him to get up the courage to talk to me about this by the end of the week. While we were walking to breakfast from our cabin to the dining building, he said, "What do you think about serving overseas?" The first thing I said, "We'd just have to sell our stuff and go." Now truly that was an amazing statement for me because I had always been rather of an insecure person, not liking new situations very much. But God had been working on me for a couple of years, and I was ready to support Howard in what God was doing in his life.

Where to Serve?

We didn't particularly care where we would be sent, though we did have one stipulation: we wanted to keep our children with us and not have to send them to boarding school. So that limited us to an English-speaking area. The Congregational Church of South Africa was in need of a treasurer. The central office of the church was in Durban, Natal. Natal was settled by the British (in the mid-1800's) so was English-speaking. The United Congregational Church Board of World Missions assigned us to Durban, Natal, in South Africa in September 1961.

Getting Ready to Go

Our assignment came through the first part of October 1960. We had three months to try to sell our home before going to Missionary Training School in Stony Point, New York, the first part of January 1961 for six months, and then to Linguistic Study in Meadville, Pennsylvania for three months. A man who owned a real estate agency was a member of our church. He wanted to sell our house and not take commission as a gift to us. The housing market was a bit depressed at that time, and it didn't sell until just before we left for overseas. At least we were able to sign all the papers before leaving.

Howard had mixed reactions to his announcement at work that he was going to be a missionary. Some thought he was absolutely irresponsible to expose his family to unknown dangers, and others were in awe and envy that he could give up a lucrative income.

We made a few trips to a missionary supply store in Chicago to buy office equipment and supplies, tape recorder, audiovisual supplies, shortwave radio, transformers for the 220 electricity in South Africa, and a pretty set of plastic dishes. Whirlpool gave us a new refrigerator, upright freezer and a washing machine to take with us. Howard was treasurer of the Whirlpool Credit Union. They had a going away party for him and gave him a very good camera which was extensively used in South Africa. I think we took about 3,000 pictures during our missionary years.

We had an auction of our household supplies and furniture at the end of December 1960. We had most of the furniture out on the lawn. Fortunately, it wasn't too cold and it didn't snow. We sold all of our breakable dishes too. We had packed up and crated all of our personal things, and had them sent to our church office warehouse in Boston until we left U.S.A.

AUCTION

Saturday JANUARY 7 1961   1:00 P.M.

— COME EARLY FOR THE DRAWING —

WE ARE GOING INTO MISSIONARY WORK IN AFRICA, WILL SELL ALL PERSONAL PROPERTY LISTED BELOW AT OUR HOME LOCATED AT 3739 NILES AVE. ST. JOSEPH, MICHIGAN. (ABOUT 2 miles SOUTH OF ST. JOSEPH on U.S. 31, by RIVER VIEW CEMETERY)

— BOAT & CAR —

14' YELLOW JACKET RUN-ABOUT BOAT. MARK 55 ELECTRIC STARTING MERCURY 40 H.P. MOTOR AND TRAILER. (This boat must be seen to be appreciated) 3 pairs of WATER SKIES. BOAT CUSHIONS, TANKS, SKI ROPE, CASE OF OUTBOARD MOTOR OIL. Other boating accessories.

1952 4 door PLYMOUTH CAR, with all new tires, radio, heater, runs good. JACOBSON RIDING LAWN MOWER. 2-32' Extension ladders, 1 wood & 1 aluminum.

— HOUSEHOLD GOODS —

10' ADMIRAL REFRIGERATOR. DINING ROOM SET, COMPLETE with 6 upholstered CHAIRS, CHINA CLOSET & BUFFET. LIGHT BROWN LIVING ROOM SET. RED LIVING ROOM SET. COMBINATION DESK AND BOOK CASE. 2 sets of twin HOLLYWOOD BEDS. BED ROOM SET complete with CHEST OF DRAWERS, COMBINATION DESK & BOOK CASE 17' BLOND T.V. OFFICE DESK. 9 X 12 RUN (floral). SOFA COUCH. MAPLE ROCKER. ROCKING CHAIRS. WASHBURN PIANO. STUDIO COUCH. APARTMENT SIZE ELECTRIC. STOVE. TABLE. WESTINGHOUSE ROASTER. FULL SIZE HOLLYWOOD BED & CHEST. 2 DRESSERS. BABY BED. 4 CHROME CHAIRS. RECLINING CHAIR. TABLE & CHAIRS. 2 STEP END TABLES with FORMICA TOPS. SEVERAL NICE LAMPS. SOME DRIFT WOOD PIECES. CORNER TABLE. COFFEE TABLE. 4 CARD TABLES. FOLDING CHAIRS. MIRROR. FIREPLACE SET & GRATES. TEA CART. WORK BENCH. SUN LAMP. CHRISTMAS

DECORATIONS. FRUIT JARS. OTHER MISCELLANEOUS ITEMS.

"ANTIQUE" CHERRY WOOD CUPBOARD. MARBLE TOP CHEST OF DRAWERS. FEW OTHER COLLECTOR ITEMS.

****

CRAFTSMAN POWER JIG SAW. OUTDOOR GRILL w/rotisserie. PICNIC TABLE. BOYS BIKE. 2 GIRLS BICYCLES. SMALL GIRLS BIKE. OUTDOOR GYM SET. WHEELBARROW. PILE OF 22' FIRE PLACE WOOD. WHIRL TYPE POWER MOWER. CAMPING ICE BOX. HAND & GARDEN TOOLS. OTHER MISCELLANEOUS ITEMS.

"TERMS" CASH — NOT RESPONSIBLE

FOR ACCIDENTS OF GOODS AFTER SOLD.

(NOTE: HOUSE IS ALSO "FOR SALE"

contact LUDWIG REAL-ESTATE)

MR. AND MRS. HOWARD W TRUMBULL: OWNERS

3739 NILES AVE. ST JOSEPH. MI

JOHN M GLASSMAN

"AUCTIONEER"

DOWAGIAC (PH) ST 2-7729

"THE AUCTION IS THE BEST WAY"

Dave was 11-1/2 when we made the decision to go overseas. He was looking forward to the new adventure, but Pam was concerned and unhappy about missing her many friends. Mike was in the second grade and Ginger was 4; both were too young to voice any strong opinions.

We rented a small U-Haul trailer for our eight months of winter and summer clothing, then hooked it into the back of our Ford station wagon. We were off for five months of Missionary Training School in Stony Point, New York.

Missionary Training School

The training center was owned by the United Presbyterian Church in U.S.A., but beginning with our class it became ecumenical and is now under the management of eight denominations. Our group consisted of 31 adults and 21 children. We represented six denominations: Presbyterian, Canadian Presbyterian, Reformed, Methodist, Disciples of Christ, and Congregational, that were sending us to Taiwan, Congo, Brazil, Sarawak, Indonesia, Iran, Arabia, Thailand, North Sudan, India, Nigeria, Korea, and South Africa.

The training center consisted of seven buildings. The administration building housed the offices, classrooms, chapel, a 6,000-volumes library, large lounge area, dining hall, and a kitchen. There were three student residence halls consisting of four three-bedroom suites, a small lounge room, kitchenette and laundry room in the middle of the building.

We had classes five and a half days a week consisting of Christian Community and Related Training, Biblical and Theological Bases of Mission, and World Issues and Practice of Mission. We were visited and lectured to by a Secularist, Buddhist, Muslim, Hindu, Roman Catholic, Communist, and labor leaders. We had to study at least two and a half hours a day. We students had duties in the kitchen, dining room, library, prayer and worship services, which were assigned and rotated. The duties had a two-fold purpose; not only to help with work, but the staff were watching us to see if you could work in a team effort. Three of the candidates didn't go overseas because they had trouble working with other people.

The children were well taken care of by a wonderful staff. Dave, Pam, and Mike went to the local public school. The school-aged children received Missionary Training on Saturday mornings.

We are so thankful to have had this training before going overseas. After Stony Point, we all went to Meadville, Penn., for two months training in Culture Area study and Linguistics. Then we had a couple of weeks to go back to Michigan for our final goodbyes with family and friends. We stayed with my mom, and I think Dot and Jack took one of our children.

Our Boat Trips to Europe and Africa

It was a beautiful sunny day on August 16, 1961, when we boarded the Queen Mary ship bound for England. A few friends and family were there to see us off. A few tears were shed when we realized that we wouldn't be seeing them for seven years. We had a lifeboat drill immediately while we were passing the Statue of Liberty.

The boat trip to England was calm, cool, and damp. Even so, some couldn't eat their meals because of sea-sickness. In the dining room, we had a hard time understanding our waiter. I never would have thought that he was really speaking English. The meals were delicious—three or four choices. We were assigned to a table for the entire trip. We couldn't quite get used to the spoons. There were two sizes; one small demitasse size and then a tablespoon. No size in between. Maybe that's always what the people in England use. We went swimming in the ship's pool. It was the first time I had swum in ocean water. It smarted my eyes a little and tasted like a saltwater gargle, but it was wonderful to swim in.

Pam, Mike, and Ginger all won prizes in the Children's Fancy Dress contest. We were to use anything we could find in our cabin. They did furnish crepe paper. I believe I dressed Pam and Ginger with the blue silk bedspreads, draped like a Chinese lady, and using the pillow covers as sashes. Mike wore a diaper made out of a Turkish towel, and I made a baby bonnet out of crepe paper. He crept across the stage on his knees with a blown up balloon held in his mouth because we couldn't find a baby bottle with a nipple. They all won a small-sized replica of the Queen Mary. The older children played bingo and won a prize.

Can you imagine? It was a bottle of champagne which was turned in for cash. Oh, yes!

The ladies had a Fancy Hat contest. We were supposed to make a hat that represented a song. I took a piece of light cardboard and shaped it into a cone shape, and I put Ginger's small teddy bear half-way up the cone. It was supposed to represent "The Bear Went Over The Mountain". I won a prize—a travel alarm clock.

Our boat docked in Cherbourg, France, on the morning before we landed in England. We had a few hours to walk in the quaint city on a cobblestone road with two-story buildings right next to the sidewalk. We went into a shop to buy David a pair of thongs. What a problem trying to communicate. Both Howard and I took French in high school, but it didn't help us. It was a frustrating experience.

We docked in England on August 21. It took us five days from U.S.A. We had two days of sightseeing bus trips and tours of the wax museum and children's museum of science and industry. Later in the evening, after we got the children bedded down in our hotel, Howard and I walked through the Trafalgar Square and Soho districts which were interesting and different.

It took us two weeks to get from England to our destination in Durban. We sailed on the Athlone Castle ship. Temperatures averaged about 70 degrees, and it was only 65 degrees the day we crossed the equator. The hottest day was the third day out of Southampton when we spent four hours at the Madeira Islands. As our boat anchored, there were many small boats surrounding us, hawking their wares of toys, dolls, woven and lace products, and diving for coins that were tossed to them. When we went ashore in the sweltering heat to take an auto tour of the city, we and all the other tourists were constantly hounded by begging adults and children. Groups of them would even run along side the car, tossing in limp, bedraggled flowers for which they expected coins. We were all glad to return to the safety of the ship.

The mission folk in South Africa sent us a welcoming letter and telegrams to the three ports prior to arriving in Durban. That made us feel warm and safe. I thought about the early first missionaries with no one to greet them. What a gift to us that we were being received by an existing missionary group. It was wonderful to see them smiling and waving at us from the dock as we stood at the railing of the boat.

As we caught sight of Durban, it looked like a Miami beach coastline. Many large hotels and apartment buildings were along the coast area. Were we really in Africa?

Ready to serve are
Howard and Marge, Dave and Pam, Ginger and Mike

CHAPTER 4.

Our South African Mission Begins in Natal

Our First Living Quarters in Durban

We arrived in Durban on September 12, 1961, at 6:30 a.m. The ten folks that came to greet us came onboard and helped us with details of immigration and customs. We got through customs very easily—only two suitcases were opened of the 23 pieces of luggage that got off the boat with us. Our possessions we packed in St. Joseph, Michigan, were shipped on another boat and arrived a few days later. We finally fitted all of us and our luggage in the several cars that our mission colleague came with, and set off to have lunch in Dr. and Mrs. Taylor's garden. Dr. Taylor was a missionary who served as the administrator of McCord Zulu Hospital. He and his wife lived in a home next to the hospital. It was beautiful as we drove up the street. The street was lined on both sides with beautiful big jacaranda trees. The trees met in the middle of the road high over head. It seemed like we were traveling under a flowering lavender archway.

We were housed in three hospital staff bedrooms for five months while the home we were to live in a block away was being remodeled.

Directly across the street from us was a 330-bed, all black and Indian hospital. McCord Zulu Hospital was established in 1923 by American missionaries. The only street (McCord Road) that lead to the entrance of the hospital was the one in front of our three staff rooms, and it was barely wide enough for two cars to pass. There was only parking space for about ten cars. Can you imagine that little parking space for a 330-bed hospital? The reason this little street wasn't involved in a real traffic jam is that an African cannot afford to own and run a car. It was really a rarity to see an African who owned a car. Many Africans drove cars, but only as chauffeurs or truck drivers.

We faced the tuberculosis wing of the hospital. There was an open porch that the patients used to come out on for fresh air and sunshine. Much of the time they sang, and the patients that were fairly strong did interpretive tribal dancing to the singing. We enjoyed watching them and marveled at their cheerfulness in spite of their illness and the constant worry of how their families were being taken care of while they were in the hospital.

McCord Road was teaming all day with Indians in saris and Africans in all variety of dress—from typical western type clothing to gunny sacks to native Krall attire which was very colorful. When the native rural African woman came into the city, she draped colorful Turkish towels around her chest and hip areas. Many times their hair was fixed with red clay which gave the appearance of a hat. They used a block of wood for a pillow so as not to harm their hair-do. On their legs and arms were at least 6 inches of wire bracelets. Their ear lobes had been stretched and slit so that an ornament as big as a half dollar fit in the lobe. You would see their faces light up when we would say, *"Saubona"* (hello). They weren't used to white people showing friendliness and respect for them.

On one side of our abode was a one-court tennis court for the nurses. It wasn't a cemented court, just hard dirt. In the back of the tennis court was the hospital laundry drying yard. They didn't have big tumble dryers like in America. Can you just visualize the lines and lines of laundry that was put out for the good old sun and wind to dry everyday? The laundry drying yard was enclosed with brick walls and wire fencing to eliminate theft. There was some theft here, mainly due to the fact that the Africans weren't paid a living wage. Howard had one of his best sport shirts taken from our laundry line in the back yard.

In front of our living quarters was a lovely jacaranda tree. It looked very oriental in shape, covered with lavender blossoms that bloomed for at least two months or more each year. Also in the front yard was a large bush about the size and shape of a large lilac bush. It was called, "Yesterday, Today, and Tomorrow". When the blossoms first appeared, they were white, then gradually turned blue, and then pink so the bush was loaded with some white, blue, and pink blossoms all at the same time. Their fragrance was lovely.

Visiting a Rural Mission Station

The mission assigned us a 1955 Chevy and soon after we arrived we were invited to stay for five days at Ifafa Mission Station, 50 miles south of Durban. Dick and Jane Sales and their three young children lived there. They lived in a big home that had electricity for a year. The man that Howard replaced lived there for 30 years and raised five children there. Oh yes! Another item that made an impression on us was the way homes in the rural area got their water supply. The mission house in Ifafa had a huge cement storage tank that held 1600 gallons of water which was collected during the rainy season from the roof of the home. This water was used for everything, including drinking, and the water was not boiled for drinking.

The home was in a remote, isolated area with African neighbors living a mile or more away on the hillsides in their thatched roof huts. Everyday Howard and I went with Dick Sales as he went to visit the different churches and African pastors in his territory. The beauty of the country side was magnificent. The rolling hills and blending colors were breathtaking.

On Sunday, Howard and I went with Dick to a rural church 150 miles away where he installed an African pastor. Most of the churches were built on the top of a high hill so that its members could see their church from long distances and hear the church bell when it was rung for church meetings and worship services. The service was two hours long, and it was cold, windy, and rainy. The church was made out of cement blocks with a corrugated tin roof and a

47

floor made of cow dung. It makes a good hard surface with no odor and is warmer to the feet than cement, which is important because many Africans do not have shoes, especially the children. The seats were wooden benches with no backs. The temperature inside the church was 45 or 50 degrees.

There were several barefooted children who wore little short-sleeved sweaters over their dresses for warmth. I was freezing with two sweaters and a raincoat on. The women sat on one side of the church and the men sat on the other side. Dick said most of the African Congregational churches have more women than men because most men are away in big cities for months at a time, trying to make enough money for their families. The church also had strict rules for membership: absolutely no smoking or drinking, that most men weren't willing to give up entirely so they stayed away from the church, and making it rough on their wives who were sincerely trying to live a Christian life. When their husbands were home, many women couldn't come to church because they had to stay home and cook the dinner. This very serious problem of a divided home made it hard for the church to be vital and growing.

School Time

There was a three-week school holiday when we arrived in Durban so that gave us time to buy the necessary uniforms and get the children registered. The morning session of school was from 8 a.m. to 12:15 p.m. and the afternoon session was from 12:55 to 2:15 p.m. We lived only two blocks from the school so they could dash home for lunch. They were assigned quite a lot of homework. Pam had to study from after school to supper time. Her teacher seemed to expect more from her than Dave's or Mike's teachers. We had to sign all homework so that we knew they accomplished what was assigned to them to do.

Progress in school here entirely depended upon exams at the end of the fourth term in school. They are examined on the whole school year's work—an entirely different concept of schooling from U.S.A. All students were required to know both of the official languages of English and Afrikaans. This meant our children had to learn Afrikaans. Normally the language was taught in the third year, so they were all behind. They were all a little behind in math too. Of course, history and geography took a different emphasis so they had that to contend with too. We were all pleased that they buckled down and worked hard to catch up. We got them each tutoring in math and Afrikaans during vacation time from December 8 until February when the next school year started.

Zulu Language Study

Howard was to spend half-time for the first two years on Zulu study and the other half-time on various treasury duties, and I was to do as much Zulu study as I could fit in. Living five months in the hospital staff rooms gave me lots of free time to study. It was a long, slow grind. We had grammar lessons at the University and also employed a Zulu woman who came to our house three days a week for two-hour sessions in drills for pronunciation and tone.

Zulu language has about 12 tones. Many words are spelled the same, but the tone you put with it gives it its meaning. Neither of us became Zulu speakers. Howard was more realistic than I was and gave up on it long before I did. Work for him became more time-consuming and most of his Zulu contact, such as pastors, knew how to speak English. Our biggest drawback was when we went into the rural areas, and we couldn't speak Zulu well enough to talk with local people.

First Christmas in South Africa

We enjoyed living next to McCord Zulu Hospital during this Christmas season. We heard all the many groups who came to sing carols to the patients. Dave, Pam, and I joined the Zulu student nurse choir (30 in number) one evening that went to all the wards in the hospital and sang carols in English to the patients. Even if they didn't know the words we were singing, I'm sure they sensed the spirit of Christ through our voices raised to Him. On Christmas Day, Santa gave what seemed like a luxurious present, not a necessity, to each patient in all the wards: a bar of soap to the women and a hanky to the men.

The older children and I also helped wrap Christmas presents and sack fruits and nuts for the 200 African employees who worked for the hospital. At the noontime party in Dr. Taylor's garden, the white staff served them a nice meal and one of the doctors dressed as Santa distributed presents, something special they looked forward to each year.

We spent our first Christmas with a missionary family at Maphumulo Rural Mission Home, 70 miles north of Durban. On Christmas Eve, we set out on foot over the countryside with flash lights when eight Africans joined us. They had such good voices and were more familiar with the hilly countryside than we were. No one fell in crossing the river on stepping stones, and Howard carried 5-year-old Ginger across the river. Folks were so surprised and appreciative that we trudged through the countryside to sing beautiful carols, all in Zulu, to them. That was a night for remembering—far different and the most rewarding from any caroling we had ever done.

We all went to the Sunday church service in Zulu at the Mission Station church from 11 a.m. to 1 p.m., and again on Christmas Day from 11:30 a.m. to 2:30 p.m. Our children did real well sitting so long. Christmas entertainment after the service included different groups that sang songs and brought presents wrapped in newspaper or brown sack paper for distribution. Many gifts—like a cabbage leaf, beet leaf, or fowl feather—came from their gardens. Gift tags with someone's name on it said that the giver wanted to give that particular gift for whenever they had need of it in the near future. I thought that was a really nice way of helping each other out. Sometimes they would run short of food, and then they could go and collect their gift.

Indian and Native Markets

One day we took the children to the Indian market to show them what it's like. It was a huge place. One part of the market had meat and smelly, smelly fish, and all kinds of grains and spices. The other section had many stacks of souvenirs. The Indian clerks came out at us from all different directions, urging us to come look, "Make you a good price." They made huge profits during the high tourist months.

The Native market was over a bridge, a block away. At the time we decided to go over the bridge, 600 or 700 others decided to go too. So we really got caught in a walking traffic jam. We were packed like sardines as we inched our way across with small shuffling steps. We were worried about Ginger stumbling and being trampled on, so we managed to get her up on Howard's shoulders, and we all got across safely with a big sigh of relief.

At the Native market there were many, many stacks of flowers and fruits and vegetables. After we moved into our remodeled house and I had to start cooking again, I went to that market every week. I bought two market baskets. Everything you buy is dumped loosely in the baskets, so you had to remember not to buy tomatoes and grapes first or anything that would be squashed. As I drove up to the market, there was a deluge of Indians and African boys that surrounded me, begging to carry my baskets for 6 pence (5 cents) or a shilling (10 cents) and believe me, it was absolutely necessary to have help. Those full baskets are very heavy.

I also would purchase a large, mesh bag holding four or five dozen oranges which the young boy would hand over his shoulder. I soon bought a large wicker basket on wheels to put all my fruits and vegetables in. It took quite a bit of time for shopping because of having to go to a number of shops to buy different types of food. We had plenty of good food all year long because of the tropical climate. It was a big relief not to have to do canning and freezing like I did in the U.S.A.

51

Getting Used to Natal Climate

Spring (March 22 to June 22) was the nicest season of the year, neither too hot nor too chilly. Winter (June 22 to September 22) were the coldest months. It could get down to 45 degrees at night and then rise into 70's in the daytime. We didn't have any heat in our home so we just wore more winter clothing. Fall (September 22 to December 22) was the rainy season, but it wasn't too cold during that time. Summer (December 22 to March 22) was hot and humid. It usually didn't get over 85 degrees, but the humidity matched the temperature so it would have been almost unbearable if the temperature was any higher. We had a big fan on wheels that we rolled to the different rooms. Fortunately, evenings and nights were cool. Most always we used at least a sheet over us.

The biggest battle we had to contend with that first year was skin trouble. Mike had lots of bites most of the time. We thought it was flea bites. Naturally he scratched the bites until they bled and then some places became infected. He started using medicated soap and that helped keep the infection down. David had several bouts of sandworms. They enter into the skin when barefooted. The worms travel and make tunnels just under the skin, and it was itchy. The treatment was to spray with ethyl chloride to kill the worm by freezing. We finally had a rule: no more barefooted Trumbulls when outdoors. When we first arrived, Pam had some Natal sores which were similar to impetigo.

We all had quite a few colds, and Howard had sore throats that he couldn't seem to get rid of. It seemed to be not the healthiest of climates for us. We didn't have any crisp frosts to kill the germs, so we were battling the first year. We gradually built up resistance and began to be a healthier family.

LETTERS, 1961

Friday, January 20, 1961

Dear Mom and All,

We drove as far as Fort Wayne the Wednesday night that we left your house. We were fortunate to have stopped at a motel where the proprietor was sympathetic with the number in our family. Ordinarily, children are $2.50 apiece and an adult room $6, but he gave us two rooms, each with two double beds, for $10. When we got up the next morning we discovered our trailer had a flat tire, so we didn't leave there until after 11:00 a.m. We arrived in Columbus at 5:00 p.m.

The next morning we started out again about 10:30 and we did stop overnight at Fernie's. We finally made up our minds as we were approaching Greensburg at 6:30. Seemed such a shame being so close not to stop. So we called from a gas station and found out they were at the Presbyterian church in Greensburg about a block away from where we were calling. She left word to her baby sitter that if we called, we should call the church and that we did. They had reserved two places for us at their dinner just in case we did come. Everett took our children out to his house while I found my suit to change into. And wouldn't you know, I let the children take the suitcase that had my silk hose in, so went to dinner with bare legs. I had been traveling in slacks. Anyway, the dinner and fellowship was real nice.

Next morning we got up at 5:00 a.m. and were on our way by 6:30. We had good weather and roads all the way from Fern's to Stony Point. We arrived here at 4:00 p.m. and were practically unpacked by dinner time—5:00 p.m. There are 31 adults and 21 children. Eleven of the children go into town to school and ten go to the nursery school in one of the residences here. The teacher is from the Philippines. We've been told that the children cry and cry when they leave Stony Point because they can't take Mrs. Guerreos with them. The children do not just play all day. They are taught finger painting, water colors and crayoning.

They sing and dance to music and they have rhythm bands. They are also taught to say grace before their snack of juice in mid-morning and afternoon, and their manners are particularly guided. They meet from 9:00 a.m. until 4:00 p.m., so I'm free all day for classes. Ginger loves her nursery school. The older children find it a little more advanced here, but they seem to be adjusting fine and they love it here as we do.

Our living quarters are superb. We're going to be very spoiled. We have three connecting rooms—each has two twin beds, built-in desks, drawers, book shelves and lamps, and each has a sink. Our private bathroom facilities are across the hall; there are three rooms. The middle room has the stool and sink, and on either side are rooms with a tub and shower. Back to back with our bathroom facilities is another set of bathroom facilities like ours for the folks on that side of our building, and the other end has the same set-up with laundry, kitchenette, and lounge separating the two ends. There are three such residences, each housing 24 people.

The administration building is where we have our classes and worship and have our meals. There is also a good-sized library in the administration building. We all are responsible for keeping our own rooms and bathrooms clean. We take turns helping in the kitchen, setting tables and putting dishes in the dishwasher. We also have rotating jobs in the library, and we each have to take our turn preparing the daily morning Liturgical worship service and noon intercessory prayer time, and Tuesday and Thursday evening free worship. It was decided that the Tuesday and Thursday evening free worship time would be a good time to share with all how the Holy Spirit has touched our life and how we felt we were called to be Missionaries. I had it Thursday night and had to plan the service, which means to pick out the hymns and scripture reading, and our prayer and our testimony. Howard said I did fine, but I was sure scared.

We are going to have a very intensive five months of study. Howard and I are very pleased with the curriculum. We are looking forward to our learning. There are five major elements in our program:

> *Christian Community and Related Training*
> *Biblical and Theological Basis of Missions*
> *World Issues and Practice of Missions*
> *Cultural Area Study*
> *Linguistics.*

There is extensive reading for all five of the above. We have to have four books read by Monday for our beginning Bible course—I've got two read and two to go.

There are five denominations represented here—Methodist, Presbyterian, Disciples of Christ, American Reformed, and Congregational. We'll have a wonderful opportunity to learn from the others—their ways and traditions. We've got quite a few different vocations represented—M.D.'s, registered nurses, physical therapist, teachers, ministers, secretary, business manager—and the destinations are Taiwan, Congo, Brazil, Sarawak, Indonesia, Iran, Korea, Arabia, Angola, Thailand, North Sudan, India, South Africa, and Nigeria.

There's no Congregational church in town so we've decided to go the Presbyterian church on Sunday, mainly so the children can sing in the choir. It's only a ten-minute walk from here.

I don't know how often I'll be writing. I'm a very slow reader, and there's so much of it, and I do want to learn as much as I can.

Love, Marge and All

Saturday, January 28, 1961

Dear Mom and All,

Mom, your birthday card arrived Thursday right on my birthday— that was good timing and the first word from home, which was gratefully received. Mail call is much looked forward to here. It's not that we aren't content and happy with what we are doing, it's just that binding unity of loved ones that we all need. Marion and Madelyn's, Dot and Jack's, and Caryl and Herman's cards arrived the next day. We are in sympathy with your weather comments as we were going through the same conditions here. However, since we didn't have to battle the elements by driving our car, we could sit in the warmth and comfort of our classroom and admire the beauty that the out-of-doors was clothed in. Birthdays are celebrated here on the last Thursday of each month. It just so happened I was the only one celebrating a birthday in January—which also fell on the day, Thursday, that is set aside for this occasion—so I was treated royally with much recognition and a beautifully lighted and decorated cake. Howard took some slides which will keep the memories vivid. He's also taken slides of the buildings and grounds too. I thank you all for your birthday cards and notes—hope I can do as well as you did.

This past week has been extremely interesting and enlightening to me, a beginner in the knowledge of our Christian faith. Dr. Bernhard Anderson, Dean and Professor of Drew Theological Seminary, stayed here in one of our residences all week and lectured two hours in the morning and two hours in the afternoon to us, Monday through Friday. We had a terrific assignment to fulfill in a week's time, "A Synoptic View of the Whole Bible," which he entitled "The Unfolding Drama of Salvation." I sometimes wonder at the present time how I thought I had anything to back me up. When I made the statement—I have faith—with my small smitterings of revelation. It makes me realize that one truly has to carry on with "faith" no matter how shaky and feeble the foundation may be, and to know that greater and stronger faith and assurance will be given as the need arises. I feel as if my cup is truly overflowing now, as if I know the secret of the ages and you feel like no one else knows and you've got to tell the world. Did you ever feel that way? The thing that subdues me is that I know that my cup that is overflowing now will be replaced by a larger one to fill, and then I'll look back after the larger one overflows and thoroughly shake my head at myself.

Well, anyway, there's one thing I'm sure of which is a great joy to me—that there is a purpose to our existence which gives life meaning. Dr. Anderson's Bible. I wish I had time and space to tell you—and above all I would covet that you all would be interested— I mean with heart as well as mind. I'm saddened with the thought that it's taken half a life time for me to realize what a horrible sinner I am—to think of all the years I've wasted.

A week ago on Saturday we also had a very informative day. Dr. George Cressey, Professor of Geography from Syracuse University, lectured morning and afternoon on geographical aspects of the world, which includes population, agriculture, climate, rainfall, soil, minerals, and politics. Now if only I could retain all this information.

All week each day we had a four-hour reading assignment to prepare for all the lectures. Did my eyes ever get tired, as did everybody else's, and needless to say my brain ceased to absorb after a couple of hours. Maybe after we get used to this pace we'll gradually be able to concentrate longer. Howard and I are grateful for this opportunity to study and grow before we leave for Africa.

Mother, I am enclosing an air mail stamp, and would you please write back the same day as we need some quick information for our sailing visas. I need to know yours and dad's place of birth and date of birth. The latest information we have on our sailing date is June 7 on the S.S. Queen Elizabeth of the Cunard Line, due in England at Southampton on June 12, and we leave England June 15 and arrive in Durban, South Africa July 4th.

Love, Marge

March 11, 1961

Dear Mom and All,

Sorry that so much time has elapsed since last writing to you. Today the children have been taken into the United Nations building for tour and orientation of the functions of the United Nations. They were real excited this morning waiting to take off.

Dad called last night from New York saying he would come to see us this afternoon. We are hoping he can stay a few days. It's really quite inexpensive to stay here. The first night is $2.00 and thereafter $1.00 a night. Breakfast is 75 cents, lunch $1.25, and dinner $2.00. There is a stove and refrigerator in each unit so guests can fix their own meals if they prefer, and would only have the expense of buying their own food. We have an interesting week coming up and Dad would probably enjoy the lectures. Our speakers this week are going to attempt to Communist brainwash us—to show us how it is accomplished and to alert us to signs as we work in foreign lands.

Three or four weeks ago we had a whole week devoted to group dynamics. We were divided up into three groups of ten people in each group. We stayed in the same group for the week. We had no structure and no given agenda from which to work. We met four or six hours a day for a week. We finally discovered by the end of the week the purpose of the "D" groups. "D" meaning diagnostic. We had each member of the group thoroughly diagnosed or pegged as to what role each of us played as a member of the group. Therefore, we were able to objectively see ourselves and improve our contributions to groups that we may participate in, in the future.

It is 3:30 and Dad just arrived, so will continue later.

Sunday, March 12, 1961

Last evening one of the candidates here, who has served five years in Hong Kong, showed us some slides of different countries they had visited on their way home on furlough.

Dad left after breakfast as he had been away from home for two weeks and felt he should get back home to see his family and attend to personal matters.

Two weeks ago we had our first seminar section on all the reading we had assigned to us so far. It was on Basic Issues in a World of Rapid Social, Economic, and Political Change. We will have twenty-four seminars by the end of our course. Three people are in charge of each seminar, which means they have to be well prepared to give a summary and lead the group in discussion. We all have five seminars that we are responsible for.

Since last writing to you we have had several lectures on Communism, scientific revolution, occupational evangelism, and a lecture by Rev. James Lawson, a Negro who has been the initiator of the Negro sit-in in the south.

Last week was a week of personal revelation and insight to all of us. We are grateful to the directors here for providing us with a week of professional psychiatric guidance. Dr. Richard Cox, University of Illinois, College of Medicine, was our lecturer and counselor. He gave five lectures:

"Psychological principles of interpersonal relations"
"Husband-wife relationships"
"Parent-child relationships"
"The Christian home"
"Problems peculiar to missionaries"

And we all had personal counseling with Dr. Cox throughout the week.

If any of you see John Burns March 16 as he speaks to Bonnie's class, give him and his family our best regards.

We haven't had any offers on our home as yet. Things are pretty tight around St. Joseph; quite a few people out of work.

Our Board is considering sending us to Meadville, PA when we finish our course here, to get area cultural study and linguistic study. Meadville is in the northwest part of PA, about a hundred miles north of Fern and Everett's. We will be through here June 3 and will not go to Meadville until June 22. As our plans stand now, the children and I will stay here so the children can finish their school term. Howard will go to Boston for a couple of weeks to get first hand information from our Board as to what they expect of him while he works in Africa. The course at Meadville ends August 9. We are hoping that we will have enough time before our sailing date to make a trip home to see everybody. We haven't been told our sailing date as yet.

What did Caryl find out about Nickie's teeth from Dr. Noble in Benton Harbor? I was glad to hear that you've had help with keeping your driveway plowed out. Thank you for you nice informative letter of February 26th. I suppose you've been wondering what's been happening with us—time seems to have a way of slipping away to easily from me. Do hope we can make it home in August—five or six years is beginning to feel like a long time.

Love to all,

Marge, Howard, Dave, Pam, Mike, and Ginger

April 6, 1961

Dear Mom and All,

It seems as if one thing after another comes up to keep me from getting a letter off to you. I had to participate in leading a seminar yesterday. The subject was Crucial Factors in the communication of the gospel in different religions and cultural situations. Two others who participated in leadership presented a debate on the uniqueness of Christ, which got quite a discussion going. I presented four different well known theologians' approach to Christianity. That was a real struggle for me. But well worth the time I put in trying to understand what they were saying—never would have tackled that deep reading on my own volition.

I looked at the schedule today and discovered we've got three seminars coming up the first of next week and are supposed to have seven required books read by then. But decided to take time out and let you know we are thinking of you all.

The children have been on Easter vacation since last Thursday. On Tuesday, Howard and I and two other couples took the afternoon off and took three carloads of children into New York at Madison Square Garden to see the big three-ring circus. They are different than when I was a little girl—lots more dancing girls and costumed parades. The idea is to attract the adults as well as the children. Yesterday the children presented a hobby display in the administration building—rocks, dolls, stamps, science experiments, favorite books, maps, post cards, and a newly found turtle and snake. Today they were taken in to see a Walt Disney movie "One Hundred and One Dalmatians." Tomorrow two of the ministers are going to skip classes and take the children on a hike, over to a lake. They are going to take a picnic lunch. Tomorrow evening the children are going to present their puppet show that they have been working on in their Saturday morning class. The adults are planning a square dance for tomorrow evening.

We had the surprise of our life last week—Tuesday evening. Howard and I were standing by the office desk next to the front entrance of the administration building, and in walked Uncle Dick and Aunt Iva. As I saw them, I only thought I was thinking about them. It took a few seconds to register that they really were there. Uncle Dick had been attending a National Superintendents' meeting in Philadelphia. They stayed overnight and left after breakfast. They were sorry time didn't permit them to stop and visit with Fern and Everett.

After coming out on top from our Communist brain washing and once more found firm footing, we were again confronted and found ourselves struggling. We had a lecture by a Secularist, who believed only in man and what man could reason and achieve. He wanted us to challenge him, but we knew what we could say about faith would have no meaning. Some people will not or can not accept Special Revelation (meaning beyond man's logic and reasoning). A few days later we had a lecture by a man of Islamic faith, a Buddhist, and a Hindu. This was a time of more soul searching. Fortunately, at this time we had required reading for a seminar that presented the positiveness of the Christian faith. You might be interested in a couple of books I found easy to read and full of meaning: "A Faith for the Nation" by Charles Forman, and "That They May Have Life" by D.T. Niles.

We've started our series of shots for entrance overseas. Dave had a few days of fever from smallpox. We had a typhoid shot Tuesday—

61

only reaction was sore arms. We have two more typhoid shots to go, and then cholera and yellow fever. Actually our place of destination is very healthy, so we've been told, but since we are going through countries where there is typhoid, yellow fever and cholera we have to be protected.

We took the children to the planetarium and Natural History Museum last Saturday. We had the whole day off since it was Easter weekend. Last Thursday afternoon we had a whole afternoon of working outdoors in silence (monk style)—raking, picking up sticks and rocks, etc.

Did Dr. Noble say that it was necessary to take out a couple of teeth before he could straighten Nickie's teeth? I know Martha will enjoy her electric organ. She will have many hours of enjoyment and relaxation. Is Jody's head all right? Has Jim left for California? Still haven't heard about our sailing date yet.

These stapled sheets of paper are statements we presented on the Relationship of the Christian Mission to other Religions. We were put in groups of three to make the statements. The theologians were together, and people of like abilities were put together, etc. I was with a couple of other housewives with no biblical training.

Thanks for your letter, Dottie—likewise, only a small part of these lectures is absorbed. I had three-day measles when I was in training, so I must have missed them in my childhood, too. I'll be anxiously waiting to hear how Bonnie came out in the beauty contest. Thanks for her picture. I can so easily picture Bonnie as a medical technician; do hope she enjoys it. I bet she loves her jalopy. The Tredoux's didn't stop.

Love to all,

Marge, Howard, and children

P.S. I've been sending Fernie a carbon copy.

Sunday, April 9, 1961 [several days included]

Dear Mom and All,

We thought of Bonnie yesterday. We are anxious to hear how she made out.

Friday evening the nursery children entertained us with their songs and band instruments that they have learned in nursery school. The older children had made puppets and made up a skit about the Good Samaritan in their Saturday morning class. They presented their skit after the nursery class performed. They seem to all enjoy showing off their accomplishments. Do hope Howard's pictures turn out good that he took.

Last night eight of us were invited to the director's house for an evening of fun playing parlor games. They are inviting groups of eight to their house periodically with the intention of having all of the candidates in their home before we leave.

We've been attending the Trinity Methodist Church in Stony Point Sunday mornings. When we arrived here, we had decided to visit around at the different churches, but it wasn't working out very well that way. There were just too many new situations facing the children all at once. So out of all the ones we visited we let them choose the one they liked best. The Sunday school is before church, so Howard and I have been attending the adult Sunday school class which is taught by candidates from here. We get into some stimulating discussions at times. We like the minister. He seldom uses notes for his sermons. He gives very simple sermons that give a powerful message. During lent season he presented sermons on the Ten Commandments. Today he did something a little bit different. He explained to the congregation what the word worship means, and why we have a certain order or form to our Christian Worship. He explained that denominations differ in their order. The Methodists have the first part of their service for the confessional, the middle part is instruction through the scripture and sermon, and the last part is the offering—giving praise to God with our gifts and song.

Monday, April 10

We all want to wish Nickie a Happy Birthday today.

We had heavy rainfall all morning; was a good morning to get reading done. We didn't have any lectures or seminars this morning, so could devote the whole time to study. Still have two more books to go for the seminar for Wednesday.

Tuesday, April 11

Today was a free day, so I almost got caught up on my reading. Howard went to New York and purchased a movie projector and a slide projector, and a tripod for his camera.

After supper one of the couples asked us to go to a nearby movie with them, which was a welcome change for me after reading all day. It was a double feature: "Hell Is a City," full of vice and crime. We were glad we walked in the middle of that one and didn't have to see it all. The other one was "Cry for Happy," oriental picture, nothing to rave about.

Wednesday, April 12

We heard from our Board today and our visas have arrived. We leave from New York on the Queen Elizabeth August 23, and dock in Durban September 19. Our visa expires September 26, so we have only one week grace. Do hope we aren't delayed by bad weather. Our course at Meadville is over August 9, so will plan to come home at that time. We don't know exactly how long we will be staying. It will depend on how many details we have to attend to in New York before sailing.

Mom, isn't our reunion the first weekend in August? We are sad that we can't make it home in time for it.

Love,

Marge, Howard and children

P.S. How's the organ playing coming along, Marty?

We've been quite disappointed in our Saturday morning Bible lecture class. We haven't really got too much out of it. Dr. Vander Kock is used to teaching college seminar students who are about ready to become ordained ministers, and his lecturing was geared at too high a level for about half of us that haven't had any Bible training. So we discussed it with him, and from now on he is giving us an assignment for each week to help us get more acquainted with the Bible. Thought I'd send you one—real good questions, aren't they?

Thursday, April 13, 1961 [several days included]

Dear Mom and All,

Seminars are over for this week. They were on the early Missionary Movement, Development of Churches in Other Lands, and past, present and future patterns of Mission–Church Relationships.

Had another typhoid shot tonight. I helped give the shots this time; seemed like old times. It's hard to believe that it's been ten years that I last did any nursing.

Saturday, April 15

I took Pam to a nearby shopping center this afternoon to get what she wanted for her birthday. She decided on dress shoes and a purse. She doesn't like the pointed-toe shoes, so we did quite a bit of shopping around to find what she wanted. Can you imagine Pam taking an 8-1/2 double A?

Sunday, April 16

At 4:30 p.m. all of the adult candidates went into New York City to attend a Pentecostal service. This was a requirement for our course here. The children were taken care of by baby sitters. I had never been to a Pentecostal service before. They certainly do get up a fervor when they sing hymns. Several of the people in the audience played banjos and tambourines. It does seem odd to me to hear so much noise and utterances during prayer and the sermon. The service was entirely in Spanish. Most of the people were Puerto Ricans. It was explained to the congregation that we were visiting them, and what we would be doing in the future. Many greeted us warmly after the service and told us we would be kept in their prayers.

Monday, April 17

Mothers of the fifth grade girls were invited to attend a movie with their daughters at school on menstruation. I had a free hour at one o'clock so went with her. I think it is a good way of informing the girls, and doing it together is beneficial so that they can talk about it intelligently without embarrassment.

Tuesday, April 18

We're really living it up lately. Six of us went to the local theater tonight and saw two very good movies: "Elmer Gantry," written by Sinclair Lewis, is about old-time revival tent meetings. Burt Lancaster won the Academy Award for the best actor in playing the part of Elmer Gantry. The other one was called "The Apartment." We had heard that it won the Academy Award for the best movie. Jack Lemmon played in it. It was very entertaining but rather tragic, because it revealed the actual goings-on of some executive married men in our world of today.

Thursday, April 20

Ginger had her birthday today. Howard and I made her birthday hats out of newspapers—enough for all her nursery classmates— and I bought balloons and animal cookies for her to take over to her school. They had a fun time celebrating her birthday with her. The cook forgot to make her a cake, so she will celebrate again tomorrow with an extra special beautiful cake (says the cook).

Friday, April 21

We wish you a very Happy Birthday, Caryl, and you too, Madelyn.

Ginger received your card, Mom, on Wednesday, and she took it to nursery school. I thought sure she would lose it, but she hasn't yet. She's very proud of it. She had Daddy put her money in a corner of his wallet, and we promised her we'd take her downtown and let her pick out something she would like. She had a real nice birthday.

Love,

Marge and Howard and the children

Friday, April 21, 1961 [several days included]

Dear Mom and All,

For this evening one of the candidates planned an around-the-world program, which we all participated in. The little children did a Japanese dance that their teacher taught them in school. Ginger wore Pam's nightie with a silk head scarf tied over her shoulders, and we made flowers out of crepe paper for their hair. They all carried little paper fans to fan themselves as they danced. Two of the candidates danced an Italian dance. Our one Negro candidate was dressed in a Philippine costume, and she told a Sunday School story to the children. Two of the candidates, who have been in Hong Kong for five years, had Chinese outfits and they sang "Jesus Loves Me" in Chinese. I found a book of games of the different countries we are going to, and we picked out games that we could all play for the rest of the evening—so we had an evening of fun for all.

Sunday, April 23

Yesterday we got a phone call from a minister of a Congregational church in Park Ridge, about 25 miles from here, inviting us to their church service as Rev. Christofersen and his wife were the guest speakers. They have been home from Africa since last September and are retiring from the mission service as soon as their speaking tours are over. They had been in Africa 46 years, working in the same place we are going. In fact, we are replacing them in a sense. He had been doing the work of a treasurer plus his ministerial duties. The minister and wife of the church invited the Christofersens and us to have dinner with them after church. The Christofersens came back to Stony Point with us and stayed a couple of days. They had another speaking engagement Tuesday evening 200 miles north of here. We had a very nice time with them, and Howard learned a lot of information from them that will be useful to him.

Wednesday, April 26

This week's seminar was on the small sects in America, dealing with the possibility and obstacles in working with non-ecumenical Christians. We talked a great deal about the power of the Holy Spirit. The small sects claim to have recovered "the living presence and power of the Holy Spirit." We agreed that our attitude must not be condemning or critical, but an attitude of sharing and learning with each other to enrich our spiritual growth.

Monday, May 1

Just received Fern's letter. She had so many interesting things to say; thought you might enjoy reading all the news in case she doesn't get around to writing to you soon. I bet she's thrilled with her furniture.

Mom, do you suppose we could impose upon you in August when we come home, and stay with you? Maybe the children could stay at Dottie's, Marion's, and Caryl's part of the time. I know we're an awful big group to stay for any length of time.

Madelyn, thank you so much for your letter. My mind is muddled from all this reading; don't know if I can decipher and catalog it for future use or not. I guess time will tell. Congratulations on your leadership awards in Camp Fire work. Why don't you send us the picture in the paper if you've got one floating around—got to see that mustache. By the way, Howard shaved his mustache and left only a goatee—looks rather distinguished. Mike was envious about Marion and John going sucker spearing. Thanks again for your letter.

Love,

Marge and All

P.S. Mom, could you give me the birthday dates of the following: Van, Rommie, Julie, Aunt Soliel, Aunt Lilly and all of the Berhman's children, and Diane?

We still haven't taken Ginger downtown to buy a birthday gift yet. She asks to look in her Daddy's wallet every now and then to see if it's still folded up in one corner.

Friday, April 28, 1961 [several days included]

Dear Mom and All,

This evening we were entertained by a young student from Union Theological Seminary. He presented a one-man act called "A Sense of Salvation." It was certainly different and your imagination had to be stretched quite a ways to get the drift of what he was trying to get across. He used motion, song, drama, art and poetry to portray the title of his presentation. He wanted us to be aware that God is in all activity and creativity. After he graduates he intends to teach college students creative art through drama. After the program, eight of us piled into our car and took him back to his residence in New York and then went on to Greenwich Village (beatnik section) to view the non-conformists, but there were so many tourists like us doing the same thing. We went into a coffee house which likewise was serving mostly tourists. However, we gave the other people something to gawk at, as they thought we were beatniks since Howard had a beard.

Sunday, April 30

This morning Howard and I and the three older children went to a Pentecostal church, a few miles from Stony Point, called "The Full Gospel Church." During the service the minister recognized that we were strangers among them and asked us to stand and introduce ourselves. Their informal ways are refreshing and give a feeling of warmth. I can see where some of our Protestant churches have been thought of as being cold and impersonal. I remember the first day we went to our Congregation church, only one person came up to us and welcomed us in their midst. If we were really looking for Christ that day, we certainly wouldn't have found him in the witness of these so-called Christian people; but then that was in the day before our awakening and we weren't too critical as we would be now.

Tuesday, May 2

Our seminar today was on "Cultural Shock," orienting us on what we might expect to happen to us as we live in a foreign atmosphere. I will share with you a good explanation of cultural shock that I ran across in my reading. Skip this if I am boring you.

Cultural shock is brought on by the anxiety that results from losing all our familiar signs and symbols of social intercourse. These signs or cues include the thousand and one ways in which we orient ourselves to the situations of daily life: when to shake hands and what to say when we meet people, when and how to give tips, how to give orders to servants, how to make purchases, when to accept and when to refuse invitations, when to take statements seriously and when not. These cues—which may be words, gestures, facial expressions, customs, or norms—are acquired by all of us in the course of growing up and are as much a part of our culture as the language we speak or the beliefs we accept. All of us depend for our peace of mind and our efficiency on hundreds of these cues, most of which we do not carry on the level of conscious awareness. When an individual enters a strange culture, all or most of these familiar cues are removed, and he or she is like a fish out of water. No matter how broadminded or full of good will you may be, a series of props have been knocked out from under you, followed by a feeling of frustration and anxiety.

People react to the frustration in much the same way. First, they reject the environment which causes the discomfort: "the ways of the host country are bad because they make us feel bad." Another phase of cultural shock is regression. The home environment suddenly assumes a tremendous importance. To an American, everything American becomes irrationally glorified. All the difficulties and problems are forgotten and only the good things back home are remembered. It usually takes a trip home to bring one back to reality, so-o-o I hope you will understand when we get overseas that my letters will no doubt be expressing a longing to be with all of you and familiar surroundings. We are told that none of us is immune to this cultural shock—at least maybe we will be aware of what is happening to us since we've had this opportunity of discussion and will be more aware of the apparent signs which are causing our state of depression.

Wednesday, May 3

Received your letter this morning. We look forward to hearing all the everyday happenings of everyone We didn't get any of that bad snowstorm that you did.

Do hope Shirley and Jim enjoy their new location. There was certainly a large group of girls in the beauty contest; couldn't see Bonnie too clearly.

I imagine Martha will enjoy playing her organ by ear better than going through all the trouble of learning by note reading. I wish I could have played by ear. What with no musical ability at all, it was extremely difficult for me to learn by note reading, too.

You must have planted your peas quite early, to have them coming up.

Love,

Marge and All

Friday, May 5, 1961 [several days included]

Dear Mom and All,

Today all the fathers and single people left at 7:00 a.m. on a bus to West Virginia to visit rural church development. It's in the coal mining district where the people have been unemployed for a long time and are living mostly on welfare. They will be back next Tuesday night. I'll be anxious to hear of their experience. Howard is going to take pictures. He also took the tape recorder to tape lectures they will be having. All of us mothers had to stay home and take care of our children. We are enjoying ourselves too—just not having an organized program is a welcome change. In the evening all the school age children went to a Walt Disney movie, "The Absent Minded Professor." Dave, Pam and Mike all slept in different rooms with their special pals since all the Daddies were gone. All the moms got together and showed slides we had taken of all the children and social functions and scenery around here; also had a good old-fashioned women's gab fest.

Tuesday, May 9

Our vacation ends today—we gals have thoroughly enjoyed our leisure. During lunch we thought up something silly to greet the returning gang with. We got a long piece of brown wrapping paper and wrote on it, "Welcome to the Convent." Then we bought some packages of black crepe paper and white tissue paper and made nun outfits. When the bus came about nine o'clock we all dashed under the sign with our outfits on and stood there reading our Bibles. Do wish we had a moving picture of that sight, especially when all the nuns ran into their husbands' arms.

Last night I went to the school music festival. David sang in the choir and also played his trombone in the band.

Sunday, May 14

Happy Mother's Day and Happy Birthday to Van.

We've had a weekend of relaxation, mainly due to the first weekend of beautiful weather. Saturday afternoon we were all out in the yard playing badminton, cricket, volleyball, and some were just sunbathing. Saturday evening another couple and Howard and I went to a drive-in movie, "The Great Imposter," with Tony Curtis. Sunday after church and dinner, a carload of us went riding and ended up at Bear Mtn. Park. It's a beautiful rambling park, which appeared to hold all of New York City's residents Sunday.

Monday, May 15

Had a free day today, so went to a shopping district and bought myself a dress for a Mother's Day present.

Received your letter, Mom, and thanks for sending Shirley's letter. I'll send it on to Fern. Thanks for writing; do know how busy you are with your garden now. Thanks for saying we can all stay at your house. I think the best way to do is take a day at a time and see how you're able to stand the troupe.

Martha, we're sorry to hear you're having so much trouble with your car. Do hope our car holds out until we get ready to leave.

You asked when Howard would be going to PA? All of us go to PA. I take the course there, too—of area and linguistic study. Starts June 21ˢᵗ and ends August 9ᵗʰ. Our training period here is over June 3ʳᵈ. Howard will be going by himself to Boston where the "American Board" is located. He will spend two weeks there finding out the ins and outs of his job that he will be expected to be doing overseas. While he is in Boston, the children and I will stay here. Their school lets out the 23ʳᵈ of June; they will have to have their exams a few days early as we will probably leave June 20ᵗʰ or 21ˢᵗ for Meadville, P.A.

We haven't heard from the Burns either. I don't blame Marion for not wanting to build. It takes a lot of time and excess energy. Maybe they'll find a real good buy on another home that will just fit their needs.

Love, Marge

P.S. Thought maybe you'd like to read this little booklet. One of the candidates gave this as his talk in one of our worship services. Send it back when you're through.

Sunday, May 28, 1961 [several days included]

Dear Mom and All,

Time is drawing near when our little Christian community will be disbanding into the outermost parts of the world. This coming week will be our last week when we will all be together. Everybody is taking pictures of everybody else for the years to come, to sharpen our memories of this wonderful five and a half months of learning and fellowship together. Our family gives Thanks for the many Blessings we have received here in this atmosphere of Love.

"Unless one is born anew, he cannot see the kingdom of God," John 3:3. This was the text for the sermon at church this morning. We rejoice that this has meaning for us. I can remember when it was just a group of words which might just as well have been in a foreign language.

Our group was very honored and blessed to have in our midst for three days Bishop Newbigin. He was the Bishop of the Church of South India for a number of years and is now the General Secretary of the International Missionary Council. He lectured to us on Friday and Saturday, and Sunday afternoon the public was invited to hear his talk. Our group sensed the spiritual depth and humility and humbleness as he talked to us individually or in groups, and we enjoyed his presence at our meals.

Sunday evening we had our last Communion Service together—our thoughts were filled with joy and sadness.

Monday, May 29

An outdoor picnic was planned for the supper meal, a steak fry. Yes, you guessed it—rain. The children still got their relay games completed before we had to go inside. We had a wonderful picnic inside. We cooked the steaks over charcoal outside under the overhang of the building.

After the pre-schoolers were tucked in bed we had an evening of entertainment that one of the candidates had creatively organized. She used a Sullivan Song Book and changed some of the wording of the songs to fit the experiences we have had here the last five months. About half of the group here have extremely good singing voices, so there were quite a few solos. We all performed. Howard and I sang with two other people "Merrily Rings the Luncheon Bell." That was pertaining to the bell that is rung before each meal. The program lasted two hours. We have it all on tape, but it's so full of roaring laughter that only we who participated in it would know what it is all about.

Tuesday, May 30

All is not play yet this last week, however, we are finding it hard to settle down to serious thinking and study. Today was the last seminar that I had to participate in leadership. I got real enthused reading up on my subject. I was reading all of Dr. Frank Laubach books on teaching illiterates to read by picture letter charts. His "each one teach one" campaign in the underdeveloped countries is proceeding at a fast pace and is teaching millions the basic principles of reading. Eighty percent in the Union of South Africa are still illiterate.

We are going to Cheshire, Connecticut, this weekend to be commissioned. We are going Saturday afternoon and join the church in their family picnic held late in the afternoon. The church has reserved motel rooms for us Saturday night. After the commissioning and reception in the afternoon we'll be dashing back here to see the Presbyterians be commissioned at eight o'clock in the evening. There are about 13 Presbyterians. They decided they wanted to be commissioned here in the Administration Building. Next year they are planning to commission all the denominations together at one time, which we wanted this year, but quite a few of the candidates had plans to go back to their own church. Cheshire is only a couple of hours drive from here, so some of the candidates say they are going to drive over on Sunday.

Love, Marge

P.S. Just got a letter from Shirley Chase; says her mom has been visiting you and really enjoying herself.

Friday, June 9, 1961

Dear Mom and All,

Howard left for Boston last Monday. He took a carload of our possessions, things we won't be needing at Meadville. The Board will crate them for us. He took the typewriter, so I will have to write my letters now. Howard called me Tuesday night to let me know we will be going by boat. Our sailing date has been changed from August 23rd to August 16th. We are still planning to come home but will know more after he gets home tonight.

We had a very nice weekend last week. We got to Cheshire, Conn. in time for the church picnic Saturday afternoon. We stayed in a motel overnight; T.V. in every room—the children enjoyed that. Sunday morning Mr. Shaw came after us at 8:00 to take us to his home for breakfast. We were at the church at 9:15. They have two services; their membership is about 1,200. From four to six was the reception, and I was amazed at the number of people that came, especially since it was a beautiful day and they could have been off picnicking or out riding. We started home about six o'clock. At seven we stopped at a service station to take Ginger to the bathroom. As she was running across the parking lot she was bumped by a car that was backing up. Fortunately, she was near the edge of the bumper so was thrown clear of the wheels. We took her to the hospital to have her checked and all is well. She just had a scratched knee. We were a mighty thankful family.

Tuesday, June 13

Howard went back to Boston yesterday and will come back on Friday. He's learning how the American Board functions. He's staying in a retired missionary home and is enjoying talking to them and hearing of their experiences.

We are hoping that we can leave school a couple of days early and get home in time for the reunion on August 6th, but we'll have to wait until we get to Meadville to see if they will allow us to leave. We have to be back in New York on the 14th.

Love, Marge

Thursday, June 22, 1961

Dear Mom and All,

We left Stony Point about 10:30 a.m. Tuesday. we pulled a U-Haul trailer, not only for our own baggage but a couple of other families' large trunks that they couldn't get in their cars. It was a pretty heavy load for our car. We had to stop about four times to fill up our radiator with water—it kept boiling dry. No leaks were found. Howard is going to flush the radiator and tubes; we might have some blocked tubes. Anyway, we arrived safely and on time.

Another single girl rode with us. We received a letter from Fern the morning we left Stony Point inviting us to stay overnight at their house. We weren't sure we could get that far the first day, but we made it to Fern and Everett's by 9:45 p.m. in spite of the many stops filling the radiator. The first time was on the express highway. All of a sudden we smelled something hot so had to stop, and no gas station in sight and the radiator steaming. We saw a far house in the distance and had to walk through a big field of oats to get to it to carry a couple of pails of water back. That delayed us about 45 minutes. We had a long, leisurely breakfast with lots of chit-chat. Everett stayed home from work until 9:30. We are hoping that we can get together some weekend. We packed a lunch at Fern's and were off at 11:30, and arrived at this college at 2:45 and were all unpacked by supper time. It's amazing how quickly unpacking goes; it took me a week to pack up, fitting and refitting to get it all in.

We are living in a beautiful dormitory. We have three rooms—two to a room—but no sink in the rooms like at Stony Point and only big community bath facilities and stools a jaunt down the hall. We started our first lectures this morning by Eugene Nida, well known author and linguistic specialist. He's terrific! One of those dynamic people that has a way of knowing how to present his information with all kinds of clever dramatic gestures and examples. Ginger went to her preschool class this morning; it's quite similar to Stony Point but with lots more children. She seemed to enjoy it. Dave, Pam and Mike are with children from ages seven to fourteen, supervised by a recreational director. I think there are about 15 children in that group. All in all there are 80 children from a few months old to 14 years of age, and 130 adults. There are far more denominations represented here than at Stony Point, like Church of God, Baptists, Seventh Day Baptists, Reformed Lutheran, etc.

We are free to study after lunch until two o'clock, and that is when the children are all in their own rooms either napping or reading. We have class from two to four this afternoon. The older children will be going swimming at three o'clock in the indoor pool. There is a life guard. They like it here very much. This college has very beautiful grounds, beautifully landscaped and quite a large area. We have to walk a block or so to the building for the preschoolers, but our lecture building is right across the street from the preschool building. In the afternoon, the preschoolers play outdoors with supervision from two to four o'clock. The meals are very good, cafeteria style. Children under ten have to be seated at a table and the parents have to carry their food to them. Eight of us sit at each table. Our new address is:

> *c/o Missionary Training Conference*
> *South Hall, Allegheny College*
> *Meadville, Pennsylvania*

Love,

Marge and All

Wednesday, July 12, 1961

Dear Mom and All,

Time has gone very fast here. We studied the land, people, culture, and history of the Christian Mission of all of Africa. So you can see we really only scratched the surface in such a short time; it's really a vast complicated continent. Today was our last day of area study. Tomorrow we begin linguistics; will let you know in my next letter what it's like.

It's been very cool here. The local residence people say this is a typical summer—high has been about 75 for the last couple of weeks. We're not complaining a bit—it's easier to study in cool weather. However, the weather seems to be hard on the children's health. All of the toddlers have had temperatures for the last few days, and I know troubles are starting in the preschool class. Ginger didn't go to school yesterday or today. She started having diarrhea and a chest cold with slight temperature. I just gave her water and vitamins C and P yesterday and added orange juice today and she seems to be improving, but I'm going to watch her closely as three of the children have been taken to the hospital with pneumonia. She seems quite her normal self this afternoon, but think I'll just give her water and juice and vitamin C and P for another day yet. I haven't had to miss any school as the older children have been taking turns staying with her. This is the first time she's been sick since she had her tonsils out two years ago.

We hope to start home Saturday morning, August 5th. We will be going to St. Joseph for the ten o'clock service Sunday morning. Dr. Lewis has asked us to give the sermon. Where is our reunion this year? We probably won't have time to make anything but will plan to buy something. Have you any suggestions? We probably can get it Sunday morning. We think we will probably have to start back Saturday morning, August 12th. We plan to stay overnight at Fern's that night and go on to New York Sunday. We are going to need Monday and Tuesday in New York to finish up last minute details. All of us are getting real anxious to come home; little Ginger talks about it every day.

Pam received your letter today. She remarked to me last week that you hadn't written to her and was worried that something was the matter. She looks forward to your letters. To get one addressed especially to her means a lot. Your letter from Stony Point was forwarded here to us. I've been wondering if you are still doing as much work as other years. It's really wonderful that you have such stamina and vigor to keep the pace up, but do hope you won't keep it up when your body says to slow down. Is Dick Jordon still in Africa? Seems to me Marion told me once that he was in Ghana. We would like to buy a second-hand foot locker or trunk. If you still deliver your garden produce, perhaps you could ask some of your customers if they have one. It seems we just keep accumulating things. I will ask Dora, too.

Love, Marge and All

Sunday, July 30, 1961

Dear Mom and All,

We've had a very pleasant day. Fern, Everett, Dough and Diane came in time to go to Sunday school and church with us. We spent a quiet afternoon chatting while the children played. Fern mentioned she had written about coming to Dowagiac on Friday for the reunion, but hadn't heard from anyone and was hoping that it was all right to come. Perhaps we could stay at a motel for a couple of nights if it's inconvenient. Whatever you decide is fine with us. Herbert didn't come with them today as he was earning money on the golf course being a caddy. He has bought a motorcycle and has to earn money to finish paying for it.

David is taking the linguistics course with us. I know he will find the information valuable when he starts to learn a foreign language. I had no idea how much our tongues move to make all the different sounds that we speak. We speak our language so automatically that we pay no attention how it is done, but learning another language is another story. We have to know how each vowel and consonant is spoken by the position of the lips and tongue, and then on top of that, many languages have words that have different meaning but are spelled the same. The only way you can tell the different meaning is by the pitch or tone. Dave is doing well. We've had two tests so far and his grade both times is right between Howard's and mine, and he doesn't do any studying at night like we do.

Pam and Mike have attended the Christian Alliance Church's vacation Bible school, a few blocks down the street, for the past two weeks and they have enjoyed it.

Mom, please don't overdo for the reunion. If you find time running short we'll just buy something in the store. We'd rather not have you tired out for the reunion. We hope to leave here Saturday morning by 8:30, so if all goes well we should arrive late afternoon.

So far we have two days planned while in Dowagiac. Monday we'll be in St. Joseph all day. Howard has much business to tend to and Dave has to go to Dr. Noble to get his braces adjusted, and I'm hoping all the gals I used to know will get together for a chit-chat in the afternoon. In the evening Howard and I are invited to the Upton home, and church members are invited for questions and answers about our training experiences, etc. We plan to spend Friday with Howard's folks, as Al and family are coming on that day.

We will leave Saturday morning, August 12th—see you soon.

Friday, August 18, 1961 (several days included)

Dear Mom and All,

We're having a wonderful experience. We were so surprised to have anyone come to see us off. Fern and Everett and Doug and Diane came, and also the Haskins, who we ate dinner with while in New York, and Marge Harvey. She was in training with us at Stony Point and is sailing this Saturday for the Far East. We received two telegrams: one from a girl in Stony Point and one from Howard's sister Mary, and also a special delivery letter from the Lewises (our minister), and a lovely bouquet of flowers from a member of our church in St. Joseph. They are holding up beautifully. The sea has been calm so far, however, today we notice more rolling, small whitecaps on the ocean. It's too cold and windy to be out on deck today; no sunshine.

The meals are delicious—three or four choices to a meal. We were assigned to a table for the entire trip. We can't quite get used to the spoons. There are two sizes—a small demitasse size and then a tablespoon—no size in between. Maybe that's always what the English people use. We are also having some difficulty understanding the stewards and stewardesses. All the help on board is British.

We went swimming for the first time yesterday in the pool. First time I've swum in ocean water. It smarts the eyes a little and tastes like a good salt gargle, but it's wonderful to swim in. We've gone to a two-hour movie every day. The same movie is shown three times a day. We went on a tour of the ship today to see the accommodations of cabin class and first class facilities, very nice indeed, and it should be for the amount of money those passengers have to pay. The children were invited to a tea party and games this afternoon. Pam and Mike won prizes—a bear puppet and candy.

Saturday, August 19

Pam and Mike entered the children's swim race and contest this afternoon. Dave doesn't like salt water to swim in.

Sunday, August 20

We attended church service in the first class lounge. The Captain leads the service, very Anglican, all liturgical. In the afternoon the children entered the costume parade contest. It was fun for all; we had to make costumes out of what we had on hand. Mike got the most applause. He was a baby. I used the hand towel as a diaper and made a crepe paper bonnet (the steward found me some crepe paper). He crept across the stage with a great big balloon in his mouth, as we couldn't locate a baby bottle. Pam and Ginger dressed as Japanese maidens. I used the bed spread for Pam's dress and the material was perfect, a printed heavy satin. I used two pillowcase covers for Ginger's dress; it was the same material as Pam's dress. They wore crepe paper flowers in their hair and looked so cute. Howard took pictures. Six children won prizes. Mike and Pam got a "Queen Mary" model and Ginger a puppet.

I entered a "make your own hat" contest in the evening. The theme was song titles. The steward found me a piece of pliable cardboard, which I made into a mountain and pinned one of the children's bear puppets to it. "The Bear Went Over the Mountain." Six winners in the hat contest—I won a traveling alarm clock, much appreciated. I was amazed so few entered the contest, only fifteen.

Monday, August 21

This morning we docked at Cherbourg, France to let some passengers off, and they let us off for two hours to see the city. It's such a quaint place. The streets and sidewalks are very narrow, cobbled streets, no super markets, individual shops—one for meats, another for fruits and vegetables, and another for pastries and breads. Bread isn't wrapped; people carry their loaves of long French

83

bread right under their arm. We were told that the bread isn't wrapped in Africa either.

I've just finished packing to have our baggage picked up by 4:00 p.m. We expect to get to Southampton by 8:00 p.m. and catch a train for London at 9:30, arriving there at 11:30. Beastly hour to be traveling with children, isn't it?

Love to all,

Marge

Sunday, August 27, 1961:
Atlantic Ocean, Athlone Castle Ship

Dear Mom and All,

What a life! This is a real vacation—don't even have to make our own bunk beds. We are enjoying the boat trip more than the Queen Mary. This ship is about a third the size of the Queen Mary. Most of the passengers are Tourist Class and we have a lot of sundeck space. The Tourist swimming pool is up on the sundeck. Yesterday was a beautiful sunny day, the first sunny day since we left New York. Today is another gorgeous day and it seems so good to be warm enough up on the sundeck wrapped in a blanket. The meals are even better. They are served in about six-course stages. The children eat breakfast and lunch with us, but in the evening all the children are served their dinner at 5:30 and the adults at 7:00. Yesterday the children had an organized Bingo game in the morning and a children's movie in the afternoon.

We arrived in Southampton last Monday at 7:00 p.m. and couldn't get off the ship until 8:00, so we went up on the high deck and watched them unload all the luggage. A big lifting crane from the dock is used. Luggage is put in a big rope basket with a wooden platform, and then lifted from the ship to the dock where it is separated into last-name alphabetical order. We found ours under the 'T' and so far haven't had any trouble with our baggage. We got

the train to London right at the dock and were all in bed at our
hotel by midnight. The hotel is much like those in America.

Howard had to attend to business all day Tuesday, so the children
and I went on a city tour. The only two places we got out of the bus
were St. Paul's Cathedral and the Tower of London. They were
both very interesting but very trying because of Ginger. What a mob
of people! I didn't dare let go of Ginger's hand a minute. One other
little item I had to cope with was English currency. We went to a
bank and got some money converted into English currency and a
little folder explaining their system. I got along all right. The people
were very friendly and helpful. After we got the children in bed for
the night, Howard and I went for a long walk around the town.
Piccadilly Circus is much like New York's Times Square. We got
quite acquainted with London from our long walks both evenings.
Howard still had some business to attend to Wednesday morning, so
I took the children to Madame Tussauds wax museum—a most
fascinating place to spend a few hours. It's England's historical
famous people in wax, extremely life-like. We met Howard back at
the hotel for lunch and then went to the British Museum of Science
and Industry. We also walked through Kensington Park and Hyde
Park. Oh, what aching feet!

The ship stops at Madeira Islands this afternoon and we can go
ashore for a couple of hours and take a tour. Will have to close—
must get this posted before noon.

Thinking of you all, with love, Marge and All

Sunday, August 28, 1961 [several days included]

Dear Mom and All,

The stop at Madeira Island was quite an experience for Howard
and me and the children. As our ship approached the island we
could see many small boats coming toward us. They were full of all
kinds of wares that the island people make—wicker furniture,
baskets, lace tablecloths, handbags, hats, jewelry, silk embroidered
blouses, etc. They come aboard to sell to the passengers.

More than half the passengers went ashore to take a tour of the island. We were taken ashore by boats from the island, and as soon as you got on the dock many taxi cab drivers were there to nab you for a tour. The lowest price, we were told, was two pounds, which is almost six dollars in our money—for the six of us. We decided to walk a little ways towards town and look around, and while in town a cab driver came up to us and offered to take us for three dollars. Someone told us not to take the tour from the dock, that we could get it cheaper if we walked farther into town, and sure enough. A big percentage of the island population makes their living from the tourist trade.

The island is 35 miles long and about 15 miles wide; population is 300,000. It is a Portuguese island. The language spoken is Portuguese, but the people that own shops and tour drivers speak English to accommodate the tourists. The island is extremely mountainous. Every bit of the land is tiered and used for growing food and flowers. Their main products for export are bananas, paw paws, and grapes. Their homes are all built on the mountainside. Everywhere were people trying to sell you something. Little children would throw a flower at the passing car and keep running after the car, yelling for money. If the taxi stopped to let you out to look at something, someone would always be there to open the car door and expect money for it. Another interesting spectacle to watch were the boys that kept diving for coins that the passengers would throw over the boat railing into the ocean.

Thursday, August 31

We've been having glorious weather. We spend most of our time up on the sundeck near the swimming pool, except during the hottest hours from 11:30 to 2:00. We're all getting good tans. Howard and I signed up for a bridge tournament and discovered we don't play with husbands and wives. Howard played off one of his games yesterday, and he and his partner won so they have to play winners of another set. I haven't played mine yet. Yesterday the children had organized deck games—relay races, etc. Last night all of us went to the movie, *Walt Disney's "White Wilderness." There are only two movies a week on this ship.*

This afternoon the children enter the dress-up parade. They dressed up in the same costumes as on the Queen Mary but didn't win any prizes this time. There were at least a hundred children that entered, and there were many clever original costumes.

Friday, September 1

Today we crossed the Equator Line at 10:00 a.m. It is traditional for passenger boats to put on quite a ceremony when crossing the Equator. The event was held on the sundeck at the swimming pool. Eight passengers were selected ahead of time to participate. One of the ship's crew was dressed as King Neptune and read a decree accusing these people of some misconduct or other. One by one they were placed on a table under a sheet, and some fellow dressed up like a clown and carrying a wooden saw gets under the sheet and pretends to saw the victim up, then throws a hunk of liver into the pool and also some links of sausages (supposed to represent intestines). Catsup is smeared on the victim and then he is led to an ejection chair over the swimming pool where he is painted with colored flour and water paste and a few raw eggs rubbed in his hair, and then ejected into the pool with no warning. Ginger kept crying through most of the affair. She thought it was for real instead of just cutting up in fun.

I started my bridge tournament today, and also ended it today. I was assigned to a partner who hadn't played much bridge. He didn't even know the fundamental rules of bidding, so we were beaten royally by our opponents. Tonight was the dress-up parade for the adults. Howard and I didn't enter. We thought it would be more fun to watch.

We've had interesting chats with lots of people. We've discovered that a lot of the passengers are teachers who have been on holiday with their families. Can you imagine our teachers in the U.S.A. making enough to take a holiday in Europe? A lot of the teachers, especially from Rhodesia, are recruited from England by the Rhodesian Government for a three year contract. Traveling expenses and paid to and from for the first time only.

Tuesday, September 5

The last few days have been cloudy and cold. Good days to stay in the lounge and play bridge. The children have been having a fine time on this ship. They've made lots of friends and have had organized functions every day. This afternoon was a doll dress-up parade for just the girls to enter. Pam doesn't have a doll with her to dress up, so we asked the dining room steward for some raw vegetables and fruits and made a doll out of them. She won a prize for the most original and got a little Scottish boy doll dressed in kilts.

We have really started rolling and rocking today. We were told that we would be entering the Cape rollers today. So far we are all doing fine. I think we've gotten used to the rocking gradually so this isn't affecting us. We will get to Cape Town at 6:00 a.m. Thursday and will leave again Friday morning at 10:00. We will have all day Thursday to tour Cape Town and will mail this while in town.

Happy birthday to Marty on September 22nd. We are anxious to get to Durban and get settled. I dread getting all our possessions through the customs officers.

Love to you all, Marge

Friday, September 22, 1961

Dear Mom and All,

We approached Cape Town September 7th in disappointing weather. In fact, it took almost an hour for the pilot to board our ship to take us into the dock. No big ship is allowed in the port unless a licensed pilot steers the ship into the dock. There is a licensed pilot at each port who comes to the ship in another boat and boards the big *ship by a hanging ladder. Every time the boat rolled with the waves the ladder disappeared five or six feet into the sea. He finally made it and we were exhausted with anxiety, but not seasick. Aren't we six good sailors? We had a marvelous boat trip full of wonderful new experiences. Mike's most recent desire is to someday be a ship crew member.*

As we walked into town at Cape Town, we hardly realized we weren't on American soil. There were several factories near the dock. Table Mountain was covered with a cloud for the entire time we were at Cape Town. In the shopping district were many fine department stores, Woolworth's, and drug stores (called Chemists). The weather was so cold and rainy that we finally ended up going to a movie in the afternoon to get out of the cold and wet. So-o-o, our introduction to sunny Africa wasn't at all sunny.

Two days later we docked at Port Elizabeth in beautiful weather. We were comfortable in our summer clothes. Howard, David and I went on a tour of the city; the other three wanted to stay on the boat. Our last stop was the snake pit where an Indian was demonstrating how gentle snakes are; he didn't convince me in the least. We went to church on Sunday at a Congregational church in Port Elizabeth. After church the minister and his wife invited us to their house for tea. They came from England five years ago to serve this church.

On September 11 at 6:30 a.m., we docked at East London until 4:00 p.m. We took a tour here also, which was by far the most interesting tour. This one was of the scenic countryside whereas the one in Port Elizabeth was mostly of historical places and monuments.

And now—the big day, September 12—we arrived in Durban at 6:30 a.m. It's a beautiful country, just like the pictures we've seen, many tall pastel hotels. It is truly the land of the vacationers. We strained our eye to see if we could recognize any of the mission folks who came to welcome us, but we weren't very successful. They found us first; we stayed on the boat and they came aboard. Ten of them came to greet us and help us with the details of immigration and customs. It was good to have such a fine welcome by so many of the mission family. We got through customs very quickly—only two suitcases were opened. We had 23 pieces of luggage that got off the boat with us. Our possessions that we packed in St. Joseph were shipped on another boat and arrived a few days ago.

We had lunch in Dr. Taylor's garden. The folks that met us at the boat were there also. Dr. Taylor is the senior missionary and will be retiring in two years. They live right next to the Zulu McCord Hospital. Two of the other missionary doctors and their families live across the street from the hospital, and one missionary minister and family a block away from the hospital. We will also live a block away from the hospital. The mission bought the house while we were en route on the boat. The house has to be enlarged and remodeled to accommodate our size of family. At the present time we are living in three rooms of the hospital property and eating our meals with the hospital staff. I don't know how long we will be living here. It may take two or three months to finish our house.

However, we may live there while they are remodeling—time will tell. We will at least stay here another two or three weeks until the plumbing and wiring are done. African homes do not have any built-in cupboards in the kitchen or closets in the bedrooms. People buy their own wardrobes and kitchen cabinets and take them with them when they move. We will be using boxes and crates for cupboards until we can get around to getting something made or bought. I think the thing that surprised and shocked us the most was, there are no screens on the doors and windows of any of the homes. All windows are the casement type windows, and they haven't figured out how to put screens on windows that open out. Flying insects do come in the open windows in the evening when the lights are on. Everybody tells us we will get used to it. Strangely enough we haven't noticed any insects or flies in the daytime, not even around food.

Last Friday we were all invited to stay five days with a missionary couple who are in charge of a rural mission station at Ifafa. Ifafa is 50 miles south of Durban. We had a very interesting five days. They live in a big old home. They have had electricity in their home for a year. The man that Howard replaced lived there about thirty years and raised five children there. The home is in a remote isolated area with African neighbors living a mile or more away on the hillsides in thatched roof huts. Every day Howard and I went with Dick Sales as he visited the different churches and African pastors in his territory. The country is magnificent. The rolling hills and blending of colors is breathtaking. We've taken many pictures.

On Sunday we went with Dick to a church 150 miles away where he installed an African pastor. The service was two hours long and it was very cold, windy and rainy. Inside the church the temperature must have been 45 or 50 degrees. The seats were wooden benches with no backs. The floor was made with cow dung. It makes a good hard surface, no odor, and warmer to the feet than cement, which is important, because many of the Africans do not have shoes, especially the children. There were several children barefooted and with little short-sleeved sweaters over their dresses for warmth. I was freezing with two sweaters and a raincoat on. The women sit on one side of the church and the men on the other side.

There were only a handful of men, but about fifty women. Dick says this is true (the high percentage of women to men) in most of the Bantu (African) Congregational churches. There seem to be several main reasons for this. A great majority of the men are away for months at a time in big cities trying to make enough money to buy food for their families. Another reason is that the church has very strict rules for membership—absolutely no smoking or drinking—and most of the men aren't willing to give that up entirely. So men stay away from the church, and many make it rough for their wives who are sincerely trying to live a Christian life. Many of the women have told the pastor that they can't come to church when their husbands are home on Sunday, because they insist they stay home and cook their dinners. This is a very serious problem for the church. It is very hard for the church to be vital and keep growing when the home is divided.

The first few days we were in Durban the weather was lovely. The temperature was about 75 degrees, but most of the other days have been cloudy and rainy and chilly. This is the start of the rainy season; the last time it had rained was in June. We certainly miss not having heat in the homes. Most of the homes don't even have

91

fireplaces, including ours, to take the chill and darkness out. We are getting used to wearing more clothing indoors to keep warm.

The country roads are very bad during the rainy time, and many times can't be traveled on. Only main roads between cities are paved.

Oh, yes, another item that made an impression on us was the way homes in the country get their water supply. The mission home at Ifafa had a huge cement storage tank that held 1,600 gallons of water. The water is collected during the rainy season from the roof of the home. This water is used for everything, including drinking. The water is not boiled for drinking.

The children are all registered for school. They will start October 11th. There is vacation time right now. They will all start in the class they finished last June, and will go in the next grade in February when the new school year starts. We've bought their school uniforms. Ginger and Pam wear green dresses with white collars, and Dave and Mike wear navy shorts with white shirts and ties. The school is only three blocks from our home.

We start our Zulu study October 2nd and will also be getting an old car that day, assigned to us by the mission. We are all well and getting along fine so far.

Love to all,

Marge and All

Saturday, October 21, 1961

Dear Mom and All,

It's been almost a month since I've written. This letter may reach you before my other letter, because I sent it sea mail which takes about five weeks. From now on I will write less and use this kind of stationary. This letter should reach you in five days.

We've gone so many places and have done and seen so many interesting things that it seems as if we've been here for a long, long time. About a month ago we stayed for three days at Inanda

Mission Station. It is a high school for 300 African girls. It is the only school in our whole mission that the government hasn't taken over. On Saturday afternoon our children played games all afternoon with about 50 of the girls. Our children think they are very nice. Miss Scott, the missionary principal of Inanda, gave our children a very fine compliment. She said the African girls mentioned, "How lovely it would be if there were more children like the Trumbulls." Just plain friendliness is tremendously appreciated by the Africans—especially in this land where they are treated in a sub-human manner. Inanda is 18 miles north of Durban.

A week later we drove to Maphumulo Rural Mission Station in our 1955 Chevy that was assigned to us. Maphumulo is 70 miles north of Durban. The Kaetzels have two children, Carol, 12, and Marsha, 7. The children had a fine time playing school and other activities children indulge in. One of the most interesting events of our stay was taking a hike to the bamboo forest. The trees grow in clumps 50 feet tall. The ground is covered with a thick layer of crunchy dry soft bamboo leaves. Mike found some good natural clay which he brought home. He has been having fun making dishes and baking them in a makeshift outdoor oven that he concocted out of bricks.

The children have been in school for a week and a half. The morning session is from 8:00 to 12:15. The afternoon session is from 12:55 to 2:15. They like getting out of school so early in the afternoon. They are assigned quite a bit of homework. Pam has had to study from after school to supper time. Her teacher seems to expect more from her than Dave's or Mike's teachers. This next month's progress will determine whether they will stay in the grades they are in now or advance with the class in January to the next grades. If they all advance, it will mean they have jumped a grade, according to U.S.A. grades. Instead of being put in the tail end of the grade they had just completed, they were all put in the next grade up. Which means Mike would go into fourth, Pam into seventh, and Dave into eighth. The teachers think by another month they can tell whether they will advance them. The mission families here tell us not to worry about the skipping of a grade, because they often lose a grade coming home on furlough.

This past week Howard, Ginger and I drove to Johannesburg, 450 miles north of Durban, to pick up the mission treasury books that Howard will have to get working on soon. Five American Board mission families live in and around the great gold mining city. It is a tremendous sight to see the huge mountain piles of sand extracted from the mines. On a windy day the whole city is bombarded with a mist of sand.

While we were in Johannesburg we met Dr. and Mrs. Braxall, a white couple, who started the first African school for the blind and deaf in 1938. They had deep compassion for these handicapped African folks, so set out on a speaking tour to raise money to start the school. After it was well established, the government has subsidized them each year for a part of their expenses, but well over half of their expenses are met by money gifts to the school. It was a humbling experience to visit the school. We also visited a Baptist mission hospital for Africans in a rural remote area. In the children's ward there were about 15 to 20 cribs with at least three children in each crib. Sometimes five have to be in one crib. Most of the children in the hospital were suffering from malnutrition. They were a pitiful sight.

We were gone away from home for six days. The three older children stayed at home because of their schooling. A nurse lives in the same building we live in, so they weren't completely alone. They had their meals in the nurses' dining room. Pam cried when we left and was very homesick for us, but other than that all went well.

Our Zulu study is going to be a long, slow grind. We've had five grammar lessons at the university. We have also employed a Zulu woman, who comes to our house three days a week for two hour sessions and drills us for pronunciation and tone. Zulu language has about 12 tones. Many words are spelled the same, but the tone you put with it gives it its meaning.

We are still living in the hospital staff house, and it appears that we will live here way past the first of the year. It's going to take quite awhile getting used to the slow pace of this new land of our. We are all well and happy.

Do hope everyone is fine. We'll be anxiously waiting to hear from you. We got a letter from Dora a few weeks ago. Dave, Pam, Mike and Ginger send their love and kisses. They like it here so far. Everyone has been so kind, and made us so welcome and comfortable.

Love,

Marge and All

Sunday, November 5, 1961

Dear Mom,

We just received a cablegram telling of Herbert's death. We felt great sorrow and shock, and we know how hard it must be on you to accept this loss and to share Fern's and Everett's grief. The cablegram just stated that Herbert died Saturday, November 4th, due to injuries from an auto accident on November 2nd. Was he alone in the car? We are concerned as to whether the whole family was in the car.

I wrote to Fern and Everett and tried to comfort them. How terribly hard it is for us humans to understand why these tragedies have to befall us. I am so thankful that I'm getting a deeper spiritual insight of God and His eternal Love for each of us. Our Christian faith is truly tested at these times of tragedies. It is comforting to realize that God knows of our loss and our heartache, and is there to give us strength and courage to carry on in this earthly life. Can we look to God and trust our lot in life to Him and let him be our guide and consoler? Can we carry on with our duties and responsibilities, and still give our praise and thanks to God even after tragedy has struck? The chapter of "Job" is a beautiful illustration of Faith and Trust, after having all the tragedies and pitfalls of life that any human being can possibly have. The reason why true, deeply sincere Christians can weather their tragedies of life with apparent lack of depression and discouragement and bewilderment, is that they know

95

they are sojourners and strangers in this land, and that their true citizenship is in Heaven, and they know that their purpose in this life on this earth is to be a witness and a bright shining light for Jesus (our salvation).

When this spiritual insight finally breaks into our pit of darkness and purposelessness, and frees us from ourselves—frees us to be willing slaves for Christ—then this life as long as we live is lived in Trust and Faith unto the Lord. That's why death to a Christian is a peaceful exit, free from fear.

We must, as adult Christians, have trust in God and know that Herbert is at Home with Our Father, for didn't Jesus say: "In my Father's house are many mansions. Where I go, I go and prepare a place for you. If it were not so, I would have told you."

We hope you find quietness and peace in prayer at this trying time.

Thanks, Dottie, for your letter.

Love,

Marge and All

Sunday, November 24, 1961

Dear Mom and All,

We hope you all had a fine Thanksgiving dinner with friends and relatives, and gave thanks for all your many blessings. The three missionary families living here in Durban decided to get together for an American Thanksgiving dinner with all the trimmings, down to the pumpkin pie which has to be made from scratch as you can't buy canned pumpkin here.

It appears that we will be living in our three hospital staff bedrooms until February, as contractors and their workers take a three week holiday in December which will delay the finishing of our house considerably. Since we will be living here at the hospital for a few more months, I thought you might be interested in visualizing our physical surroundings. Directly across the street from us is a 330-bed all black and Indian hospital. The only street (McCord Road) that leads to the entrance of the hospital is the one in front of our place. The street is barely wide enough for two cars to pass. There is only parking space for about ten cars. Can you imagine that much space for parking for a 300-bed hospital? The reason that this little street isn't a real traffic jam is that an African cannot afford to own and run a car. It's really a rarity to see an African who owns a car. Many Africans drive cars, but only as chauffeurs and truck drivers.

We face the tuberculosis wing of the hospital. There is an open porch that the patients come out on to get fresh air and sunshine. Much of the time they sing, and the patients that are fairly strong do interpretive tribal dancing to the singing. We've enjoyed watching them and marveled at their cheerfulness in spite of their illness and the constant worry of how their families are being taken care of while they are in the hospital.

McCord Road is teeming all day with Africans of all variety of dress—from typical Western type clothing to gunny sacks to native Kraal attire, which is very colorful. The native dressed African, when she comes into the city, is fully clothed with wrap-around style of many colors of material and beadwork. Their hair is fixed with red clay, which gives an appearance of a hat. They use a block of wood for a pillow, so as not to harm their hairdo. On their legs and arms are at least six inches of wire bracelets. Their earlobes have been stretched and slit so that an ornament as big as half a dollar fits in the lobe. You should see their faces light up when we say to them, "Saubona" (hello). They aren't used to white people showing friendliness and respect for them.

On one side of our abode is a one-court tennis court for the nurses. It is not a cemented court, just hard dirt. In back of the court is the hospital laundry drying yard. They don't have big tumble dryers like in America. Can you visualize the lines and lines of laundry that is put out for the good old sun and wind to dry every day? The laundry is enclosed with brick walls and wire fencing to eliminate theft. There is lots of theft here, mainly due to the fact that the Africans aren't paid a living wage. Howard had one of his best sport shirts taken from our laundry line in the back yard.

In front of our house is a lovely Jacquaranda tree. It looks very oriental in shape and is covered with lavender blossoms that bloom for at least two months or more. Many of the city streets are beautified with these Jacquaranda trees. Also in the front yard there is a large bush about the size and shape of a large lilac bush. It is called "Yesterday, Today, and Tomorrow." When the blossoms first appear, they are white, and then gradually turn blue, so the bush is loaded with some white and some blue blossoms at the same time and the fragrance is heavenly.

Last week we were invited to Umnini Camp with 14 McCord Zulu Hospital student nurses, to have a weekend of fun and relaxation. Umnini Camp is on the Indian Ocean and is the only camp for the African in the whole of South Africa. Dr. Taylor, the senior American Board missionary here, was instrumental in its existence. It was started about eight years ago, with one building being erected with money that was donated by friends and business establishments who were in sympathy with the need of such a place for the Africans. At the present time there are four sleeping buildings and one main big dining room, and several showers and bathroom facilities. Electricity was put in this year. The facilities can accommodate 160 at a time. A slab of wood on the cement floor with a thick piece of felt for a mattress is used for beds. Howard and I had our camping mattresses with us that we inflated for more comfort, but the children got along fine on the camp beds.

The camp is reserved one weekend a month for a group of McCord student nurses. About 15 or 20 at a time come out. So in a year's time, each nurse goes to Umnini Camp twice. Umnini is 26 miles from here. The nurses and their bedding are taken out in the back of a truck. Dave, Pam and Mike rode with them on the truck and had great fun, singing most of the way. Africans love to sing and have good voices. The nurses are organized in work shifts. Half take Saturday's shift cooking and doing dishes, and the other half take Sunday's work shift. Saturday evening is spent in singing or playing games. Sunday worship is held outdoors overlooking the ocean by a big white wooden cross. The chaperones who go with the nurses lead the service. Another missionary family was in charge this time. The

*nurses look forward to their weekend at Umnini with great
expectation. The camp is in much demand and has a waiting list for
groups who want to use it.*

*Thanks so much for your description of Herbie's death. It must be
horribly hard for Fern and Everett now that quietness and routine
has settled upon their lives. Every waking moment must be of
Herbie's last days of struggle for life.*

*I think your idea of putting money aside for the children's
Christmas and birthdays is excellent. It's far too expensive to send
things here, and besides that we have to pay duty on what we receive.
We don't know when we'll run across something to send you. You
may get your Christmas and birthday gifts in the middle of the
summer. We are all well and very happy, but we missed not being
together for Thanksgiving.*

Love, Marge

December 4, 1961

Dear Mom and All,

*We Trumbulls are speeding this letter to you in time to wish you the
"Happiest of Birthdays," Mom.*

*I received a letter from Fernie a couple of weeks ago and I felt quite
encouraged about her rising above her sorrow. She was able to pour
her heart out in writing how the accident happened and the horrible,
anxious hours spent by his bedside. She said, now we have only the
empty bed to look at, the empty chair, the clothes still hanging in the
closet, the food not eaten, the noise not heard, the many friends not
calling. She went on and said—yes, you guessed it—I'm feeling
sorry for myself, but I think I have a right to for awhile, anyway.
However, God is working all the time too, with His healing Grace.
She said their two ministers and a minister friend who lives 30
miles away have helped them a lot, and also the love and prayers of
all of us.*

We are beginning to receive Christmas cards. It does seem odd to us to be nearing Christmas with this beautiful warm and sunny weather.

Last week I received a letter and check of $25 from the Alumni Association from the hospital I graduated from, to use in our work. So we are putting it in our work fund to use for the Africans as the need arises. Last week there was a tornado about 75 miles from here, and quite a few of the Africans lost roofs off their huts, and one Bantu Congregational church and pastor's home was completely destroyed. There was a great response to these people from all the Congregational churches in Natal, European and non-European.

I've been doing quite a bit of sewing lately. I've made drapes for three rooms so far; at the same time I listen to Zulu phrases on the tape recorder. We still cannot understand very much Zulu when we hear it spoken, but we are working hard at it and hope that in two years we can converse with a native Zulu.

The children will be through with school this Friday and go back again January 30th. I'll have to get Ginger outfitted in a uniform next month. She's very excited about starting school.

Tell Bonnie we hope she finds her new learning very challenging and interesting.

Love to all,

Marge and All

December 26, 1961

Dear Mom and All,

Thanks for your Christmas letter, Mom. Well, we have experienced our first Christmas season away from our homeland and in spite of being away from home, it has been a blessed time for us all. We vividly realize the universal significance of Jesus' Birth for all peoples of all lands.

We've enjoyed living next to the hospital during this Christmas season. We heard all the many groups that came to sing carols to the patients. Dave, Pam and I joined the Zulu student nurse choir (30 in number) one evening last week, and went to all the wards in the hospital and sang carols to the patients in English. I don't think many of the patients knew the words we were singing, but I'm sure they sensed the Spirit of Christ through our voices raised to Him.

The older children and I also helped wrap Christmas presents and sacks of fruit and nuts for the 200 African helpers who work for the hospital. The hospital had a Christmas party for the help one day at noontime in Dr. Taylor's garden. The white staff served them a nice meal, and then one of the doctors was dressed in a Santa outfit and distributed presents to all the workers. They look forward each year to this special event. On Christmas Day, Santa goes through all the wards giving a present to each patient, a bar of soap to the women and a hanky to the men. Soap and hankies are a real necessity and a luxury to them.

We spent the Christmas weekend (Saturday through Tuesday) with a missionary family at Maphumulo Rural Mission home, 70 miles north of here. The Kaetzels are both ordained ministers; they have two daughters, Carol, 12, and Marcia, 8. Saturday evening we went caroling by car; four African ladies went with us, 14 in all. We also went again Christmas Eve but on foot this time, over the countryside. Eight Africans joined us, for which we were glad as they have such good voices. Our caroling groups really sounded good, and it was easier finding our way around as they were familiar with the countryside and led us on the beaten paths. We went down and up hills and across a river on stepping stones (and no one fell in). We only had time to go to four different African dwellings. We really surprised the folks, and they were so grateful that we would trudge through the countryside with our flashlights to sing the beautiful carols to them. We all had Zulu hymnbooks, so we sang all the carols in Zulu. Ginger kept up with us real well. Howard carried her across the river, though. That will be a night to remember, far different from any caroling we've ever done and by far the most rewarding.

We all went to the Sunday church service at the mission station church, from 11:00 to 1:00. It was all in Zulu. The children did real well sitting so long. We also went on Christmas Day, from 11:30 to 2:30. After their Christmas religious service they have a Christmas entertainment. Different groups sing songs, and many bring presents to be distributed. All gifts were wrapped in newspaper or brown sack paper. Many gifts were produced from the garden, like a cabbage leaf or a beet or fowl feather with someone's name on it, saying that the giver wants to give them that particular gift whenever they have need of it in the near future.

I'm glad Fern is coming home during the holidays. We think of them so often.

I've never heard of the sausage tree you described. It sounds most interesting.

Love to all,

Marge

CHAPTER 5. Home Away from Home

Moving into Our Own Home, April 1962

It was wonderful to have our own home and to have our own style of cooking again. Dave (13) and Pam (11-1/2) were experimenting with many new dessert recipes, which pleased me to no end since we had a freezer that I could put them in and use as we needed them. We became very accustomed to having morning and afternoon tea (something to drink and a dessert) while living in the staff house of the hospital. I noticed that the children were beginning to get cavities, so we went back to our old way of having fruits between meals.

Our home was very adequate for us. I felt quite guilty when I thought of many Africans, Indians, and Coloreds who had to live in one- or two-bedroom rooms. I seriously doubted that there was another home in South Africa that had as much storage space as we did. Most of the homes did not have built-in closets in bedrooms or cupboards in the kitchen. No basements or attics either. Since our home was to be remodeled, we were given permission to design the remodeling as we wanted it. It took from September until April to complete the remodeling, so you can imagine what a treat it was to finally have our own home again.

In our yard we had a number of fruit trees—mango, guava, paw paw, lemon, grapefruit, and avocado. Our avocado tree was huge and the avocados were about the size of cantaloupe. We bought an avocado picker, which was a long pole with a mesh basket and clipper on the end of the pole. The clipper was operated from the handle of the pole. It worked well in taking the ripe avocados off the tree. We had so many avocados that Mike, our naturally born salesman, decided to try to sell some in the neighborhood.

103

He sold them for 3 cents apiece to whites, so he had no problem selling them, and to blacks he would sell two for a penny, especially if he thought they looked hungry.

Paw paws were about the size of cantaloupe too and about the same color inside with black round seeds. The texture of the fruit was similar to cantaloupe, but the taste was quite different. I don't even know what I could compare it with. The mango was about the size of a pear. The fruit was bright yellow and stringy and very juicy. It was best to be outside to eat them or bend over a sink. We tried hard not to get any of the juice on the outside of our face because it would cause the skin to become reddish, as if you might have an allergy to the fruit. Guavas are round and a bit smaller than a tennis ball, with pale pink fruit under the skin. Again, I can't compare the taste of a guava to what fruits we were used to in the U.S.A.

My First Assignments for the Church, 1962

I was asked to get materials ready for the Bantu churches' vacation bible schools. It was a long tedious job. The theme was on the "Church". I had to sort out stacks and stacks of pictures, and use only the ones that pertained to the lessons on "Church". I divided up crayons, pencils, and paper (which were sent from the churches in the U.S.A.) to send with the pictures. There was one consolation to this job that no one liked to do, and that was getting more familiar with pastor's names and the names of towns and districts where I had to send the papers.

Another assignment I was given was to lecture on nutrition in the rural churches. A new, inexpensive powdered food (like wheat germ) had just come on the market. I bagged it in pound packages and loaded up my car. It was a high protein food. Almost 50% of the African children suffer from kwashiorkor (a protein deficiency) and almost half of those 50% die. The other half is often permanently mentally affected.

I used a flannelgraph to demonstrate the different food groups. It was quite frustrating to talk about the necessity of eating a varied diet because the average person couldn't afford much boughten produce. Their gardens only produced if there was adequate rain. They didn't have long water hoses like we were used to. They carried their pails of water from the river on top of their heads back to their dwelling.

I took a gallon thermos of hot water with me and some brown sugar. I mixed up a big bowl of ProNutro with hot water and a small bit of brown sugar. I made it rather thick so I could drop a bit in each persons hand so they could taste it. We used ProNutro at home because of its good nutritional qualities, but sometimes it is hard trying to promote an inexpensive food substance especially if the African thinks it's only for them and that whites wouldn't use it. Ginger, 5, usually went with me. She was beside me while I was mixing up the ProNutro. She was apparently very hungry and took a bite. I reprimanded her and finally found a little bowl to put some ProNutro in so she could eat some. Guess what! That was the best thing that could have happened. Every bag of ProNutro I brought with me was sold that day.

After that I always took a bowl and spoon for Ginger whenever I did talks on nutrition. It kept her hunger pangs under control and sold my ProNutro.

The Cruelties of Apartheid

We felt a deep sense of frustration as we witnessed the cruelties and injustices of apartheid. We realized we could do nothing about the conditions publicly because we were only guests of South Africa and could be easily asked to leave. However, there were little ways here in the city that we could show kindness and thoughtfulness towards the Africans—like insisting that the store clerks not wait on us first if an African's turn was next. We instructed our children to ride only in the lower part of the double-decker buses because all the other races of people were allowed only on the upper deck. Even if the bottom part was only half-full and the upper part was occupied by thoughtless whites, the driver would not stop to pick up more black people. So often when an African was not on time for work (buses being their only means of transportation), he or she would be severely reprimanded. Without an understanding boss, money would be deducted from their meager paychecks.

Since we lived in a white neighborhood, we decided to put up a cement fence around our home. We wanted to remain friends with our neighbors. We thought it might be a hindrance to our relationship with our neighbors if they saw a lot of black people coming to the front door of our home. That wasn't very common in the African way of life. Blacks were expected to come only to the back door. The more we were around our black friends, the more we respected and admired them for their ability to accept their assigned lot in life and still not let hate and revenge play havoc with their inner spirits. Our personal contacts and relationships with blacks was our main channel of witnessing to the love of Jesus, but it seemed so little. We trusted that God could magnify our effort, perhaps in ways unknown to us.

Dave Becomes a Published Author

Dr. Lasbrey, a lady doctor at McCord Zulu Hospital, sparked David into writing this little story each month. The American Board for World Ministries publishes a letter to the boys and girls of the Congregational Sunday Schools of America. The letters are written by missionaries of different countries and sent to the "American Board". We sent Dave's letter in, and they accepted it for publication:

> *McCord Zulu Hospital*
> *28 McCord Rd.*
> *Durban, Natal*
> *Republic of S. Africa*
> *July 1962*

Dear Boys and Girls,

I am David Trumbull, aged 13 years and the son of the newest missionaries to join the American Board Mission in

South Africa. We sailed from New York on August 16, 1961, and arrived in Durban on September 12, 1961.

Now that we have settled down to life in South Africa, I would like to tell you about Themba, an African boy. He is only 6 years old and his home is 20 miles from Durban in the Umzinyathi Reserve, where only African people live. There is nothing that he and his brother like more than to run down the grassy hill from their kraal (home) to the roadside; there to watch the occasional car go by and to wave to the passenger. Sometimes it is a missionary from Inanda or Durban, sometimes a tourist and often an African gentleman who drives that way. Once it was the Trumbull family!

Busses are plentiful. They are big and noisy and their oily back fire smells terrible and big double wheels churn up clouds of dust. So when a bus comes into sight, the children quickly run uphill, and sit down, breathless, on the clean swept earth near the wattle and mud hut which is their home. There they sit, playing with stones, watching for the next car. I think travelers enjoy seeing those little dark faces, with such bright eyes, breaking into a lovely smile. It makes me, at any rate, feel nice inside, and I smile too, and wave even though I've never met them.

One day Themba's father and mother took him to Durban. They traveled by bus and unfortunately on the return journey there was an accident, and the bus was damaged. Themba, who had been sitting near the door, was thrown down and badly injured. He could not walk at all. His leg was very painful and when his father picked him up, he could not help screaming out loud. He was carried home. It was a long, long way, and the pain became worse. They laid him down on a grass mat on the hard earth floor of their dark hut. All night long, Themba cried and moaned. He could not sleep and was glad he could see the red glow of the coals of the little fire under the black three-legged pot, which always stood in the centre of the hut. There was no chimney and the smoke escaped through the thatch.

Next morning Themba's father said, "You must be brave, my son, you must not cry." But even biting his lip, he could not repress a cry of pain, as he was lifted, and carried to the witch doctor kraal. The old man sat on his haunches under a flat-topped tree. He wore very little clothing except for a skin apron, a crown of animal bones and a necklace of teeth.

107

Calabashes and hide bags contained his herbs and charms.
The fee of R2.00 ($3.00) was paid. Themba opened one
eye and saw the inyanga, and was afraid, terribly afraid. He
was forced to drink something bitter and then his leg began
to hurt even more than before, because the witch doctor
made tiny holes in the skin of the injured leg—to let our the
evil spirits, I suppose. This was too much. Themba fainted
away, and the inyanga danced around him waving his hands
wildly and shouting queer words.

Themba was very weak as they laid him down again on the
floor of his home. He could not even talk. Then a visitor
came to the kraal and spoke quietly to his mother. She was
an African woman dressed in ordinary clothes, quite in
contrast to the tribal costume Themba's parents wore. The
visitor said, "I am Nurse Goba. I was trained at the McCord
Zulu Hospital and live down there near the store. My
children told me that Themba had been injured and I
wondered whether there was anything I could do to help
you."

Presently she knelt beside Themba and smiled at him. "I'll
try not to hurt you." She felt the leg carefully, and then told
his parents that it was broken and, if Themba was ever to
walk again, he must have his bones set and the leg put into
a plaster cast. "The child is very weak", she said. "Would
you not like to take him to the hospital? Shall I go with you?"
Using some long smooth sticks and rags, she carefully
splintered the broken leg and tied it to the other. That was
better, it didn't hurt quite as much when they lifted him into
the hired car, and drove towards Durban.

An hour later they drove up at the entrance to the McCord
Zulu Hospital which stands on a hill overlooking the city.

Then Themba was examined by a real African doctor, Dr.
Ntsepe M.D. An X-ray was taken, and the nurse gave him a
shot in the left arm. Then he was wheeled to the operating
room and he saw green shiny walls, a machine with bright
metal parts, and Dr. Christoferson, an American missionary.
Presently he found himself breathing something rather
strong smelling, and that is all he remembers, until he woke
in the ward lying in a bed, on a mattress between sheets for
the first time in his life. He felt his leg, it was encased in
concrete!

Three days later Mrs. Goba (the nurse) came to the hospital to see Themba, and was glad to see him smiling and quite comfortable. His mother was sitting on a bench next to his bed and was talking to an African lady dressed in a green uniform. This was Miss Nyebezi, the Evangelist. She smiled at Mrs. Goba and said, "I have just been telling Themba that we must thank God for bringing him here and helping the doctor to make him better. But, I find that neither Themba nor his mother know anything about Jesus and His love." Everyday after that Miss Nyembezi stopped at Themba's bedside and told him a story about Jesus. He also learned to sing, in Zulu, a hymn which children everywhere know, "Jesus loves me this I know, for the Bible tells me so . . . ." Themba's father promised that he would allow him to attend the Sunday school held by Mrs. Goba in her home, down in the valley near the store, every Sunday morning.

If you were to visit Natal you might meet Themba by the roadside, and he would smile and wave, and you would smile and wave back to him. When you say your prayers, will you ask God to bless Themba and other little boys like him? Perhaps you would like to make a collection of good pictures of Bible stories for the Umzinyathi Sunday school children. Please post them to me.

Your missionary friend,

David Trumbull

NOTE: Themba is a child of David's imagination, but the picture portrayed in the story above is a true one of day-to-day occurrences in the area served by the McCord Zulu Hospital. David has spent his first months in Africa living at the hospital,* seeing ambulances and cabs driving up the hill and patients carried into the OUT Patients Department. He has become acquainted with the doctors and nurses and has operated the elevator. Miss Nyembezi, lives on the sixth floor of the hospital and so he has taken her for a ride! He has driven with his parents through Umzinyathi area, and waved to boys like Themba and has seen their homes.

*At least twenty percent of patients are non-Christian people.

Dr. Aldith Lasbrey

Rural Roads

When I gave talks on health and nutrition in the rural churches, I was always glad it did not rain. I don't think I could have managed those hilly dirt roads in the rain. There wasn't much money spent on the up keep of rural roads, as not many Africans could afford cars so there really was not much travel on the roads. When a road has to cross a river and it was about ankle deep, they didn't bother building a bridge over the river. You just have to plough through it and hope you can make it to the other side.

One time, when our family was traveling in the rural area, it started to rain. We came to a river several hours later. We got out of the car to investigate the depth of the water and decided it was too deep to cross because of the rain. So we bedded down in the car and hoped the rain would stop. It did stop and by morning the river was back to its normal depth, and we were able to cross to the other side. However, the river was a bit deeper than usual. As we were going down a hill which wasn't very steep, we discovered we had no brakes because they were too wet. We soon were able to downshift into second gear which kept us at a manageable speed. Fortunately, we didn't have to go far to our destination. The brakes worked all right the next day.

LETTERS, 1962

Monday, February 5, 1962

Dear Mom and All,

I think this is the longest span of time that I haven't written. Were you wondering about us? The old egos crop up to say, "We hope so."

The first week in January we were at Inanda home (our mission high school for 300 girls) on vacation, attending our first Mission Council meeting. It was a strenuous week with meetings morning, afternoon and evening, and still not getting through all the agenda. I learned a lot about the mission and the various personalities that week. The biggest issue for the future to be worked out is the integration of Mission Council with Bantu Church. There was much discussion, but very little progress. Out of 31 missionaries, 28 were present and 26 children. An African arts and crafts teacher kept the children busy during the morning.

The children started back to school last Tuesday. Ginger settled into school routine easily, but disturbed because she doesn't have homework to do, as the older children do. This is first grade for her. They don't have kindergarten here. Pam took her to her room the first morning, but she's been on her own since. She finishes at 12:15. The other children come home at 2:30, so take their lunch. They all like their teachers. Dave and Pam have men teachers.

During the summer holidays, Dave was invited to watch several operations in the hospital—two appendectomies, two Caesarean sections, a tonsillectomy and an excision of a facial tumor. His latest comment is, "I think I'll do my internship at McCord's Hospital." It will be interesting to see how many of his decisions later in life will be influenced by these early experiences. Also, the older children have had permission to go up to the non-contagious

111

children's ward to play with the little children, so they are learning many new things and a few Zulu phrases.

When we wrote our Christmas letter back in the middle of December, we thought we would be in our home by now, so that's why we put our new address on our letter. Either address will reach us. It looks like it might be April now before we get in our house.

Last Sat. we took the children to the Indian market to show them what it's like. It's a huge place—one part of the market had meat and smelly, smelly fish and all kinds of grain and spices, the Indian clerks coming at you from all directions urging you to come look. "Make you a good price."

The native market is over a bridge and a block away. At the time we decided to go over the bridge, about six or seven hundred others decided to go, too, so we really got caught in a traffic jam, packed like sardines. We inched our way across with small shuffling steps. We were worried about Ginger stumbling and being trampled on, so we managed to get her on Father's shoulders, and we all got across safely. At the native market are many tables of flowers, fruit and vegetables.

How is Marion feeling now? I received a letter from Aunt Iva. She said Carol is feeling much better. Received Caryl's letter today. Many thanks for all your good birthday wishes. The children gave me a desk pen, and Howard gave me a lovely tea pot with cream and sugar on a tray. You just don't live in S. Africa without a tea set.

Love, Marge

Tuesday, March 6, 1962

Dear Mom and All,

No doubt Dottie told you from her letter I sent her that Ginger has been ill. She is fine now, and fatter than ever. I must limit her bread and potatoes, I guess. Howard has been bothered with sore throat that seems to be hard for him to get rid of—in fact all of our neighbors have been ill with sore throats and colds lately.

Our biggest battle since we have arrived in this tropical land is skin troubles. Mike has had lots of bites most of the time—we think it's fleas. He's been using medicated soap lately, which is helping to cut down on the infection. Naturally he scratches the bites until they bleed and then some have become infected. He seems to be a little improved lately. David has had 2 bouts of sand worm. They have entered into the skin while he was barefooted. They travel and make tunnels just under the skin and it's itchy. The treatment is to spray with ethyl chloride to kill the worm by freezing. The last one was very stubborn, and he was sprayed too much with ethyl chloride and got a bad frost burn, but it's gone—so no more barefooted Trumbulls. When we first arrived, Pam had some Natal sores, which is similar to impetigo, which we cleared up eventually, and she also went through a period of time with having to be uncomfortable with some insect that enjoyed biting her.

The children have had quite a few colds here. Seems to be not the healthiest of climates. It's only 500 feet above sea level, and with no crisp frost to kill the germs and insects. We probably will become accustomed to the climate change in a few years and will be more resistant. I seem to be the only one that hasn't been affected adversely by the change, and I'm enjoying this warm, sunny weather so much.

Each Sunday evening we attend the nurses' evening church service in the nurses' home. Last Sunday a Mr. Flemming, a missionary of the Plymouth Brethren Mission, showed a filmstrip that was narrated by tape recorder on the five missionaries that were killed by the savage Auco Indians in Ecuador in South America in 1956. This filmstrip was mainly on Betty Elliot and her little daughter. Mrs. Elliot is the wife of one of the men that were killed. She and her daughter and Rachel Saint, a sister of one of the men killed, had been living with the Auco Indians since 1958, hoping to tell them and bear witness to the love and life of Christ. Mrs. Elliot said the Auco Indians are not sorry they killed her husband. She is just another woman to them whose husband has been speared. The Aucos do not trust anyone outside their own kin.

The Aucos have no word in their language for "love." They have a phrase for "I believe", but the same phrase can also mean "think about", so they are having a real struggle trying to translate the Bible to the Auco language. Mr. Flemming who showed us the filmstrip, is a brother of Pete Flemming—one who was killed by the Auco Indians.

Love,

Marge

Tuesday, March 6, 1962

Dear Mom and All,

Do you remember when I wrote to you about taking the children to the Native and Indian markets? Not long ago this picture was in the paper, telling about two men being trampled on. This picture doesn't directly show the bridge where it is so congested, but you can get an idea of the masses of Africans and Indians that have to do their shopping on Saturday.

The other newspaper clipping is about a new protein food that is being produced here in Durban. The man, Mr. Hinds, who is responsible for its research and production is chairman of the Zulu McCord Hospital Board. Besides making this protein food, his factory also makes all kinds of cereals, spices, Kool Aid powder, etc. He has been working on perfecting this protein food for almost five years now. He plans to make no profit on it. It is his contribution to the African people.

The health of the African has been going downhill for some years now, mainly due to the change of their living—so many coming to the cities to find work, leaving their kraals and little vegetable gardens and cattle and chickens behind them. And then they find that the wages they receive aren't adequate to buy the right foods for health, and of course some of their selection of wrong food is merely not having been taught what foods they might have to keep their bodies strong and healthy.

It really makes your heart bleed to see the many babies brought into the hospital with a disease called "Kwashiorkor." It's a disease of malnutrition. The condition usually appears from three months of age up to three years, usually after the mother stops breast feeding and the extent of babies food is "mealie meal," which has almost no protein, only starch. The Africans have no refrigeration so can't buy fresh milk, and when they buy canned or powdered, they don't understand the right proportions they have to use. If putting a little in water makes it look like milk, they think the baby is getting milk, and they use such small quantities to make it stretch, because they can't afford to buy it. So you can see why I have gotten very interested in this new protein food. It looks something like fine flaked, pre-cooked cereal, but can be kept without spoiling, and only 2½ ounces or 10 tablespoons a day will keep a child from Kwashiorkor and death. Two and a half ounces costs a penny, whereas to give them the same amount of milk per day for protein would cost 7½ cents. So you can see, where there are a lot of children in the families, they just can't afford milk.

So the important step ahead now is to get the African to see the importance of this new food and to use it. I am meeting every Thursday morning with a few other people at the Hinds factory to discuss ways and methods of informing the general public. One flannelgraph set has been made (using pictures with flannel backing, which stick to a flannel-covered board) for lecturing to groups. I'll keep you posted as to our progress.

Love,

Marge and All

April 3, 1962

Dear Mom and All,

It's been almost a month since I last wrote. We moved into our own home March 17, on a Saturday, but still ate our meals at the hospital staff house until Monday, March 19. I went shopping Mon. for staples and fresh fruit and vegetables. It's quite different shopping here. I usually go right downtown to a department store which has a grocery department, and I get all my canned goods, coffee, tea, sugar, flour, cereals, soaps, etc. I order it one day and it will be delivered the next day with no extra expense (labor is cheap here.)

I get up at 5:30 one day a week and drive to the Indian Market and buy fruits and vegetables to last for a week. I bought two market baskets. Everything you buy is dumped loosely in the basket, so you have to remember not to buy tomatoes and grapes first, or anything that would be squashed.

As one drives up to the market, there is a deluge of Indian and Native boys that surround you, begging to carry your baskets for a six pence or a shilling (five or ten cents), and believe me it's an absolute necessity. Those full baskets are very heavy, and on top of the two baskets full of produce, I usually get a large mesh bag of oranges which has about four or five dozen oranges in it. The boy puts the oranges on his shoulder, and carries the two baskets on his arms.

You'd probably be interested in some of the prices for the food. This is the beginning of the cheap season for oranges. I paid 55 or 75¢ American standard for the bag of oranges, but a few months ago they were expensive, about double that price, but other fruits were in season at that time, like litchis and paw paws, peaches and mangos.

Litchis grow in bunches like grapes, but are the size of huge Robinson strawberries. They have a semi-hard shell which you peel off, and the fruit is whitish-grey in color, and inside is an oblong pit. I can't begin to describe the taste. We all like them, except Ginger. Mangos are another fruit we enjoy. They are the size of a pear, and the thick skin is easily peeled off. The fruit is yellow gold in color, with a pit the size of a pullet egg. They're terribly messy to eat. It's best to stand over a sink so you can wash right afterward.

We were told if we didn't wash, we'd get a rash around our mouths.

Going back to prices again, apples are 25 or 35¢ a dozen, which to me is very expensive, since I used to get them by the bushel to last through the winter. Potatoes are 3¢ a pound. Green peppers, five for 10¢. Pineapples (small), 7¢. The foods that I notice being cheaper is bread at 10¢ for delicious, very solid brown bread; butter, 30¢ a pound, and meats ranging from 20¢ to 45¢ a pound for steaks. I have to go to a butcher for meats, which isn't going to involve too much time because I can buy ahead and put it in the freezer. I'll write real soon again and tell you about our home and surroundings.

Howard has gone to Johannesburg for ten days to the Bantu Congregation Pastors' Conference.

Ginger was ill all last week again. Dr. thinks she had 3-day measles. She had a temp. of 104.4 for a day and night, and then slight temp. for a week. She's back to school again.

Tell Marion we've been thinking of him and hope he's found employment.

Thanks so much for your newsy letter of March 12, Mom.

Love,

Marge and All

April 10, 1962

Dear Mom and All,

Happy Birthday today, Nickie.

See, I'm keeping my promise about writing soon to tell you about our home. It's lovely and we are very proud of it. It's wonderful to have our own place again, and to have our own style of cooking. Dave and Pam have been experimenting with many new dessert recipes—which pleases me to no end since I have a freezer that I can put them in and use as we need them. We aren't having morning and afternoon tea (something to drink + a dessert) as is the custom in this country, as the children are starting to get cavities, so we'll go back to our old way of fruits between meals.

Our home is very adequate for us. I feel quite guilty when I think how many Africans and Indians have to live in one or two rooms. I seriously doubt that there is another home in Africa that has as much storage space as we do. The homes here do not have built-in closets in bedrooms or cupboards in the kitchen. Since our home was to be remodeled, and there was a carpenter who works at the hospital who said he would build it the way we wanted it if we made him a blueprint—so we have built in closets on one end of each bedroom (12 ft. long and up to ceiling, 10 ft.). There is eight feet of hanging space and four feet of wide drawer space in each bedroom, so we don't have to buy dressers.

And our kitchen cupboards are wonderful. The kitchen is about 17 ft. by 11 ft. and the cupboards go all the way around on three sides, of course leaving space for washing machine and suds-saver sink, stove, refrigerator and upright freezer. But the cupboards above the counter go all the way around the three sides, excluding windows and up to ceiling (10 ft.). They are stained a natural dark varnish. A marbleized green ceramic tile is put on the wall between the counter and top cupboards, and that tile is also put on the wall half-way up that doesn't have any cupboards. The counter tops are a cream and light brown tiny brick design. It's similar to Formica, and Howard laid our plastic tile floor (cream and light brown marbleized effect).

The living room, dining room and what's left of kitchen walls and Pam's and our bedrooms are painted a beautiful soft pale pink (my favorite color), and Howard's office and Dave's, Ginger's and Mike's rooms are painted a pretty light teal green. Baths are tiled with green marbleized ceramic tile and floor is brown and cream ceramic tile. The outside of the house is being painted a pastel blue (Howard's favorite) and window trim and doors are terracotta to match the roof tiles.

I have an African girl that helps with the work. She comes five days/week (from 8:00 to 3:00). I pay her five pounds/month

($14). She speaks very good English. The children like her very much. She would like to live in our servants' quarters out in back, but that would mean she'd be working every day plus the weekends. They usually work from 7 to 7:30 with two hours free in the afternoon and two afternoons free during the week. But I don't want anyone full time, as I've got to keep the children in our old routine of helping around the house. I'm really appreciating the help with housework, especially as I will get more involved with church work.

I have my first speaking engagement April 26 on nutritional health. I will demonstrate nutritional health with the aid of a flannelgraph to a large group of church women at their annual conference. I'll need your prayers.

I do hope Marion has found a job, especially one that's easier on his nerves.

Love,

Marge

May 7, 1962

Dear Mom and All,

Our time of year and weather are probably quite like yours now, except we have sunshine most every day. The nights are cool, 50 – 60°, but by noon it warms up to 70°. Howard and I really appreciate our electric blankets. We wish we had bought them for the children, too.

Ginger had a nice birthday party—ten in all, her first party. We celebrated Pam's party on April 27 from 8:00 – 10 p.m. Sixteen nurses came, and we had a jolly time playing games. It's fun being with Africans because they're so responsive and full of gayety.

Last weekend we chaperoned 21 nurses at Camp Umnini. They were a group of new girls that have only been in training for three months. We are glad we got real well acquainted with them when they have so newly started their training. Whenever we go to camp with the nurses, Howard takes pictures of all the girls, and after they are printed, they come to our house and order the ones they want (5¢ each). Then Howard takes the negatives down and gets them printed for them. Pam takes care of all the orders. They only come from 2:30 to 5:30 when she is home from school. The nurses are only allowed to stay 45 minutes.

We told all the girls they are welcome to come and play records or read magazines whenever they would like to get away from the nurses' home. They were a little reluctant to come at first, thinking they would bother me, but they have learned that I go about whatever I have to do and they entertain themselves, and sometimes play with the children or talk with Dave and Pam. We are fortunate to live close to the nurses' home—only about three houses away.

This is really classified as a white area, but there are so many Africans and Indians walking up and down because of the McCord Zulu Hospital that it isn't conspicuous that we have so many Africans come to our home. If we lived in an area where there aren't many Africans, then our white neighbors would report us if they saw Africans come to visit us, so we are in a very good location and using every opportunity we can to mingle with the Africans.

I did my flannelgraph talk and demonstration on nutritional health April 26, and told them about a new dried flaked food they can buy called ProNutro which will prevent their children from getting Kwasharkor, a protein deficiency. Almost 50% of the African children suffer from Kwasharkor, and almost half of that 50% die and the other half are often permanently mentally affected. I have another talk to give on the same thing this Saturday to a small rural church women's group. I feel very green and need a lot more experience before I'll feel I'm doing a very good job. The children and Maria (our girl) are going with me to be my critical advisors this Saturday

Happy Mothers' Day, Mom. I don't know if they celebrate Mothers' Day here or not. I almost forgot about it because I haven't seen any advertisements or heard any talk about it.

Is Marion working?

Love to all,

Marge and All

P.S. Your letter of April 29th just now came. So good to hear from you. I'll answer it later. Congratulations to Jack.

May 1, 1962:   Durban, Natal

Dear Mom and Marty,

The weather here has been lovely! During the Easter weekend the beaches, hotels and parks were just packed full of holiday-makers. In fact, four extra planes and train trips were needed to take people to and from Durban. We went swimming on Easter Sunday at the Beach Swimming Pools.

I'm still struggling through Std. VI (8th grade). Afrikaans is very easy as it is very similar to English. The "R" is rolled, and the "G" is pronounced down in your throat to make a sound like somebody clearing their throat. Also, the "W" is pronounced like the "V" and vice-versa. With that in mind, try this: "Die man werk bare hard" or "The man works very hard."

We are settled down now in our house. It does not have a basement, but some houses do here. I have a bedroom of my own. Mike and Ginger sleep together; so do Inkoskazi and Umfundisi (mother and father in Zulu); and Pam sleeps alone, too.

In our yard we have a mango, paw paw, avocado pear, lemon and banana trees. Bananas cost 1¢ apiece here. Avocado pears are 2½¢ apiece. The paw paw is like a melon, and the mango is stringy and yellow. We have so many pears that Mike has to go sell some of them.

Ginger and Pam had nice birthday parties. Ginger invited all of the little missionary girls. By the time the party was over, mother was very tired. Pam invited African nurses over. They had a wonderful time as they do not get much of a chance to do those things. We weren't as tired as at Ginger's party because the nurses were very quiet and had good behavior.

Mother goes regularly to the market as things are cheaper there, but we never go on Saturday because the crowds are too great. Not too long ago two men were trampled and had to be taken to the hospital.

Also, Mother is lecturing to Africans about nutrition. There is a special ready-cooked food for the Africans called ProNutro. There is 22% protein in it. Next Saturday we are all going to Ifafa, one of our mission stations, as Mother has to lecture out there for the day.

That's all of the news I can think of now, but I am writing this letter at 4:00 p.m., 7th of May, and in Dowagiac it is 9:00 a.m., 7th of May.

Your loving grandson, David

[The following was added to David's letter:]

May 18, 1962

Dear Mom and All,

I see David's letter didn't get sent out so I'll add to it.

I've been neck deep the last two weeks in getting Vacation Bible School equipment ready to send out to the "Bantu Churches." It's a terrific job. I've had to sort stacks and stacks of pictures and use only ones pertaining to the lessons this year, which is the church, and then I have send crayons, pencils, paper for notebooks, etc. That's one consolation of this job that no one likes. I'm getting familiar with the pastors' names, and names of towns or districts where the churches are.

My lecture on ProNutro last Saturday was very successful, says my family, the critics!! I did feel a good rapport, and the women were very thankful for this new food for their babies.

We are having a "welcoming home party" for Maria tonight. (Surprise.) She is going to start living in the servants' quarters tonight. We are having six of her African friends, including her mother, who works about 1½ miles from here.

We enjoyed the picture you sent of you and the snow. We've showed it to lots of people. Now they believe us when we say, "We are glad not to have to battle the snow here."

Love to all, Marge

June 19, 1962

Dear Mom and All,

Did you notice I started out with April up at the top? I get all twisted up trying to remember which month it is. It really feels like April here, but more uncomfortable than in Michigan, that is, inside. The sun at midday is delightful, but oh! the evenings, nights and early mornings. How we wish we had a thermostat that would kick some heat into our cold rooms—55 to 60°. In the evening right after dinner I crawl into bed under my electric blanket and read, and am very comfortable. The African lady who helps me with my Zulu was appalled when I told her that I slept under an electric blanket. She worries about me, fearing I'll be electrocuted. She says she will be glad when summer comes so I won't have to use it.

Yes, I'm still continuing my Zulu language study, but Howard quit about three or four months ago. He was becoming very frustrated trying to find the time to spend on it. There are just too many demands on his time with his job. In fact, every month now he has gone back to his office every evening and weekend, trying to get caught up with all the demands. The real urgency now is getting financial statements and reports ready for Mission Council meeting next week.

Fortunately most of Howard's contact with the Africans is pastors, and they can understand and speak English, but most of my contacts will be with rural church women's groups, who will not know English. My Zulu language progress is very depressing to me. I know I could go leaps and bounds with progress if I could live with an African family for a couple of months, but that's impossible, so I'll just keep plugging away with my study at home.

This past weekend we accompanied another group of nurses to Camp Umnini. Saturday was cloudy and cool, but Sunday was lovely. It was at least 72 at midday, and many of the girls and our children went swimming in the ocean. We go with a group of nurses every other month.

Maria, who works for us, has been living in our servants' quarters for a couple of months now. The Indian home in which she was living was raided by police. She was told she would have to live in an African location, or get police permission to live where she is employed. The day she moved in the servants' quarters we had a surprise welcome party for her. We invited six of her African friends for the evening. I thought she was going to cry, she was so overwhelmed. I guess things like that are just not done for African servants in this country.

Last month David and Mike went on an overnight campout with the Scouts and had a wonderful time. Their first experience with Scout camping. David has plans for going camping for a whole week down the South Coast with five other Boy Scouts in July, when school is out for three weeks. Dave has changed a lot since he started Boy Scouts two months ago. He used to be home every night after school by himself reading, but now most every afternoon he's at the Scout Hall with other boys working toward getting his badges.

David seems to have grown the most since we left the States. He's as tall as I am now.

I was given the job of getting the supplies to the Bantu churches who have Vacation Bible classes in July. It's been a very time-consuming job. I had to sort thousands of pictures and pick out ones pertaining to "the Church." I had to sort out crayons, scissors, paper and pictures and send to all the different Bantu churches.

I'm getting discouraged trying to make cakes here. They fall every time. I've tried all kinds of different methods from advice from others, but no luck. I've even had a man come here to check my oven, and it seems to be all right. We don't have double-acting baking powder here, so I put the baking powder in last, as everyone tells me to. Have you got any words of wisdom for me about cake troubles?

We do not own our home. The McCord Zulu Hospital bought it, and the Mission is renting it from them. Our home is all on one floor. I've not seen any homes here with basements.

No, the oranges do not taste better here. The best oranges are exported, so we local people get the poorer grade.

How do Jack and Marion like their new jobs? We've been thinking of all of you with your lovely warm weather now. Have Marion and Carol's family done any boating or camping this year yet? Wasn't that a coincidence, Wilbur bringing a friend from Southern Africa?

Is Bonnie home for summer vacation now? How is she liking her training, and what about boy friends? Is Nickie dating yet? Deb has started to date now.

Sorry I was so long in writing. I guess I'll have to do like when we were at Stony Point, write like a diary. Otherwise the days fly past and I'm amazed to discover how long it's been since I last wrote.

Love,

Marge

July 27, 1962

Dear Mom and All,

We've been very much on the go since last I wrote to you. The last part of June was our semi-annual Mission Council Meeting at Inanda (20 miles north of here). Our children were in school, so I commuted back and forth each day to the meetings. I got home in time to prepare the evening meal, while Howard remained overnight at Inanda and went to the evening meetings. There is much agenda and business to be hashed over at our Mission Council Meetings.

We were back to normal home routine for only three days and then our whole family went to Maphumulo for a week (where we spent Christmas.) The Congregational African Bantu Churches were having their annual executive conference week there; as many of the missionaries that can leave their jobs try to attend. The women and children (mission families) stay at the mission house and prepare meals. The mission men attend the meetings. There were 20 of us at most every meal.

After returning home and remaining for three days, we took off for Modderpoort, where our African theological training school is. It is about 450 miles north and east of Durban. Howard had to audit the books. We stayed there three full days. One of the days we all climbed into a ten-passenger VW Combi with the Booths (American Board missionaries who run the school) and took a trip into Basutoland. We went up a mountain 2000 feet by car—beautiful country, but oh! so dry and so little food for the cattle, sheep and goats. There are millions of animals that will die of starvation and thirst if rain does not come soon.

Most of the Africans wear Basutu blankets there, from necessity It's lots colder than in Durban. Nights were about 20°, but midday was 65 to 70°. The Basutu Africans seem to be more artistic than Zulus. Many of their huts had pretty designs carved on the mud walls.

While we were in Basutoland, the Booths took us on foot about two miles over hills and valleys and streams to a cave where there are original Bushmen paintings on the walls. Howard took many slides to show you all when we come back home.

After leaving Modderpoort, we went to Johannesburg and stayed with two mission families for three days, and then started for home on Thursday. We stayed at a hotel on Thursday right near Hluhluwe Game Reserve, about 200 miles from Durban. We spent the day on Friday motoring through the game reserve. We took an African guide with us. The only time we got out of the car to go on foot was to go to the place where the white rhino stays. We got within 30 feet of it. The guide said white rhinos don't charge, and besides they can't see, but their sense of smell and hearing is very keen. In spite of the guide's reassurance, we all felt a little uneasy.

We were fortunate to have a giraffe appear in the road ahead of our car, and he went around our car several times. He was so close we could have stuck an arm out of the car and touched him. There were no lions, elephants or tigers at the game reserve.

Mom, thanks so much for your letter. Congratulations to Bonnie and Brian. And thanks heaps to Madelyn for her letter. We hadn't heard from anyone since April, so you can imagine how we felt when a letter arrived from home. We miss you all very much.

Love to all,

Marge and All

August, 1962

Dear Mom,

During the July school holidays (27 June to 23 July) we went to Modderpoort, our theological school for African pastors. The Rev. and Mrs. William R. Booth live there, also American Board missionaries. The school is situated in the Orange Free State, north-west from Natal. Harold, their 13-year old son and I went exploring around the caves and rock paintings there. The paintings were made by Bushmen quite a long time ago, but they can be seen clearly on rock cliffs. They mostly consist of stick-men and wild buffalo.

However, soon we had to leave and traveled further north to Johannesburg, largest city in South Africa, with a population of about 1,000,000. We slept at other American Board missionaries' homes.

Just outside of Johannesburg is our Fellowship Center, called "Wilkespruit." Mr. and Mrs. David H. Rubinstein, American Board missionaries live there with their four children. Steve (12), Peter (9) and I went to the old

127

abandoned gold mine at the Centre. Inside there is a large shaft that goes straight down. We threw a stone into it, and it took ten seconds to reach the bottom! I was just about to go farther inside the mine when suddenly Steve shouted out to me to stop. He than came up to me and shone a flashlight in front of me on the ground. If I had gone one step more, I would not be here to write this letter, for in front of me was another large shaft! I quickly retraced my steps back outside.

On the return journey to Durban, we stopped at the Hluhluwe Game Reserve, a 57,000-acre area in northern Natal, set aside for wild animals. On entering, we only saw different varieties of deer and buck. After stopping at the Rest Camp to hire a guide, we went through the rest of the Reserve. About halfway down the road, we saw a giraffe. It came out to the middle of the road and stood right in front of the car. Every now and then it would flap its ears, which sounded like pistol shots. He walked around the car a couple of times and tried to look in the windows. He would not leave us. The guide told my father to go on, but the giraffe still ran after the car. When we rounded a corner, he stopped and stood looking at us seeming to say, "Why do you run away? Stay with me."

Later we got out of the car and walked across a field to a clearing to see a rhinoceros. He was standing by a tree. The guide took us up as close as 25 feet from the rhino! It turned around, faced us, and flapped its ears. Suddenly it started walking toward us and we retreated—but fast!!

Until next month, Salagahle.

Your missionary friend,

David Trumbull.

P.S. Right now it is nearing the end of winter in Durban. Since late April there has been no rain, and the dirt roads in Natal are like dust pools. I did not go camping down the south coast.

You wrote your letter at 4:00 a.m. South African time.

[Appended to David's letter was the following:]

Friday, August 10, 1962

Dear Mom and All,

David has made carbon copies of this letter to send to Sunday School departments of our three supporting churches, so that's the reason his signature is "Your missionary friend." He's been sending newsletters to the Sunday School classes each month (at least the last three months).

Our family is invited out to Inanda (our African high school for girls) for supper and games tonight with the teaching staff (African and white teachers).

This Sunday we are going on a "field outing" with members of the WildLife Protection Society. It's just a sort of a nature hike—sounds like fun, since we all like being outdoors together. It seems that the only time Howard isn't at the office is when we have planned engagements, so we all look forward to our times together. Howard has enough work to keep two or three people busy, so he's been working evenings and even Sundays that we don't have anything planned.

Write soon.

Love,

Marge and All

September, 1962

Dear Mom,

This month we have been in South Africa a year, but it seems like only a month.

Three weeks ago I obtained 30 silkworms. The worm when it hatches is from an eighth to a quarter of an inch long, and no thicker than a hair. The worms eat mulberry leaves steadily for five weeks. They grow so fast that they shed their skins four times. At the end of five weeks, the silkworm is about 3 inches long and nearly half an inch thick. Now the silkworm is full grown, and is ready to spin its cocoon. First the worm spins the outer covering, or floss of its cocoon. Then it begins to wind a long continuous thread of silk around and around its body. As the worm spins on, it shrinks smaller and smaller, and is finally hidden from view.

Two weeks later, the silk moth emerges from the cocoon. It is rather large and white, with black-lined wings. Its body is short and blunt, with stout legs. From wing tip to wing tip, the moth measures about 2 inches. The female moth lays from 200 to 500 eggs.

We have gone on several nature hikes. The first we went on was near Pinetown, 18 miles west of Durban on a private estate. As we were inexperienced, we took no water or food with us for the hike, but left it in the car. The hike began on a path sloping gently down into a forest. The party (about 40 people) split up and went different ways. My mother and I went with a small group to the bottom of a valley. Soon the telltale signs of tiredness began to slow us up. We met another group coming up from the valley, and some of our group went with them back to the top. Thinking it was not far to the bottom, we went on down.

An hour later, after reaching the bottom, we could hardly walk, and thinking of the upward climb made us feel all the worse. Puffing and panting, we started up. After a while, we were left behind the rest of the group. We had to stop every few yards to rest and as the wind had stopped blowing, that did not help at all. Arriving at the top, we just about collapsed. After a lunch and a rest, we felt much better.

The next outing we went on was to St. Thomas Bay, 35 miles north of Durban on the Indian Ocean. The morning was spent in looking at sea life in the numerous rock pools. There were sea anemones, shells, crabs, red and green seaweed and many varieties of tropical fish. Just before lunch, we went swimming in the swimming pool at the beach. We had lunch and spent the remainder of the afternoon resting on the beach.

The third outing that we went to was 40 miles south of Durban, and then inland to a small river, this time to go bird watching. Most of the group went on to a field, but we stayed by the river. In South African rivers there is a disease called bilharziasis which originates from certain snails. The parasite causes damage to vital organs. We wanted to wade, but we were afraid of catching the disease. But then one of the bird-watchers said the river was bilharziasis-free, and before you could say "Jack Robinson" we were wading in the river as it was only ankle-deep. We had a picnic lunch and went home.

That's all the news, so until next month, Salakahle.

Your missionary friend,

David Trumbull

[Appended to David's letter was this from Marge:]

Dear Mom,

I suppose you're wondering what's been happening to us, just as we keep looking for word from home. All is well with us, but we miss hearing from you.

David wants to get this sent out, so I just wanted to dash a note to you and let you know I'll be writing this next week. This afternoon I have to go to one of our rural churches and give another flannelgraph talk. It is very cloudy and cool - not raining yet. Do hope it holds off until I get back. I don't like going on the dirt roads when it's raining. Also have to cross an ankle-deep river with the car. I'll let you know how I make out.

Love,

Marge

October 2, 1962

Dear Mom and All,

Just after last writing to you, I went to another health demonstration class geared for teaching the Africans. I met Kay Wolfson there. She is the artist who draws and makes the flannelgraphs that are used to tell the story to the Africans of how they can help themselves to better health. Kay and I liked each other right away, and we got to discussing what we did for recreation. She belongs to a wildlife preservation group and also a bird-watching group. They have outings about once a month on Sundays. On August 12 she invited our family to go with their WildLife Group on a hike. What a hike! Four hours of it—away down in a valley and up again. I thought I would never make it—how out of condition I am! I am not doing my own housework. After having our picnic lunch on the lawn of this beautiful private estate, we felt like new people again.

In the afternoon we were taken on a tour of the farm. This is a dairy, pig and poultry farm, on a big business scale. So you can see we had a most interesting day. Since then we have been on two other outings, each as interesting and very different. We are getting acquainted with parts of Africa that we never would if I had not met Kay. It's fun being with real nature lovers.

Mike decided not to have a party on his birthday as everyone else does. His one request was to be taken down to the boat dock when the Athlone Castle boat was in dock. That was the boat we came from England on. He wanted to visit a couple of deck stewards that he became fast pals with. So that we did and his birthday was complete.

On August 27 Ginger came down with the hard measles. She was very ill for a good week and very tired and no pep for another two weeks. But all is well now, and she is fatter than ever.

About a month ago, Howard had an accident with his motor scooter. An African was crossing an intersection and got confused when he saw Howard coming toward him on his scooter. Instead of continuing to cross the street, he dashed back, which made Howard swerve quickly to avoid hitting him, so he tipped over, but fortunately wasn't hurt badly. He had the wind knocked out of him, and also skin abrasions, which are healed up now. He ruined his pants, shirt and sports coat, but our insurance covered some of that expense.

I have given six health talks in the last two months, and am getting the Africans acquainted with a new dried prepared food which is made entirely from protein foods. It's so sad seeing so many of their babies dying from protein deficiency. After telling the story about health in the rural areas, I leave a 40-pound bag of ProNutro with

*the pastor at his home, and the people come to buy it from him for 8
cents a pound, which lasts one child a week. It looks as if I'm going
to have a pretty full time job keeping the pastors supplied with
enough ProNutro.*

*Last Friday when I started out, it looked very much like rain, but
fortunately it held off until after I got home. I don't think I could
have managed these hilly dirt roads in the rain. There isn't much
money used on the rural roads as not many Africans can afford
cars, so when a road has to cross a river that's about ankle deep,
they don't bother building a bridge. You just have to plow through
it and hope you make it. I had to go through two last Friday.
The second one was a little deeper than the first. I got across all
right, but as I started to go down a hill, I discovered I had no
brakes. The hill wasn't steep, and as soon as I could, I shifted into
first gear for the rest of the trip. I managed all right in spite of the
steep hills. It's beautiful country there—hills and valleys as far as
the eye can see.*

*The children are on school holiday this week. Dave and Pam are at
a Christian non-denomination camp. It's up in the Drakensburg
Mountains about 150 miles north of here. They left on a train
Friday night, 1520 boys and 72 girls. The girls' and boys' camps
are 15 miles apart. We thought the camp fees are reasonable—$14
each. That includes all their food and train fare and one all-day
excursion trip. Pam was packed a good week ahead of time, packed
and repacked many times, much to David's amazement. He packed
the night before leaving, and no repacking. He's beginning to
realize that boys and girls are quite different in their thinking and
attitudes.*

*Maria doesn't work for us anymore. She is getting married. Seems
quite nice to have our home to ourselves for a change, but of course
the work is always to be done and by us. We haven't decided what
to do about hiring anyone else yet. If I didn't have outside work
(church) to do, I'd like to keep up my own home. Of course that's a
little hard to convince yourself that that's the right thing to do when
so many people are starving because of no work.*

Received your letter yesterday, Mom, and as you can see, that's all it took to get me inspired to sit right down and write back. I certainly would have liked to see your garden and taste the produce. Sorry to hear about Malcolm and Julie. Be sure and tell me next time you write how they are doing.

We haven't heard a word about whether the American Board is going to accept David's letter for publication. Sparkie and Jodie are nearsighted, and our children are farsighted.

We miss you all so very much.

Marge and All

Tuesday, October 9, 1962

Dear Mom and All,

I picked Dave and Pam up from the train Sat. evening by taxi, as Howard and five others drove our car to Rhodesia. They went to meet with Dr. Marcus, our field secretary from New York, who is a Negro. He was not granted a visa to enter South Africa, so some had to go to Rhodesia to meet with him and discuss problems.

It was good to have Dave and Pam home again after their week away at a camp. Pam said that she was a little homesick at first until she was there a day of two, and then made lots of friends. By the end of the week, it was a sad departure for all the campers. Pam was so anxious to tell us all that they did and her impressions of the campsite, her tent mates and camp councilor in each tent. She was spiritually refreshed by being with such wonderful, dedicated leaders. Dave's impressions come out little by little as the days pass. I'm very glad Pam likes to chitter-chatter so much with me. It will be a great help to us as she goes through the ups and downs of her approaching teenage years.

One afternoon while Dave and Pam were away, I took Mike and Ginger to a downtown theater. We saw Walt Disney's "Jungle Cat." Ginger was a little frightened of some of the animal fights, but she managed to watch it all without hiding her face. The downtown theaters are very plush—soft cushioned seats and thick carpeting. Afternoon prices are adults 50¢ and children under 12, 18¢. In the evening all pay the same price, 85¢, so we don't go as a whole family in the evening. And the drive-in theaters aren't so very reasonable for us any more either as we have to pay for Dave, Pam and Mike now. All children over 10 have to pay. On the weekends the tickets are 60¢.

Last Thursday, Mike and Ginger went with me to give my flannelgraph talk to one of our churches at KwaMashu. They were a big help to me. They passed out leaflets on ProNutro (a dried, flaked prepared food—looks like prepared baby cereal.) They helped pass ProNutro around to the Africans in its dry form and then, after I made it into a porridge by adding hot water and a little brown sugar, they passed that around. I make it real thick so it can be spooned into the palm of a hand. We had an extra excitement that afternoon. One of the African ladies went into an epileptic seizure. Ginger was quite frightened and started to cry, and Mike was all eyes taking it all in.

KwaMashu is an African location 15 miles from here. The houses are made of brick, four rooms side by side. All the houses are alike, made by the government. Over 10,000 Africans live here. We hear that at least 10 Africans are housed in each four-room house. This is very alien to their way of living, but that's urbanization for you. The church pastor had to get a pass for me so that I would be allowed to enter the location. When we returned home (6:00 p.m.), Howard took us out for hamburgs and milk shakes and the drive-in movie "Swiss Family Robinson."

Howard will be back from Rhodesia Friday or Saturday of this week. I'm keeping myself real busy doing my own housework now that Maria isn't with us any more. I still haven't decided to get anybody else yet—seems so good to have our home to ourselves.

I'm still studying Zulu. I have one hour of grammar lesson and one hour of conversation a week. The lady that used to come every day and read Zulu readers with me has a full-time job now, so I'm practically on my own. I bought a pocket book of Basic English,

135

and am translating all the English sentences into Zulu. It's good practice because there is a lot of repetition in the translating. When I hear someone talking in Zulu, I only understand a few words of what they are talking about, and I'm still too frightened to try to converse with anyone for fear of not being able to understand what they say back to me.

Monday, October 15, 1962

Dear Mom and All,

We received your air mail letter today. Thanks so much for sending Bonnie's clippings and her both parents in the picture. It's good to have a recent picture of Dot and Jack, too. I bet Bonnie is glad she decided to go on to school and get some extra training. I sure am for her.

David was all sparkle when you were praising him for his letterwriting. I do hope he keeps writing to the Sunday School. Howard hasn't written to the church since last Christmas, and I've only written about three letters.

Howard got back from Rhodesia at midnight Thursday night. He said it was quite hot there. It's lots nearer the equator than Durban. He brought back a fruit called a monkey orange. It's as big as a grapefruit and is green and has a very hard outer skin. We haven't opened it up yet to see what it looks like inside.

Did the box of gifts I sent you cost you any money? Your letters are a blessing to all of us.

Love to all,

Marge

Tuesday, October 30, 1962

Dear Mom and All,

You should see my flowers blooming in the yard—cannas, mums, hydrangea, lilies and flowering shrubs. They were all put in about three weeks ago. Mrs. Taylor, senior missionary, is an avid gardener. She has a lovely big yard with flowers galore. She asked two of the hospital yardmen to help her thin her flower beds, and she had them bring them over here and plant them for me, with her supervision, so they were put in right, and in the right places.

Our grass is doing well that was planted last May, not by seed but by grass roots placed ten inches apart. The roots spread and eventually all empty spots are filled with grass—that is, if you can keep the never-ending weeds out. Every day since last May the children have had to spend a half hour weeding. Most families have African yardboys. White people just don't do menial work here, at least Mom and Pop can't get their children to help with the household tasks. I feel lucky to have been able to bring up our children in America where home responsibilities are shared. They seem to accept their share of the work quite willingly, in spite of the fact that their friends do none.

Two weeks ago the children and I went to Camp Umnini with the P.T.S. nurses. They are girls that have just started their training. What a difference it is going with these girls. They are really full of energy. We played all kinds of games on the beach Sat. afternoon. It was too cloudy and cool for swimming. Dr. Lasbrey (woman) also came for the weekend. She did the Sunday morning service. We had our service overlooking the ocean. It was still cloudy and cool so it wasn't too bright or hot. Howard stayed home to catch up on some of his work. How we miss him!

An Indian doctor who works at the hospital has a brother who owns an elegant theater for Indians, strictly out of bounds for whites. But occasionally when there is an excellent movie showing, he invites Dr. and Mrs. Taylor and tells them they may invite at least eight of their friends to go. Fortunately we've always been asked to go with them. Tonight we are going to see "Ballad of a Soldier". It's a Russian movie, but with English dubbed in. The Indian doctor takes us as his guests.

Ever since Fern told us about Diane getting a kitty, Ginger has been green with envy. The weekend we were out at camp with the nurses, she found a kitty to play with, and I think spent most of the weekend with it. When we were ready to come home, we found it tucked safely in the car. We didn't take it home with us, but I made up my mind to give in and get her a kitty.

The very next day, we heard that the family a few houses from us was trying to give kitties away, so Pam went over and picked out a male kitten, all black except for white paws and white under its neck like a necktie. Ginger has named it Socks. She has a story of a black kitten with white paws that is named Socks. She dearly loves it and races from school each day to be with it. We keep it in the bathroom with a box of dirt. He has learned to use the box of dirt now.

This is the time of year for firecrackers to be used here. Friday and Saturday was the Indian religious celebration called Despavali. It is the Festival of Symbolic Lights. It is the celebration of Good overcoming Evil. Many firecrackers are used in the celebration. They also exchange gifts at this time, and distribute food parcels to hundreds of poor and needy families.

While we were playing bridge Saturday evening with the Taylors, an Indian doctor who took his internship at McCord Hospital came over to bring Dr. Taylor a gift of Indian pastries which we thoroughly enjoyed during the evening. This Indian doctor has a private practice at Pinetown, 15 miles from here. He watched us play bridge for a while and said he'd like to play with us sometime. He learned to play bridge while at the University. He's a single fellow, but he knows of another Indian doctor who likes to play. We are going to give him a call one of these days and make a date to play. We think it will be a good opportunity to get to know some of the Indian people here through him.

We'd like to go to an Indian wedding sometime. The Indian people are so much more industrious and progressive than the Africans. They remind us of the Jewish race in America.

*How are Marion and Madelyn now? Is Julie still feeling good?
How's Malcolm? Tell Malcolm, Girlie and Aunt Lilly that we
are praying for them in our morning family devotion time, that they
might be comforted and strengthened through the Holy Spirit at this
most trying time for them.*

*Doesn't seem possible that Christmas is approaching so soon again.
As it looks now, I don't see how Howard is going to find time to
write our annual Christmas letter. He works evenings and
weekends.*

Write soon.

Love,

Marge

Monday, November 26, 1962

Dear Mom and All,

*Have you ever heard of Guy Fawkes? He tried to blow up the
King and Parliament in England on Nov. 5, 1605. Ever since
that day, England and South Africa and probably other countries
with English ancestors celebrate "Guy Fawkes Day" on Nov. 5,
much like we celebrate the 4th of July. But with far more
enthusiasm because firecrackers can be purchased here ranging from
teensy ones to the big jet rockets.*

*We had a real bang-up night Nov. 4. Our neighbors next door
invited us to their house for a potluck supper and fireworks. They
own a grocery shop, and decided to shoot off all the fireworks they
didn't sell. We had enough fireworks to shoot off constantly from
7:00 to 9:30. What a treat for the children!*

*Dr. Malcolm, who has been teaching me Zulu grammar for over a
year now, died of a heart attack last week. He was 77. He has
always been interested in helping the Africans. His latest project
was translating a book of Zulu poetry into English. He's been a
lecturer on Zulu at Natal University for the past 17 years. For*

139

many years he has taught missionaries Zulu grammar and with no charge.

A couple of weekends ago the children and I went to Camp Umnini to chaperone a group of nurses. Howard couldn't go, and he had to use our car that weekend, so I used one of the hospital's cars. What a time I had! It was bad enough driving a strange car, but on top of that, the rearview mirror wouldn't stay in position, and the gears locked once. Fortunately I wasn't far from a gas station, and one of the attendants came and raised the hood and unlocked the gears. I was told later that that car quite frequently had that trouble. When the attendant put the hood down, the latch didn't catch, and after I had driven about half a block down the street, the hood flew up. I thought "What next?" Anyway we arrived home safely.

Dr. Marcus, our field secretary from New York was finally granted a visa to enter South Africa. He is an American Negro. He had been a pastor for ten years at a predominately white church in Ohio. We were all very much impressed with his wisdom and deep Christian faith. We were all spiritually enriched by being in his presence. I heard him preach four times this past week in our African churches, and not once did he refer to a note. The African people were so curious about him—they were so surprised that he looked quite like them and surprised to hear the there are 20,000,000 Negroes in America.

Dr. Marcus was at our house on Thanksgiving, and we enjoyed together the traditional turkey dinner with all the trimmings, down to the pumpkin pie. We thought of you all and wished we could be with you, too.

I was kept pretty busy last week with dinner guests. I think we had someone here every night but Saturday. We do a lot of dinner entertaining—that goes with our job. We all enjoy it very much. We meet some very interesting people. Lots of folks are here in Durban from out of town to joint church meetings, etc., so Howard invites a few to dinner every now and then. This Friday we are having a couple of fellows from Cape Town stay with us. Last week we entertained two missionaries from Angola, the trouble spot.

They were on their way home to America. Their wives and children had gone home in early 1961 because of the grave danger to missionaries.

We have just discovered our home is being eaten from under us. For the past two nights in our bedroom, we were bombarded with hundreds of flying ants. We couldn't figure out where they were coming from. This the time of year when they make an appearance, so we close the windows in the evening when we have our lights on to keep them out of the house, but in spite of doing this, our bedroom was loaded. We finally discovered a mound of dirt under my desk. They had built a huge dirt pyramid under the floor and had eaten their way through the floor. Flying ants are termites. So our house is being treated and ant poison pumped into that huge pyramid under the house.

Did you go to Fern's for Thanksgiving? I hope so, because that certainly would have helped Fernie keep her mind off Herbie. This month was probably not an easy time for them. We have prayed for them every morning in our family devotions time for the month of Nov.

I don't know either of the doctors you mentioned that Malcolm is being treated by. No, there is no "trick or treating" here and the children feel cheated, too.

The children are writing their final exams this week and next. Their exams determine their whole mark—daily class work is not counted. They will be out of school Dec. 7th until Jan. 31st.

We hope that you all are well and happy and not too bogged down with work. All is well with all of us, for which we are grateful to God.

Love,

Marge

Wednesday, December 5, 1962

Dear Mom,

We all wish you a Happy Birthday. These years roll around too fast, don't they? We received a letter from Madelyn about the purchase of a power mower for your birthday and Christmas. We hope you like it. Wish we had a power mower. Dave does our mowing with a hand mower, but we thought since we'll be leaving here for home in another four years, we didn't want to put so much money into a power mower. And no doubt storing it for a year in this ocean salt air wouldn't be very good for it.

The letter I wrote to you on Nov. 26th may be six weeks in getting to you as I think I forgot to put the extra 5¢ stamp on the envelope.

The children are through with their exams now, and will be out of school this Friday until Jan. 31st.

We'll be having dinner by ourselves tonight for a change. The two fellows from Cape Town that have been with us since Thursday left today. They both played bridge, so we had a good relaxing time playing bridge each evening.

I still haven't employed anyone to help in the house. If I could get someone to do the yard work, then I wouldn't get anybody to help in the house, as Mike and Dave could do work in the house instead of outside. Keeping up the yard is a major job in a tropical climate.

Last Sunday was the first time Howard spent a Sunday with us in a long time. We went to the ocean for a swim with another family. They are missionaries from Sweden. Pam is in the same class as their daughter Irene. That's how we got acquainted with them. They belong to the Swedish Holiness Union Mission. It's not Pentecostal, but quite like the Baptist church.

Pam is going to the Baptist church now, as she wanted to go where Irene went. Irene and Pam are going to a Bible camp for a week Dec. 17 through Jan 2.

Maybe Howard will be able to spend more Sundays with us as he is moving his office upstairs in the building he is working in and he won't have so many interruptions by people coming in.

We just can't imagine it being Christmas. We are sweltering in the heat and humidity, but nights always seem to be comfortable. Christmas is quite simple for me now, as the children can ask for anything up to $5 and that's all we spend. Of course they buy each other 25¢ presents.

A very Happy Birthday from all of us Trumbulls.

12th December, 1962

Dear Mom,

Well, school is out until the end of January. Break-up day was on Friday, 7th Dec. Certificates were handed out for 100% attendance and Merit Awards for coming 1st, 2nd and 3rd in class. I came 3rd in Standard Six (eighth grade.) Pam, Mike and Ginger received their report cards and they all passed, Pam into Std. Six, Mike into Std. Three (fifth grade), and Ginger into Class Two (second grade). Next year I am going to High School.

Summer is here, and with it rain. All this week it has been cloudy, but so far two Sundays in a row have been sunny. The first Sunday we went swimming at Umhlotl Rocks, about 15 miles south of Durban. The Kaarlsons, Swedish missionaries, went with us. There was a natural enclosed rock pool to swim in and rocks to explore. We had a picnic lunch, and then returned home.

The second Sunday Mike and I took an airplane trip over Durban. It lasted 15 minutes, and was very enjoyable.

Ginger has now started to wash dishes, and she can make her own bed, but there is one thing she just can't do, and that is tie her own shoes.

This morning we cleaned out all the cupboards and drawers in the kitchen and put insect powder on them.

With love,

David

December 20, 1962

Dear Mom and All,

I see David isn't going to get around to finishing his letter to you, so I'll dash off a few lines.

The airplane ride that David and Mike took was part of David's birthday present. Mike used his own money.

Howard's birthday was yesterday. Pam baked him a peanut butter cake (41 candles), and we had a luscious baked ham dinner. We invited two teachers from Inanda Mission School for dinner. They play bridge, so we finished the evening with a bridge game.

Dr. Taylor has given David a job working along with the maintenance man at the hospital. Today was his first day. You should have seen him when he came home for lunch. He was black from head to toe. They were working inside a boiler tank, scraping it. He worked a regular day's work, 8:00 to 4:30. It really showed, too, because he tumbled into bed at 8:00 p.m. instead of 10:30 or 11. I wonder what he's going to think about a steady diet of work—it will be good for him, as he doesn't have any friends he pals around with. He reads and lies around most of the day after he's through with his assigned work at home.

Tomorrow the older children are going to the hospital to help serve dinner to all the African people who work at the hospital. It's their annual Christmas dinner. In the evening they will go to the nurses' home and help serve dinner to the nurses. And then they are going caroling through the hospital wards with the nurses' choir. Sunday evening all the missionary kids are giving the evening worship service in the nurses' home. It will be a Christmas theme about the Christ child.

David sang a solo in the Christmas church presentation two weeks ago—"While Shepherds Watch Their Flocks by Night". He did it behind a curtain. We couldn't hear him very well because the organ was too loud.

Howard almost has our Christmas letter written. We hope that you all were blessed this Holy Season by gaining a true insight into Christ's Love and Saving Grace.

Our love to all,

Marge

CHAPTER 6. Settling In

High School for Dave, 1963

Dave's uniform for school was grey long pants, black shoes, navy blue blazer, white shirt, tie, and straw hat. He was to wear the uniform at all times he left the house, except going to the beach. It was very uncomfortable when the weather got hot. So often he would come home with his shirt soaked.

Dave was quite teed off with the discipline methods at his school. The principal (headmaster) has nothing to do with making the boys behave. All discipline is done by "prefects," picked from the senior class. There were 11 prefects at David's school of 800 boys. One of them is the "Head Prefect." He's the one who doles out the physical punishment with a very thin, springy stick. The other prefects were on the lookout to catch any wrong doing of any of the students.

Things that the boys were caned for were having hands in pockets, not wearing their straw hats to school, having the school blazer unbuttoned, throwing paper on the ground, not knowing the 11 prefects' names, and many other petty things. David was caned the first week of school for not having his hymn book with him for school assembly period. It was only two strokes, but the two red welts lasted for a week. Instead of caning you could substitute the punishment of writing 200 lines, but that took at least two hours to do and there just wasn't much time to spare after homework was done. The first year the students really took a beating and, of course, the upper classmen laughed at them. We just tried to encourage David to bear with it. We knew the first year would be the hardest.

Another thing he found discouraging was that he would get no extra credit whatsoever by researching and doing extra reading other than his textbooks. Tests were graded only on what was in his textbooks and not on any outside reading.

I'm sure he would have jumped at the chance to go back to America to go to school, but despite the downers of the South African system, all our children learned the discipline of study and respectful manners. They were expected to stand when the teacher came into the room and also to address or answer the teacher with "Sir" or "M'am". When our children came back to the U.S.A. in 1966 on furlough, the teachers liked their respectful manners.

Pam's high school wasn't nearly as petty with the discipline. Maybe girls are easier to manage. Pam had a summer and a winter uniform. For summertime she wore a short-sleeved, yellow gingham dress with a belt and white-colored cuffs. In the winter she wore a black wool jumper and long-sleeved white blouse, white anklets, and black shoes. Pam's experience wasn't nearly as frustrating as it was for Dave, mainly because Dave was a vast reader and felt thwarted and limited in his search for knowledge in his South African school experience.

Christmas Eve and Christmas Day

On Christmas Eve, the staff served a delicious meal to the student nurses. Our children were invited to help with the serving. After the meal it was the custom to have a costume parade. They don't celebrate Halloween here by dressing up in weird clothing so I guess this could match for our Halloween dress up fun time.

The dining tables were put in the center of the room and all made their entrances, one by one, by striding across the tables to be judged by the onlookers, who were sitting around the edge of the big room. Pam and Ginger entered the dress up parade too. Pam was Father Time, dressed in a sheet and a long beard that I made using the coiled hair usually stuffed into mattresses. Ginger, 7 years old, walked in wearing a diaper as the new 1964 along with Pam. Dave entered the contest as a ninth-month pregnant woman, carrying a sign saying, "Anything to please you, Mr. Botha." Mr. Botha had made a public appeal for all white women to have a baby to increase the white population in South Africa. Dave got roars of laughter. I had made a wig for him out of mattress stuffing. He looked somewhat like Pam with his long hair.

We were awakened on Christmas morning, 1963, by the nurse's choir standing in our front veranda and singing carols. Wasn't that an ideal beginning to Christmas Day?

Asked by the matron if Dave, Pam, and I would go through the hospital on Christmas morning to judge the staff-decorated wards, we had a difficult time making decisions for the best and what fun too!. We met up with Santa and at least 25 nurses trailing him, singing carols and spreading joy. He gave each patient a gift, a bar of soap or maybe a washcloth, but no one was forgotten on Christmas Day.

On holiday we usually invited two staff nurses and two interns from the hospital to share our meal and to play games later. The day after Christmas is also a holiday in South Africa. It's called Boxing Day. That's the day when Christmas boxes are given to postmen, milkmen, garbage collectors, etc. Even though they weren't working, they visited each home for their Christmas box. I guess that's how it got its name, "Boxing Day".

Hindu Customs: Fire-Walking, Dinner and A Wedding

An Indian doctor invited our family to witness a Hindu fire-walking ceremony in the courtyard of a Hindu temple with benches for a paying crowd of spectators. Much to our delight, the front row seats were still vacant, but the heat was almost unbearable. The red-hot bed was about 18 by 8 ft. in size. At the end of the bed was a foot bath filled with water and two gallons of milk to soothe the feet after walking in the bed of coals. Before the fire walking began, men carrying Hindu idols walked several times around the pit in a prayer march, not for the fire walkers, but for personal pleas

149

to God. Five men walked as if in a trance through the red-hot coals. The air was tense, but no casualties occurred. They say it's mind over body!? It would be good to be in that much control of your physical body, but I can't say that I would want to walk through a bed of red-hot coals.

Howard's office was across the street from a number of Indian shops. He soon became good friends with some of the owners and employees of the shops. One of the shop owners invited our family to his home to have an Indian meal. The man of the house sat down at the meal with us, but none of the women or children did. That was disappointing as we would have liked to see how an Indian family ate their meal. The table was set as we were accustomed to. They told us they fixed the curry especially for us so it wouldn't be too hot (fiery to the tongue). I loved it because I like spicy food. In spite of it supposedly being mild in flavor, my eyes and nose started running, but I loved every bite. After dinner the family dressed Pam and me in some of their beautiful saris, and Howard took pictures of us. We did look very nice. We miss not seeing the colorful beautiful saris in U.S.A.

This family invited us to a Hindu wedding in Petermeritburg, 50 miles north of Durban. We didn't understand the ceremony, as it was all in Hindi. A band was playing most of the time that the ceremony was going on, which lasted a couple of hours. Apparently, a lot of symbolism was in the rituals, and it was really quite tiring and very noisy. People weren't paying too much attention to what was taking place in the ceremony.

The whole big crowd of people was fed after the ceremony. We sat at long tables. As soon as you were through, someone else took your place at the table. Our family managed well with no silverware and a banana leaf for a plate. We were served rice and curry, potatoes, grated carrot salad, and tapioca pudding for dessert. You probably can't imagine eating that type of food with fingers. We all did well. Ginger, 9 years old, loved it that way.

The American and Canadian Club

I decided to belong to the American and Canadian Club because it was quite active in charity work. Every Wednesday morning a group of about 12 of us went to the hospital sewing room and sewed whatever the hospital had needed. We made lots of baby flannel gowns and diapers. Each new baby was sent home in a new gown and diaper.

One time we rented a hall and had 40 tables of bridge-playing women to make money for McCord Hospital needs. The American and Canadian Club women also started many day nursery schools for blacks aged 2-1/2 to 5, to help the black working mothers.

Every year in October we had a big jumble sale. It would be called a garage sale in U.S.A. We used a Methodist church that had a courtyard. Around the courtyard was a waist-high brick wall. The people, mostly blacks, would stand behind the brick wall and we would hold up a garment until some one gave the sign that they had the money to pay for it. Most of everything was marked very low in price. We couldn't stand close to the brick fence because sometimes garments would be snatched out of our hands. So we worked in teams. One would hold up the garment and the other would collect the money, then the garment would be given to that person. Howard took some moving pictures of the scene, but we thought afterwards a tape recording would have been more revealing. The shouting is unimaginable.

Kruger Game Reserve

During our children's vacation period from school in October 1963, we took a trip to Kruger Park. The previous year we decided to buy a used VW Combi so that we would be able to travel as a family and see some of South Africa while the children were still with us. We anticipated camping in South Africa, so we had our American camping gear shipped to us when we left U.S.A. Believe me, our Combi was really loaded and since it had an engine like a small V-8, we traveled slowly going up hills. As our custom was when the children were young, we traveled at night (Howard and I took turns driving every two hours) so the other children could sleep.

Kruger Park is 200 miles long and 50 miles wide. Luckily we saw four elephants at a waterhole not far from the road before we reached our first camp, five miles from the gate. Each camp was securely enclosed with strong, high fencing. Stoves were kept going at all times for your convenience to cook on. The last camp we stayed at, the largest within Kruger Park, accommodated 385 people, not counting those with their own equipment. It had a lovely swimming pool, so we lazed around the pool during the heat of the day.

It was so hot at night that we slept under the stars, too soundly to hear animal noises that other people had told us about. Mosquitoes or other insects never bothered us, which never ceased to amaze me in this tropical country. I remember when we first arrived in South Africa, I was surprised that there were only burglar guards on windows in homes and no screens.

Each day we got up at 5:00 a.m. and went driving around the different roads in search of animals. We saw 27 different varieties of animals, but no lions up close. The baboons and monkeys climbed all over the car (windows up) in search of food that might be handed out through a crack in a window. We all enjoyed our week's vacation at Kruger Game Reserve.

Slipped Disc Again, 1963

In November 1963, one of my lower lumbar discs slipped out of place again. The last time that had happened was when Ginger was still a baby. I don't remember lifting anything heavy or doing anything strenuous to bring it on.

I was in bed at home for a week, only getting up to go to the bathroom and a few times to supervise the children. Oh! how it hurt. Dr. Taylor decided that I should come to the hospital and have Dr. Heddon (an orthopedist) see me. He put me to sleep with Pentothal (I.V. anesthesia) and did a twisting manipulation, then put me in a hospital bed with the foot of the bed tilted up a bit. The doctor put wide adhesive tape down both sides of my legs and then hooked weights to the end of the tape beyond my feet. The weights dangled over the end of the bed. I heard later that was his way of keeping his patients in bed. That suited me fine because it hurt too much to get up. The hospital had two private rooms reserved for missionaries and hospital personnel use. The twisting manipulation didn't help a bit.

Fortunately the children's school year and exams were over. I don't know how they would have had time to do the household tasks and cooking if they still were studying so hard for their exams. Apparently they got along o.k. without me—kind of put my nose out of joint a bit until I remembered—I had been teaching them all these years to be independent and know how to take care of themselves and the house in case I wouldn't always be able to be with them. Howard brought his work home so he could be around if they needed help.

I was in bed almost a month (my vacation). The doctor had decided to do surgery, but put it off for a few more days. He would test me each day to see how far he could raise my legs before I had pain. Finally he could raise it almost 4 inches before I had pain and that was a positive sign. Each day my leg could be raised a bit higher. Finally, after about a month of being in bed, the pain was gone and I haven't had any serious problems since. Only twinges now and then. I learned how to protect my back with proper stooping and lifting and doing exercises that strengthened my back and tummy muscles.

Children's Jobs at the Hospital

During the summer break from school—December 6 until February—Dave, Pam, and Mike had jobs at the hospital. They worked from 9 a.m. to 1 p.m., Monday through Friday. Dave worked in the laboratory and storeroom or library, wherever he was needed. Pam worked in the children's ward, where she was getting wonderful experience. She loved working with African and Indian children, the majority of whom are hospitalized because of malnutrition. Pam liked it so well that she went back on the ward after lunch and gave some of her own time. Mike worked with the hospital maintenance man. He was happy working with his hands in building or repairing anything.

We were paying their salaries of 10 cents/hour. They didn't know it though. The hospital paid them when they paid the rest of the workers and then we reimbursed the hospital. We were so glad that Dr. Taylor, the hospital administrator, would agree to this arrangement. Howard and I believed that kids should be kept busy and learning new things. It was a great way for them to earn a bit of money. All jobs that kids do in U.S.A. are done by Africans here so there wasn't any way they could earn money.

Umnini Camp

As a family we entered into the life of the student nurses (who lived next door to us) as much as possible. We attended nearly all of their parties, concerts, celebrations, ceremonies, and worship services. Soon after we were settled into our home in Durban, the student-nursing headmistress asked our family to accompany a group of student nurses to Umnini Camp for the weekend. Every month the student nurses' ward assignments are rotated. One group (20 – 25 nurses) is assigned for only theory and study. These are the nurses that go to Umnini Camp every month.

Umnini Camp was about 25 miles from Durban on the Indian Ocean. Dr. Taylor, the American missionary who was McCord Zulu Superintendent for over 40 years, had Umnini Camp built. It had a main building which had a crude kitchen and a large dining area with a built up stage at one end of the room. Then there were several dormitory buildings which had two private rooms at the end of the buildings for the chaperones. This was the only camp which the African, Indian, and Colored groups could reserve to spend a weekend near the ocean.

Our children would ride on the back of a lorry (truck) with the student nurses to the camp. They sang most of the way there. We got there Saturday morning and came back Sunday afternoon. Saturday afternoon was spent on the beach. I was glad the nurses were intimidated by that big expansive ocean. They rarely went in beyond waist deep. I didn't have to worry about them too much because they had a buddy system to watch out for each other.

Howard spent a lot of time taking individual and group pictures of the nurses. If one of the nurses had a nice looking bathing suit, they all would go behind a rock and exchanged suits so each of them could be photographed in that particular suit. Most of the swimsuits were donated (secondhand) to the hospital. After Howard got the rolls of film developed, he would let the nurses know. Then, one by one as they had time, they would come to our home and order the ones they wanted for 5 cents a piece. At first they were worried about bothering me too much, so we set up a time between 2:30 and 5:00 p.m. when Pam was home from school. She knew all the nurses from working in the children's ward. So they would come and spend time with Pam in girl talk and playing records.

Also on Saturday afternoon, you'd see a lot of little groups of nurses practicing for the evening talent fun time. Always on Saturday nights we could have talent time. We marveled at their ability of impromptu skits and lack of self consciousness. Our kids entered too, with songs and skits they made up. Dave and Pam liked to sing together, "There's a Hole in My Bucket". I remember once Mike made up a skit doing surgery on delivering a baby beginning with a sheet held up in front and a lamp behind him and the patient. It showed what he was doing by shadows on the sheet. He used a big butcher knife for cutting open the abdomen. That was a howling success. Ginger was good at memorizing, and she would recite poems.

I often did a riddle for which you had to guess the password to join a particular club. I would get volunteers to come up (about six of the nurses). For example, if the word was "mimic", I would start mimicking any gesture or facial expression they would make. The more I mimicked, the more crazy it became. I told them there were two M's, two I's (and I pointed to my eyes), and a C (and of course I pointed to the sea, when I said "C"). Howard had a flash camera so he took pictures of all the different skits, etc.

Sunday morning we usually had our worship service outside near a big white cross overlooking the ocean. We chaperoned a group of nurses about five or six times a year.

LETTERS, 1963

January 2, 1963

Dear Mom and All,

We are fortunate to live so near the hospital and be invited to participate in the many holiday functions. Last Friday, December 21ˢᵗ, Pam and Mike helped at the African Christmas dinner (workmen). They helped serve them their dinner and pass out sweets (candy), peanuts, and a bag of popcorn to each one. Santa makes an appearance and gives each worker a present, all wrapped up. This same evening Pam and Dave were invited to go caroling with the nurses' choir through the hospital wards.

Every Sunday evening Howard and I go to a European Church service from seven to eight, and then dash back to the nurses' home to join them in their worship service from eight to nine. It's a very informal service—in fact, most of the nurses are there in their duty uniforms. We like to go to this service to hear the beautiful singing of the African nurses. The sermon is given by a variety of different types of people—doctors, laymen, ministers of many different denominations—but on Sunday, December 23ʳᵈ all the missionary children put on a nativity pageant.

Some of the children represented different countries bringing their gifts to the Christ Child. Ginger dressed as a Japanese child. I just draped a piece of lavender material around her and put a flower in her hair, and she carried an umbrella. Mike was a boy from South America. He put a striped towel around his waist and carried a spear. Dave and Pam didn't dress up in anything as they had the talking parts. Pam recited a poem called "It Is Love." She learned it by heart. I was very proud of her; she didn't falter one bit. David did the offering part of the service. Usually, offering isn't taken at the nurses' service, but for this service an offering was taken for a patient who had been at McCord's hospital for over a year. He is

157

paralyzed from the neck down from an accident. He has endeared himself to all by his cheery disposition. After the pageant, a record was played called "The Lullaby of Christmas." It's narrated by Gregory Peck. It's about a little boy who is denied the gift of speech until the morning he looks upon the Christ Child in the manger. It's a very moving story; we bought it while still in the States.

On December 24th, Christmas Eve, the children went to the nurses' home to help serve the nurses their annual Christmas dinner. After the dinner their traditional, fancy dress parade is held. It's similar to our Halloween dress-ups. The dining tables are put in the center of the room and the entrants walk upon them. The audience is sitting in chairs back against the walls, circling the tables. Pam and Ginger entered this year. Pam was "Father Time," dressed in a sheet and a long beard. Ginger was "1963."

We were awakened on Christmas morning by the nurses' choir, standing in our front yard singing carols. Wasn't that an ideal beginning to our Christmas Day? Then the children just had time to open their gifts, and we did eat a hurried breakfast before attending nine o'clock church services. This was the first time that we have ever gone to a service on Christmas Day. Our church back home always had a midnight candle light service, which was lovely but too late for the children. We all enjoyed attending together on Christmas Day this year. Earlier in the week, the matron of the hospital called me on the phone and asked if Dave and Pam and I would go through the hospital on Christmas morning and judge the wards. Every ward is decorated by the staff working in that particular ward. Each Christmas a prize is given to the best and most originally decorated ward. So after church, through the wards we went. What a difficult time we had making a decision, and what fun, too! We met up with Santa making the rounds to all the patients, and at least 25 nurses trailing him, singing carols and spreading "Joy." Each patient is given a gift. It's not much, but no one is forgotten on Christmas Day.

Well, in spite of our busy time schedule on Christmas morning, we sat down to a big turkey dinner at 1:30. We invited four graduate nurses to share our dinner with us. These girls were off duty from one to four in the afternoon. After dinner we had time to play some parlor games before they had to go back on duty. In the evening we invited eight different graduate nurses over to have pumpkin pie and ice cream and play games with us. We all mentioned what a marvelous Christmas Day we had. We had a couple of free hours in the late afternoon, and we found ourselves reminiscing of past Christmases and wished we could be with you, too.

The day after Christmas is also a holiday here, called "Boxing Day." That's the day when Christmas boxes are given to postmen, milkmen, garbage collectors, etc. I guess that's why it's called "Boxing Day." While you were all snowed in, no doubt, we spent the day on the beach with five other families.

Pam went to a Baptist Bible Camp from December 27 to January 2. I thought she might get a little tired of just Bible study and discussion all week, but she didn't. She said she had a wonderful time and learned a lot. There were over 300 young people there.

Seems so good to hear from you more often, Mom. Shirley wrote to me and said she'd received the pictures from you, and Jim said "What, no pictures of the kids?" We forget about taking pictures of us. We must do that soon; the children have grown a lot.

I haven't written notes to Aunt Lilly or Girlie yet. I got a letter from Fernie a few days ago, and she was so glad you all came for Thanksgiving. Jack, we enjoyed your Christmas poem. We'll be looking forward to next year's Christmas bit from you. And thanks to all for your notes. Mom, Howard said when he was treasurer of the church he didn't send notes to people who sent him money, so I guess they don't do that, which was a surprise to me, too. The children are off school from December 7ᵗʰ until January 29ᵗʰ. Write soon.

Love, Marge

Monday, February 18, 1963

Dear Mom and All,

We do hope the worst of the winter is over for you. We've been hearing some pretty bad reports by letters, radio, and newspaper.

Right now we are in the hottest time of the year here. It feels just like back home in the hottest time of the summer—hot and sticky night and day. We've been enjoying the beach and swimming pool at the beach lots lately. Ginger is just beginning to swim a few yards now and attempts to dive off the side of the pool—what a plop! But she comes up for more.

The children have been in school for three weeks now in their new grades. Ginger in 2nd and Mike in 5th, still the same school three blocks from us. Pam is in 8th in an all-girls school called "Mitchell." It was pretty difficult for her the first few days of school, mainly because of tests for two days to determine which class they would be put in. There are six groups (about 30 in each) in her 8th grade. The faster and higher IQ girls get put in groups together, and the average in another, and the slow and lower in another. Pam was so anxious and tied up in knots the second day worrying that she would be put in the last group, that she burst out crying at the breakfast table. I took her to her room and calmed her and sent her off to school with a pretty good frame of mind, and when she got home she was in good spirits—she got into the middle group.

Just last week I found out from a fellow American that our kids don't have to take Afrikaans if they plan to go to University in the U.S.A. So I went to see the principal about it and told her Afrikaans would not be a University- accepted subject, and asked if Pam couldn't take Latin instead. She had to be advanced to the next higher calibered class to take Latin, but also has to continue her Afrikaans. She is going to have a very busy year with homework to keep up with the class. Fortunately, she is a very conscientious worker and does what has to be done. I hope she does well this year; it will help her self-confidence.

Dave got into the swing of his new school very easily (Durban's Boys High). This school is supposed to have the best reputation in Natal (scholastic and tradition). For every boy accepted, six are turned away. He has lots of bounce and enthusiasm these days—he likes the challenge and competition. He always seemed to be bored in the grade schools. The boys are classified according to their abilities, same as at Pam's school. He was put in the advanced group, so will have plenty of competition. He and Pam have from two to three hours of homework every day. They are having to grow up so quickly here. All work and hardly any time for relaxation and fun. Dave's school is within walking distance, but Pam has to take a bus.

Pam and Dave both have joined the "Student Christian Association" in their schools, and Dave has joined the "Debating Club." He debates this Friday on whether it's better to eat fruits or vegetables. He's debating for the vegetables. Dave also is required to be at school two hours on Saturday, either morning or afternoon, to watch the school cricket team. It's compulsory. He has to wear his school uniform whenever he leaves the house, except going to the beach. He has to have his blazer (suit coat) buttoned at all times. You should see his shirt when he comes home from school—we could wring out the water. They're very formal and English-like here. We still can't get used to being called by our last names by people here.

Last week Howard and I went to our neighbors' daughter's wedding and dinner-dance reception, held in a hotel. We had nearly forgotten how people really booze it up. We are pretty isolated from that type of association. However, we will probably be a little more exposed to that type of living now as I have joined the "American and Canadian Women's Club," mainly because they come to the hospital every Wednesday morning and sew sheets, gowns, surgical masks, baby clothes, etc., for the hospital. But once a month on Wednesday morning they have a social meeting at someone's home, usually with a speaker. Last week an artist gave a talk on art and painted a picture.

Occasionally the Club has a husband and wife social evening. That's when we will discover how the rest of the world lives. This Saturday night we are going to a box lunch at one of the ladies' homes. The box lunches are to be auctioned off, and you eat with the gentleman who is the highest bidder on you box. The money is to be donated to a charity.

Sorry I let the "cat out of the bag" about your birthday and Christmas present. I didn't realize you would get that letter before your birthday. Sounds like you all had a nice Christmas and New Year's Eve party. We were in bed on New Year's Eve about

11:00 p.m. We were invited to the nurses' home to join them for hamburgers and an evening of games.

What two clubs do you belong to, Mom? We received your letter of the 13th today. I think those high hairstyles of the Africans do have something to do with marriage. Surprisingly, their kraals are not hot inside—the thick mud is a good insulator.

Sounds like Dottie's too busy. Did you know Cherri wrote to me, and a very nice letter indeed. Did you know Al Trumbull, Jr., had a heart attack about three weeks ago? He's progressing satisfactorily, so we hear.

Thanks for the birthday remembrance, Mom. Howard took me out to dinner and a movie, "The Music Man."

Love to all,

Marge

March 8, 1963

Dear Mom and All,

I thought you would be interested in reading about the "Protest Fast" against university apartheid.

Rev. Ntlabati (African) was refused admittance to Natal University, so two other ministers in sympathy dropped their courses. The three of them decided to go on a 101-hour fast, lasting from Tuesday morning to Saturday noon, to try to arouse the public heart to the injustice of non-academic freedom. They stayed on the university steps day and night, only having water to drink. Many of the university students and professors gave them their support by sitting with them between classes, and some stayed through the night.

We read about it in the paper on Tuesday and gave them our support by sitting with them each evening. We took them our two-gallon thermos jug so they could have ice water. It was beastly hot during the day, as there was no shade on the university steps.

162

They conducted prayer and devotional services three times a day and took Communion each morning. They had lots of opportunity of witnessing for Christ during their 101-hour fast. Many of the students are agnostics, and the witness these three men were making put a lot of them to serious thinking about the void in their lives.

The first evening we took our battery tape recorder and played a tape for them that we recorded during our Missionary Training course. It was a lecture by Rev. James Lawson (a Negro) who was instrumental in organizing the non-violence student sit-in movement and the freedom ride. This lecture proved very helpful to the three men, and gave them additional strength and courage for the days ahead of them.

As far as I know, they didn't experience any difficulties from the public or police. One car drove by one evening while we were there, and the occupants yelled out "Kaffir (black) lovers." By Saturday they looked pretty gaunt and red-eyed from lack of food and sleep. The three men aren't expecting any immediate miraculous changes in the government policy, but as Christians they felt moved to protest loudly against non-academic freedom. We hope sometime in the future the universities here will once again be able to serve all those who apply for admittance, regardless of race or color.

Love, Marge

Wednesday, March 28, 1963

Dear Mom and All,

I have to think twice to remember we are not approaching spring as you are. Today is a typical March day of memories of Michigan. The trees are swaying and bending with the gusts of wind. In fact, I think it is making me a wee bit homesick. Do wish I could pop in and visit all of you. I guess I'll have to content myself with a magic carpet and my imagination, but what a poor substitute.

Pam is now wearing braces—not the kind that go around each tooth, but on removable plastic plates. She's getting along quite well with her new additions. Over a month ago she had four permanent teeth pulled to make room, to push her protruding teeth in proper alignment. She had gas for the anesthetic in the dentist's office. She got along fine. It only took two minutes from the time the anesthetic was started and the teeth pulled and the time that she was awake. And she wasn't even fuzzy—she got right out of the chair and walked to the car with me. Pam seems to be getting along all right in school. This past week has been a bit trying, as they were having month-end tests.

All parents were invited to the Overport school to visit the teachers one day last week. Ginger's teacher asked me what she could do for Ginger to make her more neat in her writing and sums. Ginger just doesn't care what it looks like. I've discovered they put a terrific amount of stress on neatness over here. In fact, every one of the children was marked down because of poor handwriting. The children are not allowed to use an eraser. They are expected to get it right the first time. At test time, if their paper looks smeared as if a word was erased and written over, then that word was counted wrong even if it was right.

Mike is doing satisfactory work. Her remark was the he's a very keen and enthusiastic worker.

David is getting quite teed off with discipline methods at his school. The principal (headmaster) has nothing to do with making the boys behave. It is all done by "Prefects," picked from the senior class. There are 11 at David's school of 800 boys. One of them is a "Head Prefect." He's the one that doles out the physical punishment with a very thin, springy stick. The other Prefects are on the lookout to catch any wrong-doing of any of the students, so they can bring them to the Head Prefect to be caned. Things that the boys are caned for are having hands in their pockets, not wearing their straw hats to school, having their school suit coat unbuttoned, throwing paper on the ground, not knowing the 11 prefects by sight and their names, and many other petty things.

David was caned the first week of school for not having his hymn book with him for assembly period. It was only two strokes, but the two red welts lasted for a week. Instead of caning you can substitute the punishment by writing 200 lines, but that takes at least two hours to do and there just isn't that much time to spare after homework is done. At least five times already this year a prefect has made David's whole class copy 100 lines (an hour's work) because there were paper wads on the floor. I've heard the newcomers (David's class) really take a beating during their first year. So we just encourage him and tell him he can laugh at the newcomers next year. Right at the present, he'd jump at the chance to go back to America to go to school.

On March 5ᵗʰ we read in the paper about three ministers going on a 101-hour fast on the University of Natal's steps in protest of non-academic freedom. Two of the ministers were white and the other was African. The African was refused admittance to the University to further his education. The two white ministers decided to drop their courses they had signed up for in sympathy with the African. They hoped their protest would awaken the public's heart to the injustice of academic freedom. They got a lot of publicity, and much of the student body and faculty were behind them and sat with them on the steps between classes. Howard and I went over each evening and sat with them, giving our support.

We received a letter from Al, Jr., yesterday, and he's doing quite well. He says he's 20 pounds lighter and a non-smoker now. He expects to go to work gradually next month.

Dora wrote and said Dad Trumbull had been down with the flu, but was better and had gone to Detroit and then planned to go to Cleveland to see Al, Jr.

The children have a ten-day vacation starting April 5ᵗʰ. David and Pam plan to go to church camp for four days over Easter weekend. Mike is looking forward to working again with Mr. Peltzer, the hospital maintenance man. I forgot to tell you that both he and David were paid a small salary for working during the summer holiday.

I bet you're all glad to know that spring is here, a wonderful time of year, isn't it? Tell Aunt Lilly thanks so very much for her letter.

Love to you all,

Monday, May 6, 1963

Dear Mom,

It's midnight now, but I'm just going to take a few minutes to dash you off a note, to let you know we've been thinking of you, and especially at this time with Mother's Day approaching.

Howard gave me my Mother's Day present today (shoes) because he is leaving for Maphumulo tomorrow and will be gone for a week. It's the annual African pastors' conference. It seems like he's been gone already for two weeks, as he has had to work almost every night until one or two in the morning, and Saturday and Sunday to get all his reports ready. He's also going to teach a simplified way of keeping books for the churches, so that has given him many extra hours of work.

I don't think I'll be able to find time in the next two weeks to write all the news, as I'm working on a talk. We're having an experimental family African weekend conference at one of the churches. My subject is the parental responsibility in the training of children in a Christian home. What a job. It sure doesn't come easy for me, especially when I'm allotted two hours. I think I'll fill a lot of the time in by having small group discussions on a variety of questions, and have the spokesman for each group present his findings to the general group.

We are all fine. I bet you've wondered why you haven't heard from me. Mainly because when I type a letter it takes me at least a half a day, and I just haven't had a whole half a day to spare.

Tell Madelyn thanks for her letter, and also Marion. Howard will write to Marion after he comes back from this conference he's going to.

We'll be thinking of you on Mother's Day.

Love,

Marge

June 6, 1963

Dear Mom and All,

What a glorious time of year for all of you at home! This is our nicest time of year, too. Sunshine every day—noon temp about 72 and nights between 50 and 60. With our electric blankets, what could be better?

We purchased a VW station wagon not long ago for our family use, as the Mission now has a policy (Howard advised it) that missionaries should have the same price-range cars as the African Church personnel are authorized to buy. They just aren't big enough for a family of six, especially on vacation trips. And since this will be our only term in Africa that we will have our whole family with us, we decided to splurge so we can take trips and show the children as much of Africa as we can while they are still with us.

I'm really enjoying having my own car to flit around in. I've had more opportunity to see Durban lately. It's opened my eyes up to how beautiful this city in Africa really is. Summer and winter there are always lovely flowers of all colors in everybody's yard. The yards are kept so very well cared for, because most homes have garden boys (salary from $6 to $10 a month plus their food—the bulk of it being "mealie meal" which looks like a white, fine-grained cooked cereal, and dried beans). I see Indian or African men sweeping the streets of the city every day, so the beauty of the city plus the cleanliness makes Durban a lovely place.

A couple of months ago, an Indian doctor took us to see the Hindu fire-walking ceremony. It was in the courtyard of their Temple. Benches were put up for spectators who wanted to pay 50 cents. That we did. There were crowds of people, but much to our delight, the front row seats were still vacant. We soon found out why; the heat was terrific. The logs were piled high and burning with great gusto. Fortunately, soon after we sat down they began taking the big burning logs out, just leaving the red hot coals. The red hot bed was about 18 by 8 feet in size. At the end of the bed was a footbath filled with water, to which was added two gallons of milk.

Before the fire walking began, men carrying the Hindu idols walked several times around the pit. This was followed by a big group of Hindu women marching around the pit. They each had a sack of camphor ice which was in inch-square pieces. They tossed the camphor pieces in little bonfires spaced about a foot and a half apart all around the pit. This was a prayer march, not for the fire walkers but for personal pleas. There were five men who walked through the red hot coals. They all appeared as if in a trance. They had pins stuck straight through their tongues and cheeks, and some had hooks on their chest and arms. Two of the fire walkers almost passed out before they reached the end of the fire bed. One fellow carried a baby in his arms. The air was tense with anxiety, but there were no casualties. One man walked through the fire bed at least three different times, apparently with no ill effects.

The children are suffering through their half-year term exams now. These are times they wish they were back in the States going to school. Pam has had a headache every day this week, just from anxious tension.

I went to a meeting last week where they had a panel discussion by teenage exchange students on the differences of educational methods of America and South Africa. Two of the students were from California, going to school here for six months. The other student was a South African who had gone to school in America for a year. Most of the criticism was given to South Africa, even by the South African student:

1) The State exams that must be passed are a hardship on the overly anxious child who does well in his daily work and monthly exams, but fails to pass the term exam;

2) Notes are passed out to students all mimeographed, which makes the pupil less attentive in class—hence more time to throw spit balls, etc.;

3) The student isn't encouraged to do research on anything other than what will be asked in State exams, which causes the enthusiastic students to become complacent and disinterested;

4) Discipline was mentioned.

The student from South Africa was quite impressed with how well American pupils behaved without any forced physical control. He liked the way that most of the teachers in America gained respect from the students. He said that if the teacher deserved respect, he got it. He thought that the link between parent and teacher in the States was the main disciplining factor. This South African went to a California school which I've heard has a good rating, and teachers' salaries are higher than elsewhere.

Did you ever get our Christmas letter? Our church offered to mimeograph them and send them out, but no one has ever commented on receiving it. Maybe our letter never reached the church.

I bet Cherrie is glad to have her braces off. Pam is going to have the upper appliances put on Tuesday.

We had two guests all last week. A missionary family arrived in Durban for a week's stay. They had been in the States for their year's furlough. They are in the mission in Southern Rhodesia, about 1,300 miles north of here. There are six in the family, so we took the two boys, ages 13 and 11, and the two girls, ages 5 and 3, and the parents stayed with another family. These two boys knew how to play bridge, so they taught our children the basic rules, even Mike. It gave all three of them a fairly good foundation after playing every spare moment for a week straight.

Love to all,

Marge

Tuesday, July 23, 1963

Dear Mom and All,

169

I am really becoming lazy with my correspondence. It seems that it's one thing that is just too easy to convince oneself that I'll do it tomorrow.

The children returned back to school today after having a three-week holiday. How we all did enjoy sleeping in until after 7:30. During school time I get up at 5:45 and prepare four lunches before starting breakfast.

The last part of June, a week before their school was out, I attended our Mission Meeting by going back and forth each day (18 miles). Several days I didn't get back until after 10:00 p.m., but all was well. Pam prepared dinner and made sure Ginger was in bed by 7:00. It is good that the children are old enough to manage on their own occasionally.

This was our last official Mission Meeting, as we are now integrated with The Church. All missionaries are now assigned jobs by the Executive of The Church. Right after our Mission Meeting was over The Church had its annual meeting which lasted a week. I only attended one day, but Howard went for about four days. We don't get much out of it because it is all in the Zulu language. I forgot whether I told you that I gave up my language study. I kept at it six months after Howard quit. I was just stubborn enough to think I could progress in it, but I finally made myself face reality and realize a foreign language is not spoken or understood just by learning it from a book. I hear very little Zulu spoken. Most all the Africans I come in contact with speak English.

The last time I wrote we had just finished having guests for ten days, a family from Rhodesia on their way home from a furlough at home in America. The two boys (Dave's and Mike's ages) taught Dave, Pam, and Mike how to play bridge, that is, the basic fundamentals of the game. So during the children's holiday we spent many hours together at the bridge table. They got quite put out with me and at times bored when I insisted on explaining all the whys of playing the game in certain ways, and I kept drilling them on rules and bidding, and I made them each keep score. They play a fairly good game now and know the game well enough to make it interesting to Howard and me when we play with them.

The first part of July we entertained guests again. A family of four from Johannesburg stayed with us for ten days, and also a fellow missionary from the Cape Province (500 miles south and west). The men attended The Church's annual meeting while we women and children had fun together going to the beach, etc.; of course, plenty of work mixed along with the fun. We had just settled back into the family routine of living again when we got a phone call last Sunday from a couple of fellows who could not find accommodations anywhere in Durban (because of tourists during the holiday). So we are now a family of eight for a few days.

These boys are between high school and university and are touring the whole of Africa. One of the chaps is from Denmark and the other from England. Prior to coming to Durban, they had been in a youth work camp near Johannesburg. A fellow missionary runs the camp, and he gave them our name to call when they got to Durban. It's really interesting to get to know folks from different countries.

I just received a letter from Mrs. Torr, Edwina's mother. She asked me if I could meet a friend of hers arriving August 6th, Mr. Trevor R. Gautier. Anyone know him? He will be here only three days and then will continue on with his tour group. Mrs. Torr said that Edwina lost her husband to another woman about two years ago, but is getting along fine and is the same sweet girl she always has been, and has many good and fine friends. I had thought that Edwina must be going through some difficult times, because I haven't heard from her for at least three years, not even a Christmas card.

I got out of that talk I was supposed to give on Parental Responsibility of Training of Children and did Nutrition instead. The whole family weekend was a real success, and they want more. They are eager to learn.

Cherrie's graduation picture is lovely. We have it on our piano. Folks that see it say she resembles Pam. Sorry to hear she hasn't been well.

171

No doubt you heard that Deb's foot slipped under the power lawn mower—seems to be healing all right. Dad Trumbull had a heart attack but he seems to be quite good now, just has to slow down.

Howard is still up to his ears in work and is only home when we have guests over. We are all very well and have so far escaped the epidemic of flu that is going around.

The Board has just set a vacation policy for all of us: $40 for husbands, $30 for wives, $30 for each child over 11, and $15 for each child under 11 per year. We are not entitled to claim it unless we take a vacation, so we are planning to do something in October when our children are off school for ten days. Aren't we lucky?

Good to hear your garden produced well. Thanks for your letter.

Love to all,

Marge

August 13, 1963

Dear Mom and All,

We have been treating ourselves royally since last I wrote. Last month we took the three older children to see "My Fair Lady," and last Saturday we saw "Oklahoma" (both musicals). We only could afford the last row seats, but with our binoculars passed among us we could see quite well. We all liked "Oklahoma" the best. Our tape recordings of the two musicals have been working overtime lately.

Last month, when we took a group of nurses to Camp Umnini, we shared the camp with a group of Africans from a Presbyterian church. There were 44 Sunday School children, plus their teachers and minister. They used only one building to bed them all down in, and did their cooking outside in big iron three-legged pots— something we see only in antique shops in America. They all walked to the camp from the railroad station a mile away.

It is amazing to see how uncomplicated they do things. They all slept on wooden platforms raised from the floor a couple of inches, with a half-inch felt mat on top of the boards. As far as I could see, they each carried one blanket with them for sleeping. You should see my car loaded up for just one night for all of us. We would freeze with just one blanket. I think it went down to 45 or 50 that night. Saturday evening we all came together in the main hall for an evening of singing and games. Sunday morning we all had our worship service together under the big white cross overlooking the ocean. The Presbyterian minister did the service (in Zulu and English). In spite of the cold that Saturday night, Sunday was a beautiful day for swimming. Five of the interns joined us for the weekend, too. They always spark the girls to a jolly good time.

Mike is strutting proudly these days with a new watch for his birthday, and going to Scouts last Friday. He will love scouting; he's in his glory when he can go hiking or camping. Dave quit about six months after he joined. He's the type who would much rather exercise his mind (with a book) than his feet.

Dave, Pam, Mike and I went to the South African Art exhibit held in the Durban Art Gallery. We bought a little book that at least gave the titles to the paintings; otherwise I don't think we could have stretched our imaginations far enough to know what some of them were supposed to be. Some abstract contemporary paintings I liked, but not of the human form. Most of them are so grotesque. Anyway, I wouldn't want one of those grotesque human forms hanging on my wall. Several first prizes went to Africans, which pleased us.

Last Sunday we went for a ride to see the new Indian Township being developed about ten miles south of here. Already 10,000 people live there in the four-room, cement block houses. Some of the buildings are four family apartments, each apartment having a living room, kitchen, bathroom (with some having regular-type stools with flush, but the cheaper rented ones having just a hole in the floor), and one bedroom. No doubt five or more might live in an apartment that size. Eventually, when the township is completed, 50,000

Indians will live there. I wonder how long this separate development will continue before the BIG FALL.

A new missionary family is arriving from the States this Thursday to join the American Board Mission here. They have one child about a year old. They will be staying at Ifafa Mission rural house during their language study. They will probably be staying with us for about a week or so until the house is ready for them. They've been waiting for a year for their visas to enter this country. We were lucky ours came through in six weeks.

Mrs. Torr's friend, Mr. Gautier, arrived August 6th. He's her neighbor in Florida, not Dowagiac. I picked him up from the boat, and he had dinner with us. Then in the evening we went to the fellowship meeting at the hospital.

Just received a letter from Aunt Iva with 11 snapshots of the reunion. It was wonderful to see everybody again, but I'll have to confess I didn't recognize some of the bigger boys. Dave and Mike had butch haircuts when we arrived here, but not for long; they were really ridiculed. So they are going through the miseries of keeping hair combed and plastered down with hair goo, just to be one of "the group." Boys and girls don't wear Bermuda shorts here, either. Both sexes wear shorts very short.

Aunt Iva has been very faithful in writing to us, at least once a month. She sends most of the letters she receives from relatives on to us, too, so helps us keep up with what's going on with everyone. Last month she sent snaps taken while you and Marty were visiting them in May. You all look just the same; makes me homesick to see you all again. Aunt Iva said Shirley and family are coming for a visit in September—give her my love.

Tell Jim: Mike still remembers him.

Love,

Marge

Monday, September 23, 1963

Dear Mom and All,

I must dash off a letter to you or it will be another week before I write.

Our Theological Seminary moved its location the first of the year and is having its opening ceremony this Thursday. It's in the Cape Province (550 miles south and west from here). Howard and I and three others are going in our car Wednesday morning at 6:00 a.m. and returning Friday. It will be nice to see that part of the country. A bus load of 55 Africans are going, too. The children are staying with friends.

The first two weekends in September we chaperoned two different groups of nurses at Umnini. We always have a good time.

Since Howard went to the office to work yesterday, I went with Dr. Taylor to the Indian College and listened to 12 speakers give ten-minute talks on Mohammed, "The Prophet of Islam." Dr. Taylor was the master of ceremonies. All the speakers were Indian people. I'm glad I went; I learned quite a bit about Mohammed. This was a speaking contest with prizes. Its aim is to try to encourage people to learn more about their religion.

Well, the flu bug finally hit our family. Ginger came down with it first, two weeks ago, then Howard and Pam a week ago, David last Friday, and Mike today. The first day they all had a temperature of 101, but by the end of the second day their temperatures were normal and they were raring to eat again. I guess I let David eat too soon because he had to stay home from school today, too, because of diarrhea. I'm the only one that hasn't had it yet. If I'm going to get it, I hope it happens before we leave on our trip to the Cape Province Wednesday. I'd hate to get sick while traveling.

Mike went on a weekend campout with the Scouts. He didn't get home until 6:30 last night, and Howard and I were just getting ready to go to a church service. Since he's pretty sick today, I haven't found out how the weekend went. Last night at the nurses' worship service from 8:00 to 9:00 p.m., I was asked to hand out graduation

175

certificates to the girls finishing their nurses' training this month; brings back memories of when I received mine.

David says to tell you, thanks for your letter.

We are going to Kruger National Game Reserve Park (600 miles north of here) from October 4th to the 12th during the children's vacation time.

Our love to all,

Marge

October 1, 1963

Dear Mom and All,

Our trip to Alice in the Cape Province was very nice; it took us 12 hours. We had a good highway except for 40 miles of gravel. We went a hundred miles out of the way in order to have good roads. The countryside is terribly dry, very hilly, and many cracks are visible on the hillside. What a trek the occupants have each day to fetch their water from the streams, and many streams were all dried up.

You will be receiving a parcel in the mail. I am sending some beads that the Zulu people make from the bean family. I have sent six— one each for Mom, Caryl, Fern, Dorothy, Madelyn, and Dora. They are in envelopes; you may open them all and take your pick. First there gets the choice. The red ones are called lucky beans and the grey is called "ubuhlalu."

Oh! I forgot to mention, I did get the flu that the rest of the family had, and I came down with it at a most inopportune time. I felt all right riding down to Alice but felt horrible the next day, so I was in bed all day while the ceremonies of the theological school were going on. And I didn't feel so good the next day riding home, either, but I'm fine now and so is everybody else.

Received your letter last week, Mom—sure would have liked to join you for Martha's birthday dinner. Chicken is one of the most expensive meats here, so we just don't have it.

We are starting to pack for our vacation starting this Friday. Ginger seems to be the most excited. At least she's more verbose than the others.

Howard had some film he wanted to use up, so he took some pictures of our house and us'ns. We will be sending them soon.

We long to see you,

Marge

October 27, 1963

Dear Mom and All,

Two weeks have already gone by since we returned from our holiday. I bet you've wondered if we had been eaten by the wild animals. There wasn't even a possibility of that though. The animals were more frightened of us and our car; they always went running off when we approached them.

We left for Kruger about 2:30 on Friday afternoon and drove continuously through the night. Ginger and Mike slept on the floor between the two back seats, and Dave and Pam used the two back seats except when they took turns sitting with the driver so one of us could use a seat to stretch out on for a snooze. Howard and I took turns driving every two hours. We drove to the top end of Kruger near the border of Rhodesia, which was 743 miles from Durban. We entered the Park about noon on Saturday.

Our camp was five miles from the gate, and we were lucky to see four elephants at a water hole not far from the road before we reached camp. We paid a $5 entrance fee—60 cents a night for a camping spot and 50 cents a day for the car. So you can see we had a very inexpensive week. We ate out only one meal at the restaurant the whole week. Each camp has a restaurant, store and gas station. It wasn't at all difficult doing our own cooking, either.

Stoves (coal) are kept going at all times for your convenience to cook on. The cooking areas have thatched roofs in case of rain. Outside grills are kept going for steaks and chops, etc. Each cooking area has a huge black pot with a spigot, which contains boiling water for coffee and tea and doing dishes, etc. The first camp we stayed at accommodated 103 people, and the last camp 385, which was one of the largest camps within Kruger. That number doesn't include campers like us that had all our own equipment, but that number means the people that use the rondovals, beds and bedding, which costs one dollar per person a night.

On Saturday when we got into camp and started to put up our tent, we very nearly had heat strokes. It was 105 degrees in the shade. We really wouldn't have needed to put up our tent, as it was so hot yet at night that we lined up our cots out under the stars and slept outside all night. We must have slept too soundly to hear animal noises that other people told us about.

We stayed at this camp one more night, planning to move south to another camp the next day. We bedded down outside again at 8:00 p.m. About midnight I woke up and it was pitch black, no stars or moon. The wind had started to blow and I could see lightning in the distance. I woke Howard and we decided to get everybody up, take down the tent, and sleep the rest of the night in the car. We just couldn't imagine taking down a wet tent the next day and trying to hoist it on top of the Combi. We were lucky—we got everything done in an hour and a half, and settled in the car before the rain came.

The next night we didn't bother to set up our tent. We bedded the children in the car, and Howard and I got our cots and sleeping bags out, and slept by the car. No rain that night. We were never bothered with mosquitoes or other insects, which never ceased to amaze me in this tropical country. You remember when we first arrived in this country, one of the things that surprised me was that there were no screens on the windows.

On Tuesday we arrived in the southern end of Kruger and set up our tent, and stayed there until Friday. Each day we got up at 5:00 and went driving around the different roads in search of animals. Early morning and late afternoon are the best time to see animals. We got back to camp about 8:30 and had a leisurely breakfast. The camp we chose to stay at had a lovely swimming pool, so we lazed around the pool during the heat of the day. This was the only camp that had a pool.

We saw 27 different varieties of animals. We were so disappointed we didn't see lions close up. Elephants were plentiful. It was quite amazing to see them eating dry dead bushes—some even had thorns. The baboons and monkeys were fun. They were climbing all over our car in search of food. Kruger Park is 200 miles long and 50 miles wide. We drove 700 miles inside of Kruger. We took lots of pictures to show you when we get home. The countryside varies a great deal in the Park. Some parts are mountainous and rocky, and other parts are flat. Some places have lots of brush and trees, and other places have hardly any edible brush, trees or grass.

We started for home at 2:00 p.m. on Friday and arrived home at 8:00 a.m. Saturday. It was a slow journey because of the mountainous country. We crept up the long hills about five or ten miles an hour. Our Combi has the same motor as the small VW car. To top it off, we weren't getting very good power because we needed new spark plugs, but all went well and we arrived home safely with very fond memories of our holiday. In fact, it inspired Pam to write to Jody right away.

Howard and David are going out to dinner together tonight. It's a dinner for all past "School and Varsity Campers" and their dads. They'll see a "Fact and Faith Film" and hear a couple of speakers. Howard was not too enthused about going but I sort of encouraged him, knowing how nice it is for father and son to go out together. Dave is really looking forward to it. Pam has gone on a Sunday School picnic for a cook-out tonight. Pam and Dave have started their year-end memorizing for exams, which start the latter part of November.

Next Saturday I am asked to give something on Health and Nutrition at a weekend conference. I've located some slides on Kwashiorker (protein deficiency) and tuberculosis. Luckily, this

Mission church has electricity. Howard will go with me so that he can run the projector. Next month I am asked to speak at the Pastors' Wives conference on "Care of the Home and Family." I had just about collected enough thoughts on the subject when I happened to see Dr. Jacobson (woman), who taught me how to use the flannelgraph on "ProNutro." I hadn't seen her for a year. She's got a new flannelgraph on tetanus. She's going to come with me to the conference and give her talk on tetanus, which is a great killer here.

Love to all, Marge

Friday, November 22, 1963

Dear Mom and All,

Have you ever had to pay extra postage on the letters that I send newspaper clippings in? I'm taking them to the post office now to get them weighed, so I will get the right postage on them from now on. I enjoyed getting your news clippings. We do get the church bulletins every month. That was a fine picture of Dr. Lewis's family, wasn't it? The folks didn't send us the article on Deb, either; that's a lovely picture of her. She's really happy at the University of Michigan this year. I bet the folks miss her terribly.

How's Caryl doing with her painting and papering? I bet the house looks much better. So glad Cherrie didn't get hurt in the car accident. I think it will be much safer living in Benton Harbor for her, especially during the snow and icy roads that will be coming soon. Is Scot still planning on going back and forth? How wonderful to have Bonnie and baby home for Thanksgiving.

The new missionary couple that came to Africa in August is staying with us for a couple of days now. It's such fun to have them. They are very interested in "Eat Right to Stay Healthy," so we have much to yak about. They got interested in preventive medicine through nutrition a few years ago when they were living with Larry's folks. Larry's dad had a heart attack and was generally not in good health, and through a mutual friend of Larry's dad who believed and lived good nutrition, introduced them to a better way of life. They are even planting soy beans in their garden.

Carol and I exchange ideas in getting better nutrients into our daily food. It makes cooking rather exciting when you know that something good will come from your efforts. I do a lot of my efforts sort of underhandedly so my family won't think I'm a fanatic—like substituting a cup of ProNutro for flour in pancakes, adding powdered milk to meatloaf, making pie crust with oil, adding peanut butter and ProNutro to fudge we make, substituting brown sugar and honey for white sugar in recipes, putting ground up liver in meatloaf and salmon loaf, etc. I use the noon meal to eat things like yogurt and molasses when I am alone with Ginger. I am so glad, Mom, that you introduced us to good nutrition. I hope our children will feel the same someday.

The children are just about through with their year-end exams now—how hard they do study! Pam went through a terribly anxious time again. She won't know if she passed for another week yet. Their school is out December 6th.

You really do well in writing to us, Mom. Howard remarked about it when we received your last letter. You write two or three times to Dora's once. Hope you all had a lovely Thanksgiving together.

Love, Marge

Thursday, December 5, 1963

Dear Mom,

Another birthday has come around for you again; the years are going much too fast. I won't let the cat out of the bag about your present because no one has written to let me in on the secret.

Received your letter yesterday. We were stunned, too, about the President's assassination, but somehow I have a feeling there is a divine plan in this tragedy and that "Good" will come of this that seems "Evil" to us.

181

Pam and Dave passed their exams. The anxious time is over again. Mike hasn't gotten his results yet.

Do you remember when Ginger was a baby and I was in bed with a slipped disc? Well, I've done it again, but don't know how. I don't remember doing anything strenuous. I was in bed at home from Wednesday to Monday, and then Dr. Taylor thought I'd better come into the hospital and let Dr. Heddon (orthopedic doctor) see me. He put me to sleep with Pentothal on Tuesday and did some kind of manipulation, then put me in traction (foot of bed tilted up and weights put on my legs), but it hasn't relieved the pain yet. I'm supposed to be in traction two more days; maybe by then all will be well. I'm certainly thankful the children's exams are over, because it's taking all their time to do household tasks and getting meals. Their school year is over for them tomorrow.

Dr. Heddon just popped in. He thinks it may be another week before I'll be out of traction. I'm in a nice private room at McCord Hospital. There are two rooms reserved for missionary personnel. Howard is bringing his work home to do so he can supervise the children. Apparently they are getting along quite well without me. Well, I've been teaching them all these years to be independent and know how to take care of themselves and the house in case I wouldn't always be able to be with them.

Your Thanksgiving dinner sounded delicious. We didn't have a Thanksgiving dinner but we thought of all of you and your full, contented tummies.

"HAPPY BIRTHDAY, MOM"

Love, Marge

Tuesday, December 17, 1963

Dear Mom and All,

Received your letter yesterday, Mom. I've been in traction two weeks today. The disc isn't completely back yet, so I will have to stay in the hospital a while longer. The way the doctor tests if the disc is back or not, he lifts my leg up while I'm flat on my back. If I can get it all the way up without pain, then the disc is back in place. I still can't do that, but it is improving and fortunately I don't have any pain while lying here in bed now. The doctor threatened me with an operation if it doesn't get better soon. If it has to be done, we will ask for consultation with another neurosurgeon first.

Ginger has been staying at Ifafa with the Gilleys, who came to Africa last August. They are the couple who I was telling you about—they believe in right nutrition for health. Ginger has been with them since December 6th. I received a letter from her and she seems quite happy, no signs of homesickness. The Gilleys are coming to our house to spend Christmas with us, even if I'm not at home. I've got a turkey in the freezer and Carol can fix that, I'm sure. I'm certainly glad they're coming. I don't think the children will miss me so much if other folks are around. They are getting along well at home without me. Pam does all the cooking, washing and ironing. This is really making her grow up fast.

Dave, Pam and Mike have jobs here at the hospital during the summer holidays; they work from nine to one in the mornings. Dave works in the lab and storeroom, Pam in the children's ward (she likes working with the babies), and Mike works with the hospital maintenance man. We are paying their salary of ten cents an hour; they don't know that though. The hospital will pay them when they pay the rest of the workers, and then we will reimburse the hospital. We are so glad the hospital will let them do this. Howard and I believe that kids should be kept busy, and fortunately here they are learning new things. They pop in and see me a couple of times during the morning.

It doesn't seem possible that you were 70 on the 13th. The older I get the younger you seem. Do you still use that liquid on your scalp to keep your hair from getting grey?

Thank you for your prayers, Mom.

Love, Marge

Saturday, December 28, 1963

Dear Mom and All,

I must dash off a note to you to let you know how nicely I'm getting along—and no operation, either. I came home from the hospital Monday, the 23rd. I'm beginning to feel like my old self again. My legs are finally getting back to normal; a whole month in bed is a long time.

We had such a nice Christmas. We opened gifts on Tuesday so that Christmas wouldn't be too rushed. We went to church at 9:00 a.m. and then had Christmas dinner at Inanda (our African girls' seminary), 18 miles north of Durban. When I have more time and space I'll tell you about our Christmas breakfast, which Carol Gilley made for us. The Gilleys have been with us since the 23rd, the day I came home from the hospital. They are going home today. Dave is going with them and coming back with them on New Year's Day when another big dinner is planned at Inanda again for all the mission families. 'Tis good that we are such a close clan— sort of takes the place of our families back home while we are away from all of you. We do have Christmas trees in our homes, much like yours.

You might not hear from me for a while as I'm going to be very busy until after the middle of January. Our mission has a training conference for church teachers at Inanda from the 3rd to the 10th of January, and I'm in charge of the Family Life division for that week. I have six hours of nutrition lectures to give, plus taking care of the recreation time during the week. And then, from the 10th to the 15th or later I'm having two people visiting us, so I don't think I'll be writing letters.

Would you let Howard's folks know that I'm doing fine? I don't know if I'll get a letter off to them.

Love, Marge

CHAPTER 7. Holidays and Crusades

Snake Bite for Mike, 1964

One of these weekend camping trips with the student nurses brought Mike the rather dubious honor of being the only person in a missionary family in South Africa to have ever been bitten by a snake. Actually, much to his annoyance, he never saw the snake.

Dave and Mike, barefooted, decided to go down to the beach after supper when it was dark. On the way back Mike thought he stepped on a sharp stick. As we were having our evening talent fun, he said his toe was sore. There was an area about the size of a quarter that was whitish. I thought maybe he was bit by an insect. We weren't too concerned. It starting swelling, and he was limping. Fortunately a mission doctor was with us. She told him to wash his foot well with soap. His feet were really dirty. Upon examining him closely, she noticed two tell-tale (very close together) puncture wounds. He was beginning to raise a temperature. At her suggestion, we applied a tourniquet on his leg and made a fast trip back to McCord Hospital. There, another Mission doctor who had seen many snake bites took one look and asked the nurse on duty for snake-bite serum. The doctor's diagnosis was that it had probably been a baby night adder bite; the snake-bite serum for a youngster was a massive dose of 25 cc, part of which had to injected near the wound, that by three or four hours after having been bitten was quite swollen and very tender. This was an excruciating pain-filled time for him.

The next day his temp was 101 degrees with rapid pulse, but the swelling gradually went down and he went to school on Wednesday. Unfortunately he was one of those rare individuals who react to the horse plasm in the snake-bite serum. About a week after he had the injection, he broke out in a complete body rash. His lips and eyes were puffy, and he had joint pains. His temp was 101.4. The doctors decided he was having a reaction to the serum. There was nothing to do but to let it wear itself out. The doctors said there would be no permanent damage after the symptoms went away. It was very fortunate that it was a baby snake that bit Mike. Sometimes, if bitten by a fully grown adder, even a 15-minute delay could be fatal.

Drakensburg Mountain Holiday, April 1964

Combi packed and everyone accounted for, we took off for Drakensburg, a range of mountains stretching across the western border of Natal about 170 miles from Durban. After going about 100 miles, we noticed that the car was going slower and slower up hills. We evidently had overloaded the Combi too many times for the motor to hold up. What a disappointment to have to turn around and go back. When we were about 60 miles from Durban, we were approaching the small township of Howick. We thought: why not camp there for a week near the famous Howick Falls? Howick is famous for its waterfall (365 ft.) of the Umgeni River.

After setting up camp, Howard drove the Combi back to Durban, which was downhill most of the way. Fortunately he was able to get a rebuilt VW motor put into the Combi right away, so he was back with it that evening.

Howick was a very small township, population about 4000, so there wasn't a lot of things to do. We did go to the local swimming pool everyday and the town had a theater so we went to two movies.

We went to Queen Elizabeth Park, a nature reserve about 10 miles away. The highlight of our stay was when we went to Giant's Castle Nature Reserve about 75 miles from Howick. An African guide took us on a hike to some Bushmen rock paintings in some caves. The scenery was very beautiful. All around us were mountains.

Because of more idleness than usual, we were trying to think of something to occupy our time. Pam said, "Let's study the Bible together." So that was what we did. We spent about two hours each day, and found it so interesting and stimulating that we continued to do it at home together. We did it for about 45 minutes after dinner. Even if we had company, they joined our study too. Each evening one of us was assigned to lead the discussion. Fortunately when we were in the U.S.A., we had bought a set of Interpreter's Bible (11 volumes) and since coming to South Africa, we bought William Barclay's paperback Interpreter's Bible (NT, 12 volumes), so we could do some research on the passages we were assigned.

Dr. Eric Hutchings' Crusade in Durban, 1964

Howard and I had attended the all-denominational Good Friday evening service at City Hall. Dr. Eric Hutchings, "the Billy Graham of Britain", was the speaker. We were impressed with his appeal to take the coming month-long crusade in all seriousness and to bring others to the crusade. Right away I thought of our nurses, so Howard and I took carloads of the African student nurses each night of the first week.

People from many different churches served as volunteer counselors about two months before the crusade started. Although 92 counselors had been trained, 250 young teenagers "stepped forward" after the first Friday youth-night service and more counselors were needed so Howard and I both decided to help out. Our Mike (12 years old) went forward on Saturday night. I had no idea that he was going to do that. He just went, never looking at any of us. He was really touched and knew that something was different for him. He said after Sunday School the next day, "I really knew for the first time what my Sunday school teacher was trying to tell the class."

All our children attended a Baptist Sunday School class while in Durban because the Congregational church's youth department was literally dead. They were getting a good Biblical foundation, but we worried about the

187

fundamentalism and dogmatism they were learning. Legalism with do's and don'ts can be so judgmental. It takes freedom out of your faith.

Our Longest Vacation (Three Weeks), July 1964

During the Winter school holidays (July, below the equator), we took a three-week trip through Southern Rhodesia (Zimbabwe) and a small portion of Northern Rhodesia (Zambia).

We chalked up over 4,000 miles mostly on tarred roads and a small section of "strip" road. The latter consists of two 12'-wide tarred strips. It's fine when there's no traffic coming towards you. On-coming traffic necessitates switching over to using just one of the "strips" while the on-coming traffic uses the other. This means that two of your wheels are on the strip and the other two on the dirt side of the road. Since these "strip" roads are used in lightly traveled sections, the sides and center between the strips are rough and stony and very dusty. Thus, each on-coming car and a passing car is a real experience in rough and blind driving (from the dust). These same conditions prevailed on many other roads listed on maps as fully tarred, but which turned out to be only 8-, 10- or 12-feet wide.

Well, anyway, we did just fine. The car was washable and so were we. Our holiday was both entertaining and informative. Our first stop was at the Zimbabwe Ruins. I remember John Burns from South Africa showing slides of the Zimbabwe Ruins before we left the U.S.A. John and his wife were studying at Andrews University in Berrien Springs, Michigan. We stayed there a couple days and pondered the ruins as many people before us had.

Our next stop was Chikore Mission Station, started by our church board, with its high school for 300 Africans. It was good to get better acquainted with our colleagues in Southern Rhodesia. The surrounding community of Afrikaner Dutch farmers didn't like the Mission very much, and we noticed a great deal of tension there. Government controls on African education are to teach them only what it wants them to know.

Next we camped at Kariba Dam, then onto Victoria Falls, and finally our last stop was Wankie Game Reserve. We bought lots and lots of curios made by Africans, while we were in Rhodesia. Many small items and a couple of big ones, such as a big drum hallowed out of a tree stump, covered with cow hide on top and sides carved and decorated using different colored shoe polishes. We also bought a 4-1/2 foot wooden giraffe which some how Howard fastened up on the inside of the roof of the Combi. It's made many thousand-mile journeys with us, and is still intact; also, the drum. We gave away many small curios and made a 6" board shelf on two of our living room walls in our retired home apartment for all of our small curios.

LETTERS, 1964

February 13, 1964

Dear Mom and All,

What a busy month January and February have been for me! I did not have to go to Inanda the first week in January to conduct my classes in nutrition. There weren't enough people signed up to take the course, so it was canceled. I was told there wasn't enough publicity about it to the churches—the chairman of the training conference just wasn't on the ball this year. I was rather glad that I didn't have to go this year, especially not knowing how I was going to hold up after just getting out of the hospital.

I've had company all through January and just said "goodbye" to our last guests last Saturday. It's good to be just a family of six again.

Mom, thanks so much for the lovely birthday wish and also your letter of January 29th. How are Cindy's plantar warts? The high protein food ProNutro has dried whole milk powder, fish flour, dried meat, peanuts, legumes, and calcium and iron added. ProNutro has proven more effective in diarrhea over milk. I haven't been doing much lecturing on ProNutro lately. I use it quite a bit though—in pancakes, muffins, candy, meatloaf, cooked cereal, cookies, etc.

Caryl, thank you very much for your birthday letter. I really appreciate hearing from you and all the news about Cherrie, Van, and Rommie. We watched our home movies last night and they really made us homesick; brought back all the memories of so many nice times when we all got together.

I mailed off a box to all of you yesterday. It contains six birds. We bought them from young African boys just along the road as we were leaving Kruger Park. They're real crude birds, but strictly African talent of the young people seven years on up. They are supposed to stand up, but most of them don't. Maybe someone could file off the bottoms straight, or put them on standards. The six birds are for Mom, Caryl, Fern, Dottie, Marion, and Howard's folks.

My back is fine, and everybody else is fine and very busy.

Love,

Marge and All

Sunday, March 29, 1964

Dear Mom and All,

The children are on holiday from school now. Dave and Pam have gone to church camp over the Easter weekend. They went Thursday and are coming back tomorrow. They went last year and had a wonderful time; it's a good opportunity for the teenage boys and girls to be together. They don't get much of this relationship since their schools are not coeducational.

After Dave and Pam get back we hope to take a camping trip about 200 miles from here in the Drakensburg Mountains. It will all depend on how Mike gets along. Last Saturday when we were chaperoning a group of nurses at Umnini Camp, Mike was bitten on his toe by a small snake. Mike, David and another boy decided to go down to the beach after supper when it was dark. They were barefooted. On the way back Mike was bitten but believe it or not, he didn't know it. He thought he had stepped on a sharp stick. As we were having our evening singing, he said his toe was sore, and it had a white area about as big as a quarter. I thought he might have gotten bit by an insect so didn't think too much of it until it started to swell and he was having trouble walking. Fortunately, Dr. Lasbrey was with us for the weekend. We looked it over carefully and decided we could see two fang marks. This was about one and a half hours after being bitten, so we put a couple of tourniquets on and dashed 30 miles back to McCord's, where he was given anti-snake venom serum. He was quite sick on Sunday with a

191

temperature of 101.6 and a rapid pulse, but the swelling of foot gradually went down and he went to school on Wednesday.

Then yesterday, a week after the serum, he broke out in a rash and his lips and eyes were very puffy. The doctors decided he was having a serum reaction; nothing to do but let it wear itself out. He's worse today—temperature of 101.4 and complete body rash with joint swelling. The doctor says no permanent damage is done after symptoms go away, but he has to be mighty careful not to get bitten by a snake again as he is so allergic to the anti-snake serum. We bought a snake kit to take with us to Drakensburg. We were mighty lucky that it was a baby snake that bit Mike; sometimes even a 15-minute delay is fatal.

Love,

Marge

April 23, 1964

Dear Mom and All,

How wonderful of Lou Lyman to call you. I'm so glad he got in touch with you to reassure you all is really well with us. We all thoroughly enjoyed being with him. We were so sorry that his wife and daughter had to remain behind in Johannesburg. His wife had gotten tick-bite fever in Rhodesia and Anne, the daughter, stayed to be with her mother. Dave was terribly disappointed that Anne couldn't come. Anne is 16.

Why don't you drop Lou Lyman a thank-you note at Lyman Chevrolet Co., Kent, Ohio. He's doing a terrific amount of work for the "Kingdom." Many times truly dedicated laymen can do much more to get the message across than ministers. He was over here on his own expense to find out what missions are doing here, so he can effectively awaken the people and groups to whom he speaks.

Mike is fine. He recovered from his serum reaction so that we could leave on our camping trip on the day we intended, but lo and behold, our car kept losing power. We finally decided to turn around after

*100 miles and go back home. What disappointments, but not for
long. I remembered reading about a camping spot at Howick Falls
which is on our way home, so we stopped off there and set up camp
from Tuesday until Sunday.*

*As we look back now our disappointment of not reaching the
Drakensburg Mountains turned into a real blessing for all of us.
Howick is a very small town of about 1,500 in population and not
a lot of things to do. We did go to the local swimming pool every
day, and the town had a theater so we took in two movies. Because
of more idleness than usual we were trying to think of something to
occupy our time, and Pam suggested studying the Bible together. So
that we did. We spent about two hours each day and found it so
interesting and stimulating that we've kept it up ever since, usually
about 45 minutes right after supper. In spite of Dave's and Pam's
heavy schedules of studying, they make time for our family study
together, even if we have company; they join us too. Fortunately, we
bought the "Interpreter's Bible Volumes" (eleven in all for $70)
and I've bought the paperback "Interpreter's Bible Volumes"
written by William Barclay. Each volume is only 65 cents. Why
don't you investigate and see if you can locate them. They are a
wonderful help and so simply explained. Once you get them you'll
wish you'd had them years ago. Just get a few volumes at a time,
whatever you're studying.*

*I wish I had more room to tell you about the Durban Crusade;
maybe next time. Sorry about Jack's father.*

Love,

Marge

Tuesday, April 28, 1964

Dear Mom,

*Howard and I attended the all-denominational Good Friday
evening service at City Hall about a month ago and Dr. Eric
Hutchings (leader of the Durban Crusade) was the speaker. He
and his team are from Britain. He's spoken of as the Billy Graham*

of Britain. Howard and I were very impressed as we listened to him that Friday evening. He made an appeal to all in the audience to take the coming Crusade in all seriousness. Each of us does our part to bring others. Right away I thought of the African nurses, so Howard and I took carloads of nurses each night of the first week. The Crusade started April 4th and will end May 3rd. Each evening there is a service.

About two months before the Crusade started, people from many different churches volunteered to be counselors to the people who came forward each evening to accept Christ as their personal Truth and Way. Counselors have an intense week of lectures on the know-how of helping people to have a better knowledge of what they have accepted. Ninety-two counselors had been trained, but after the first Friday Youth Night service in which 250 young teenagers boldly stepped forward, they made an appeal for more counselors for whom there would be a week of classes to attend in the evening.

Howard and I both decided to help out and take the counselor classes. We both learned much through these classes. It was an entirely different approach to religion than what we were used to. What with having a liberal religious background and then taking it from a Fundamentalist viewpoint through these classes gave me a fresh start with my spiritual growth. I can see much criticism for mass Evangelism and yet lots of good, too. There are some that are never really touched in their own church with a personal relationship with Christ, and sometimes it takes a powerful Evangelist like Dr. Hutchings or Billy Graham to finally have it strike home to them. Howard isn't helping as a counselor because he's too busy and never did get a chance to do all the required Biblical research of the counselor classes. It took me every free moment for a week to do the research. That's why Caryl's birthday letter was late. Anyway, we are both grateful for this opportunity to know more about Evangelism and how it works.

Mike went forward a week ago Saturday night. He was sitting right beside me and I had no idea he was going to. He just went, never looking at any of us. He was really touched and knew exactly what had come into his life. A whole new spiritual insight opened up to him. Christ tells us our spiritual eyes are opened once you truly accept, repent and believe, and that's what happened to Mike. He said after Sunday School the next day that he really knew for the first time what his Sunday School teacher was trying to tell the class. It's quite a revelation to watch someone whose soul is touched by the Holy Spirit. It makes your own faith so much stronger and gives you assurance that the Word of God is indeed Truth. It will be interesting to see how God will use him for His Purposes as he continues through life.

Dave and Pam accepted Christ rather in this fashion at a Baptist youth rally when they were 11 and 10 while we were still living in St. Joe, so they already know they are children of God and no longer belong to themselves. At the time they accepted Christ I didn't have spiritual insight to see and know what they did, so their growth has been much more gradual, but with Mike it's different. Both Howard and I know the experience he is having and are able to guide and explain. It was through Dave's and Pam's spiritual experience that I started groping and searching. Remember what Jesus said: "Those who knock and seek, they will receive." That's what I kept doing and am still doing and, little by little, small bits of Truth gradually keep opening for me. I wonder how often it happens that parents are le to Christ through their children. Jesus said, "Suffer the little children to come unto me."

All our children attend a Baptist Sunday School here. Pam was the one who started them all going. She went with a friend and was so impressed. The Congregational church that we go to has a very poor youth department, literally dead, so you can see our dilemma and concern about what the children are learning. They're getting a good Biblical foundation, but we worry about the fundamentalism and dogmatism they're learning. We have to be on the alert all the time to undo what we consider wrong concepts. We don't want them to think it's wrong to dance, play cards, wear lipstick, go to movies, go swimming on Sunday, etc. That's like putting God in a box with a nice pretty ribbon around it. I just can't see that approach; to me that's worshipping a "conditional God." If you do this and that then you'll slide into Heaven.

195

The big wrong of dogmatism is if you don't do it this way or believe this or that, then you're not in. Dogmatism is the cause of all the different denominations in Christianity. As for me, I have to live and let live, and let God do the judging. To me God is Love and all forgiving. He's the same yesterday, today and tomorrow, and He accepts me wholly as I am with all my faults, spiritual stupidity and imperfections. But the secret is after we accept and believe, God gradually molds us in His likeness, and I truly mean gradually— seems it takes eons. I finally discovered why Jesus says we no longer live by law (Moses' Ten Commandments) because when you accept, repent and believe, your heart breaks whenever you do anything that displeases God. You no longer live by law, but by love.

How thrilled I am that our children are gaining in their spiritual awareness at such a young age. As I look back and remember the void—living was merely an existence, wondering what it was all about—I'm quite resentful that I had to be so old before I realized what was the matter. But then I guess I should be very grateful. People grow old and die and never know. When I started this letter I was just going to tell you a little about the Crusade and ended up writing a chapter of my thoughts. I get carried away sometimes (as you know) and my pen flies away. We pray many times in our morning devotions that God will open up His Ways to all our Loved Ones.

I'm sending a few clippings of interest of the Crusade.

Much love to all, Marge

[There were no clippings of the Crusade in this envelope, but there was an exam form enclosed, with the following] written on the back by Marge:]

This is David's Scripture Examination questions. All Baptist Sunday Schools put these examinations out to Sunday School students, whoever wants to participate in them. Dave and Pam did last year and this year. All Baptist churches have the same day for students to write the exam so they don't cheat and look up a friend from some other Baptist church to find out what was going to be asked on the exam.

196

It took Dave three hours to do this one; Pam's took two hours. I don't know what happened to Pam's paper. Each age group has a different exam. The purpose of the exam is to make children study Scripture. I don't know when we'll know the results. Pam's friend Irene, who got Pam to go to the Baptist church, came in first of all entrants last year.

[The following letter is written to Allen R. Trumbull, Howard's father, and copied to Marge's mother in Dowagiac]

Monday, May 11, 1964

Dear Dad,

I hope you don't mind that Howard shared your letter with me. I wish that he had time to answer you. I know it would mean so much to you. This is his busy time of year and we haven't seen much of him. He's been working nights and weekends for a month now. It just so happens that so many conferences are held at this time of year, that he either has to prepare reports for or is away at the conference for a week at a time, which means he has to work on the double when he gets back to his desk. After June his work should slow down somewhat.

We humans are all alike in wanting to be understood and at the same time wanting to understand other people's thoughts and actions. I know we have created a puzzle in your mind as to why we're here in Africa, and I don't know if I'm articulate enough to really explain in black and white to help you understand, but at least I'll try and no doubt get myself in deep water and start calling for help.

Most of us are so afraid to say what we really think or believe, for fear of being misunderstood or being ridiculed. We hate to appear simple or immature in others' eyes—having others say we don't know the score yet. I'm one of those in the above paragraph, and I quake in my boots as you read this for fear of what you will think.

197

Nevertheless, I summon up courage and carry on, not yet knowing how my thoughts will accumulate.

My very first thought is, "By the Grace of God" we are here in Africa. Now I'll try to trace our lives back a few years and try to explain the above thought. I really didn't know what was happening way back then because I couldn't put it into words, but now that I'm growing in spiritual insight, God's working in and through our lives is becoming more apparent to me. In fact, I think this is the only true way to look at God's leading and not look at the present moment and say, it is "God's Will" that I'm doing this or that, because it's too hard to separate your own will out of it all.

About two or three years before we went to that church family camp I was invited to be with six other girls in a weekly study group. We called ourselves the "Get to Know Ourselves Group." We started out reading books on psychology, which was a great personal help to me, and then we started reading together books written by dedicated Christians. One evening about a year after I had been with this group I went to a Baptist Evangelical Crusade meeting and that preacher was talking directly to me (for the first time in my life)— Jesus Christ really died for me. It's taken a long time to get the full impact of what it all meant and I know I'm just on the fringe yet; but I know I really began to live from that day, not merely existing and wondering what life was all about. What a glorious knowledge it is that we don't really belong to ourselves, and that what man counts as success, God counts but folly.

Our life before coming here was one long struggle of climbing the success ladder—that big word "Pride"—keeping up with the Joneses and worrying about making more money so we can buy more possessions, give our kids all kinds of fancy lessons, and send them to the best schools so our pride can shine and say, "See what our kids can do." Never did we worry about giving them their true heritage—what God has done for them—and I don't mean what Sunday School teaches (yes, we did that). I mean living and thinking this revelation in our own home.

Now to go on with my story—I devoured Christian literature during those few years, staying up night after night until the wee hours of the morning. Howard was no doubt puzzled because always before, come 10:00 p.m., I couldn't keep awake any longer. Finally, summer came and I was determined to get my family to church family camp for our vacation. Howard was much against it. He didn't want to spend his hard-earned vacation time at any religious camp, especially since he had a motor boat to buzz around in. I even went to talk to our minister as to what to do; I didn't want to antagonize Howard with my selfish wishes anymore. I knew our registration fee had to be in at a certain time or we couldn't go, and I just didn't know what to do.

So talking it over with the minister we decided the best thing to do was to send in the registration fee and have faith, so that I did, not daring to write a check, though, for the fee. I took it out of my grocery money and we ate a little more simply that month. It so happened that there were two sessions of , one in June and one in July. Three of our very prominent church families happened to go to the one in June and they came back raving about it, especially the husbands. This was the situation which really softened Howard into going—it wasn't my doing at all—in fact I thought it best I quit talking about it. I knew I had the registration fee sent in, if he changed his mind.

So we went to that camp, and here we are in Africa today. God was using one of His servants at that camp to reach Howard. I thought the two of them were playing chess half the night those many nights, but they had many serious talks and just two days before camp was over, walking through the beautiful trail to breakfast he said to me, "What would you think of selling all we had and using our talents where they are needed in some other country?" I can imagine the fear he had in his heart as to what my answer might be. I can remember as clearly as if it was yesterday saying, "What we've got at 3907 Niles Avenue, St. Joe, is outward security" and I guess that's all the answer he needed. He started working on plans immediately to find out where best he could serve. Now, why it had to be outside the U.S.A., only God knows. He was the one who laid it upon his

199

heart. Some are called to go far from home and some work for Him right in their own backyard.

We appreciate your concern and worry about our children being in this unsettled land, but we feel that it's more important that our children's lives are right with God than that their safety is always assured. We had to get these thoughts settled in our own minds before we left America. We still don't know really why we're here rather than in the South working for the rights of Negroes, but that's not for us to question—only will the coming future years perhaps reveal His purposes. It very well could be through our children—who knows?

Do you see why I can feel God's leading through our lives? He was preparing me first, to be able to accept the fact that all that we do for ourselves is outward security. I couldn't have given Howard that go-ahead answer a few years before that. How I marvel at His workings when we truly bow before Him.

I wish you could write in simple words what you are trying to say. I'm puzzled over your last paragraph when you said it would give you a lot of pleasure if you could help complete the plans that you and your wife had, long before your children were ever born. What could be any higher than what we've found? Perhaps this sounds naïve, but I'm just comparing our lives before we found true "Purpose" and after. I know now what I want for our children— that they take the first two commandments of Jesus and know them for themselves and live by them. I think I can be so bold in my stage of development to say that there is a void in living until God reaches us and claims us for Himself. It's just the way he made us. We can try to escape from it, and many people do in many different ways.

You say there are many philosophies in life that are acceptable today; well, I guess I've expounded my philosophy. However, I must add it's my present philosophy. We mortals are ever changing as we get new leadings and insights, so don't worry about bursting my bubble. I wish you would write more often and just say what you think, fears and all. I read II Kings, but I haven't had time to study it and still don't know what it says.

Please share this with Dora. I was only addressing it to you because it was answering the letter you sent to Howard. Don't tear up so many of your letters next time—send them on. I'm wondering if I've confused or clarified? I suppose I'll be wondering for a long time, judging from the infrequency of your past letters.

We send our Love and Concern, Marge

Friday, May 15, 1964

Dear Mom and All,

I bet you wondered what happened to my Mother's Day greeting to you. To tell you the truth, I forgot all about it. In fact the family didn't think about it until Saturday, the day before Mother's Day. You don't hear so much about it here; it isn't as commercialized as it is in the U.S.A.

I just remembered the last letter I wrote to you I sent by sea mail because it was too much to get on this airmail stationery, so you probably won't get it for another two or three weeks. You will be receiving a book soon—it's on the race relations problems here, but presented in fact form so you can draw your own conclusion and try to seek an answer. The only answer I can see is everybody's right relationship to God, but that's not about to happen in our generation or probably many more to come.

We finally received a letter from Dad Trumbull (about the second since we've been here). He wrote after seeing Mr. Lyman. He said he's just as confused as ever as to why we're in Africa, and he says he stopped and spoke to you and you are, too. I wrote him a long letter a couple of days ago trying to explain; it may be helpful to you if you read it. I really don't know if I've confused or clarified but one thing I do know—if whoever reads it has had a personal rebirth through Christ will know what I'm saying, because a reborn spirit can only make sense through another reborn spirit. Paul says this doctrine of the Cross is sheer folly to those on their way to ruin, but to us who are on the way to salvation it is the power of God. And we're only on the way to "Salvation" after we've accepted Christ as "Our" Way, "Our" Truth," and "Our" Life.

201

I remember the above Scripture so well because we spent one whole hour on it a couple of nights ago in our family Bible study. We were trying to get it across to the children what it meant when it said "being saved" instead of just saved. The Revised Standard Version has "being saved," and King James, which the Baptists use, has "saved." To me the "being saved" is a continual process throughout life, not a once-and-for-all business. Look up I Corinthians, Chapter I, Verse 18—that's where I got the above verse. I took the verse from the New English Bible.

I do have a copy of the letter I wrote Dad—would you like me to send it on to you? Sorry, no more room.

Our Love to you all,

Marge

Monday, June 29, 1964

Dear Mom and All,

So sorry to hear about Dora's brother passing away; we hadn't heard about it until we heard from you. I can't remember Susie Danberry.

We had a family of five staying with us this week from our theological school in the Cape Province about 550 miles southwest from here. This week is the annual meeting of our African Church, which is held 70 miles south of here, so the men are attending that while we women stay home with the children. The family that is with us will be staying until the 10th of July in our house, but we'll be leaving on our holiday the 4th or 5th of July to Rhodesia. We'll be seeing a couple of our mission stations and many points of interest. All in all our roundtrip mileage should be about 3,310 miles.

Mom, I was very glad you said that you appreciated hearing about my inner searchings. I've been worrying about it lately, wondering what the rest have been thinking about my rambling on about my religious quest. No one ever writes anymore and I'm wondering if I've hurt anyone's feelings. I was glad you mentioned that you were sorry about leaving the wrong impression with Dad—I was sure you understood about us being here—but I know how you felt talking with him. He appears so wise with his own wisdom. I know I always feel so stupid when conversing with him, or I take that back—it's not really conversing, it's listening to his side and then feeling too inadequate to say what I really think. So I understand just how it was during your conversation.

I've sent off a sea mail letter to you of clippings and some photos that you'll probably receive while we're on our holiday. We're going to be gone three weeks, so I won't be writing to you for awhile. Anyway, you'll be getting the sea mail letter in the meantime.

So glad you are well and are still so very active with your garden.

Love to all,

Marge

Monday, August 10, 1964

Dear Mom,

It was nice to have your letter waiting for us when we returned from our holiday. Our first jaunt of the trip was 24 hours of steady driving (Howard and I take two-hour shifts of driving). We arrived in South Rhodesia at the Zimbabwe Ruins about 8:30 p.m. and had to set up the tent, etc. I remember John Burns showing pictures of these ruins. We stayed there a couple of days. Our next stop was our Chikore Mission Station. We stayed there a week, which gave us a chance to individually visit our fellow colleagues.

Our Mission runs a high school for 300 Africans there. We noticed a great deal of tension there with the surrounding community (Afrikaner/Dutch farmers). They don't like the Mission very much; they say we're teaching the Africans wrong things. Most whites in this country don't want the Africans to be very well educated (endangers the white's position too much). This is why the government has taken over all African education, so they can teach them what they want to.

203

Next we went to Kariba Dam and then on to Victoria Falls, which is beyond even describing in a picture unless you were in an airplane. We had to walk a mile along the Falls to take it all in, and with raincoats on.

Our last stop was Wankie Game Reserve. It's smaller than Kruger Park, but we saw a lot of game. We were in Kruger a week and saw 27 animals, and in Wankie a day and saw 18 different animals. We were gone three weeks in all and none of us was tired of traveling; having the big Combi makes traveling easier on everybody. Our car held up until we got to Johannesburg (500 miles from home). It didn't have the right amount of power in first gear so we stayed overnight with a mission family in Johannesburg, put the car in a garage, and got it fixed. We just had a new motor put in last April. I think we overload it for the size motor, but we do need a lot of equipment for six people. We just had to replace a couple of parts; I don't know what.

He said he thought that Jack and Dottie pretty much agreed with him, whatever that means. It was a long letter but Howard and I couldn't understand it, so we're right back where we started from. Howard wrote to him over a week ago and expounded some of his thoughts and "Faith." I wish he'd let you read it.

Keep up your Bible reading, Mom. It's food for the "Soul." Just as the body would shrivel and die without edible food, so would the "Soul" without its proper food.

Jack, why don't you write us a letter and explain to us Dad's philosophy or theory on life? We don't seem to make head nor tail of it when he writes.

Greetings to Mrs. Ames; hope she will like her new home.

Love to all,

Marge

Friday, August 28, 1964

Dear Caryl, Herman, and Children,

Congratulations, Herman, on your new promotion. Mom says you might have to move to Chicago. I hate the thought of you all not being in Dowagiac when we come home; it doesn't seem possible that we'll be home in less than two years. We are thinking and planning about it already. We've all missed our families very much and through separation realize how precious are the ties that bind.

Van and Rom might be interested in Mike's new venture. He is now taking up horseback riding and paying for it out of his own money. It costs $12 for a series of 12 lessons. He was lacking $3 so I got many odd jobs done around the house. Needless to say, we are all learning much about horses and horse stable language, which I'm learning is very crude, but I think it's good for him to be exposed. He says don't worry—he knows what's right and wrong. I wish I could be as sure. Tonight the horse riders are getting together for a cookout at the riding grounds. Howard and I plan to go after dinner and meet his friends.

Dottie sent a couple of pictures of Tammie. Mom is holding her in one picture; Mom really looks good. At first glance Tammie reminded me of Diane when she was little.

Have you met Girlie's new husband-to-be? It's good that she has found someone that she can love and have companionship with in the later years.

I have to go to one of our rural churches and give a talk on health and nutrition tomorrow. I haven't done that for almost a year. Then when I come back we're all going to "Umnini Camp" for a weekend and chaperone 20 nurses.

Greetings to Cherrie. What does she want to do after she gets her education?

With love to all,

Marge, Howard, and children

Monday, September 14, 1964

Dear Mom and All,

I just realized it's been over a month since I've written.

Dave and Pam have been without a piano since June. The Bergsman folks came back from their furlough in June, so they took their piano that we were storing for them. I finally located a used piano today; it needs tuning but otherwise it's okay. Used pianos are very high here; the cheapest usable secondhand pianos here are about $150. I hated to put out that much money, but the Gilleys said they would buy it from us when we leave for America.

Mike only wanted money for his birthday. His latest interest is horseback riding, which costs $12 for a series of 12 lessons. He lacked a few dollars so did a lot of odd jobs around the house, which I was glad to get done. We are a horse-conscious family of late.

I spoke to a rural church women's group a couple of weeks ago on nutrition. I haven't done that for over a year and it's rather stimulating talking to these groups, especially this one. Very few of these particular women had had any education, so this knowledge was brand new to them. It really gave me a feeling of being worthwhile.

In October I'm going to do some kind of cooking demonstration at the "Pastors' Wines Conference." I think I'll do it on salad making. I've discovered Africans eat very little raw food. This group I had just talked to had never eaten raw cabbage, and cabbage is one of their main vegetables, but always overcooked in too much water.

We spent last weekend at Umnini Camp with a group of nurses. We took lots of pictures of the girls as this was a senior group, and it would be their last opportunity to get pictures before they graduate. We only take pictures when we go to Umnini with the nurses, so I've been busy this week with girls coming over and ordering the pictures they want. We've been doing this ever since we started going to Umnini with the girls. Sometimes we don't go—someone else chaperones them—and then what wailing. It seems our picture taking is their only source of getting pictures of themselves. We charge them what it actually costs us for film and getting them developed.

I haven't heard from Everett. I wonder what it was he was questioning—probably some of my immature theology.

Thanks heaps for your letter, Dottie, and snaps. I really appreciated hearing from you. I'll be writing to you—won't promise when— seems I'm getting worse and worse at getting at my letterwriting.

Love to all, Marge

Saturday, October 3, 1964

Dear Mom and All,

I've come across some very exciting reading lately that has opened up some new ideas and thoughts for me. The author's name is Paul Tillich. He is one of the foremost theologians of our time and is now teaching in the Divinity School at the University of Chicago. His writings are based on a deep Christian Faith, but he presents his ideas and thoughts in an entirely new way.

Many highly intellectual people have come to a keen understanding with the problems of "being" and "existence" through Paul Tillich's preaching and writings. The three books I've read of his are "The Shaking of the Foundations," "The New Being," and "The Eternal Now." All of these three books are collections of sermons he has preached. I've just started another of his books called "The Courage to Be." I've only read three pages and have almost given up as it is too difficult for me to understand. The person who loaned it to me has encouraged me to keep wading through it and it will get clearer as I go along—I hope so. I do wish one of you would try reading one of the above books and see what you think of Paul Tillich's approach.

Another book I found very good was Fosdick's, "Dear Mr. Brown." David liked it, too. Each chapter is a letter written to a Mr. Brown, a college student who is going through a very difficult time with his faith. It's nice that our colleagues have so many books in their homes that we can borrow.

All for now . . . Love to all,

Marge

Enclosure: This was our Bible Study for our last Tuesday night Hospital staff fellowship:

John 15:1–9, The True Vine

The Old Testament frequently refers to Israel as a vine, but as a degenerate vine. Jesus says: "I am the true vine." It is not by being Jews, but by identification with Jesus that we become right with God. As Christians, we must be united with Christ as the branch is to the vine. As the vine gives life and sustenance to the branch, so Jesus gives life and sustenance to His believers.

There are two kinds of branches—the fruitful and the useless branches. There are three ways in which we can be useless branches:

Those who refuse to listen to Jesus Christ at all.

Those who listen to Him and talk as if they know Him and yet do not show it by their actions.

Those who accept Him as Master and then, in the face of difficulties or moved by the desire to do as they like and not as He likes, they abandon Him.

What does God mean when He says, "Every branch that does bear fruit, He prunes"? What would you say were some of the methods of pruning?

Trials (misfortune)

Sorrow (humbling)

Temptations

A person who is bearing fruit He gives heavier tasks and responsibilities.

What does Jesus mean when He says, "You are already made clean by the word I have spoken to you"?

Is it true that apart from Jesus you can do nothing? What is this nothing He's talking about?

What is meant by abiding in Christ? Abiding in Christ means to keep in constant contact with Christ. It is only in this way that we can defeat the evil and remain victorious through the disciplines of life.

What are the different ways of helping us to abide in Christ? Bible reading, prayer, silence and listening, obedience.

What are the results of abiding in Christ? Your own life is enriched (meaning, purpose). Your contact makes you a fruitful branch. Brings glory to God (for which we were created). Eternal Life (effectual prayer).

If then we evaluate ourselves honestly, are we fruitful branches? Do we have contempt—perhaps because he's dirty, smells of liquor, has different customs, is uneducated?

Do we feel superior or can we be self-effacing, remembering that others have different endowments, environments and opportunities?

Do we judge?

Do we reject?

Do we accept our fellow workers and patients as ones loved by God and know that they crave our acceptance?

Do we give of ourselves willingly and ungrudgingly to help others (friend or stranger) in their trials, sorrows, and fears?

What about the joy and freedom that Christ had offered us—do we radiate or feel this? If not, what is the reason? We do not have the right relationship with God. We have not wholly accepted the divine "forgiveness" that has been offered to us.

November 5, 1964:   8:00 p.m.

Dear Mom and All,

Today is Guy Fawkes Day—the children are over on the roof of the hospital to see everybody's fireworks displays. It's much like our 4th of July, except that children are permitted to buy firecrackers here. The city is threatening to outlaw it just as the States have, because of careless use.

About another ten days and year-end exams for the children—Pam is being affected already. I have noticed she brings some of her lunch home lately. Mike's horseback riding is at a standstill right now— he ran out of money. However, he continues his interest by library books on horsy stories.

I didn't have to do my cooking demonstration in October—too much rain. The roads in the country get pretty horrible at times. I've been addressing envelopes as Howard has got our Christmas letter done on time this year. I guess I really scared him last year. I was getting so put out with him for putting it off week after week, so I wrote one and told him I was going to send it out if he didn't get one written in two days. It was a pretty horrible example of a letter compared to how he writes, and I wrote it in such a way that you wouldn't know who the writer was. So that's all it took—he got his done in two days' time and that was the middle of January, way after Christmas. I've been threatening him with one of my letters since August this year.

Howard has to go to Johannesburg next week for a week to some meetings. The American Women's group I belong to is planning to have a big family dinner together for Thanksgiving at a hotel. Are you all getting together this year?

Dr. Christofersen's father died last week. Dr. Christofersen replaced Dr. Taylor as superintendent. His father had worked here in the mission for 42 years. He was a minister, but also was treasurer before Howard came. He and his wife left here for retirement in the States when we came here; he was 77 years old.

You'll be battling the snow drifts soon, and we are already beginning to feel our summer heat!

Love to all,

Marge

Monday, November 30, 1964:   9:30 a.m.

Dear Mom and All,

Our last letters passed en route; I wonder if they will this time.

I've got myself a new job for this morning and tomorrow morning. I'm keeping an eagle eye over 21 Indian boys (15 years old) in an Indian school as they write their three-hour, Latin year-end exam. I just have to see that they don't cheat or disturb each other. It's a wonder this school system ever produces any real thinkers. They get no credit for daily classroom work, so there's no incentive to do any further research work on any subject as they only get tested on what is in their own textbook. No outside project or report that they hand in during the year helps any towards their grade.

The American-Canadian club I belong to had a Thanksgiving dinner for all of its members at a hotel dining room. We all brought our families; there were 110 present. We would practically forget about American functions if it wasn't for belonging to that club.

You mentioned about Halloween. The American club usually has a Halloween party for the American children, but South African people don't have any such function. They do have fancy dress parades just for fun and give prizes sometimes. The McCord nurses have a traditional fancy dress parade Christmas Eve. When we first came here we thought that was so odd, but we've gotten quite used to it now.

The children will be through with their exams next week. School is over for the year on December 11ᵗʰ. Are you making big plans for Christmas? We are having a mission family from Johannesburg with us for a few days. Then between Christmas and New Year's Day all our mission families are meeting at Inanda girls' school for just a good old-fashioned fellowship and discussion time. This sort of helps take the place of all our relatives and friends that we've left behind, and gives us a closeness with one another.

Would you give Cheri a message for me? A nurse (Zulu), Ora Mbatha, came over to ask me if I could suggest a pen pal in America for her, so I gave her Cheri's name. Tell Cheri to please write to her. Ora is 20 years old and I think in her junior year of nurse's training. She's very interested in writing to someone outside of this country. She has an uncle teaching at Hartford Seminary in Connecticut.

Is Girlie still going to get married? The boys are getting very restless—they've been writing for two hours now and have one more hour to go!

Love, Marge

Tuesday, December 8, 1964

Dear Mom,

Do you think this will arrive in time to wish you a "Happy Birthday"? I hope so—the years roll around much too fast.

Today was our 20th wedding anniversary. I didn't have to get up at the usual 5:45 a.m. today. The children fixed their lunches and got breakfast all ready, and then called us at ten minutes to seven.

We've had some very depressing news. Lee Bergsman, one of our missionary colleagues, had major surgery for cancer a year ago while in the States and was apparently cured. He and his wife have been back in Durban since last June. Lee had a check-up yesterday and another mass was discovered low down in the tummy, so he went into McCord Hospital today and is going to be operated on tomorrow. Madge, his wife, is staying with us. Their two children are in university in the States. We're all going to have a very tense and anxious day tomorrow.

It's midnight and I'm very tired, so will close. We went to a movie tonight with another couple who has an anniversary the same day as ours. Movies start at 8:00 here and get out about 11:00 p.m. There's always an intermission about 8:45 after the shorts and newsreels and before the regular film starts.

We all send "Our Love" to you,

Marge

CHAPTER 8. Trials of Many Kinds

Pam's Birthday Party, 1965

The last couple of years Pam invited the McCord Hospital student nurses, who were in their month of study instead of ward duty, to her birthday parties. The student nurses spoke English and were taught English. There were usually about 20 nurses in the study at one time.

In 1965 Pam was going to be 15 years old and, up to this time, she didn't reveal to her white school friends that she had made some very close friends among the student nurses. She was concerned that her white school chums would look down upon her if they knew she was volunteering in the children's ward at the hospital and going to the Umnini Camp one weekend with the student nurses every other month. The nurses coming over to order snapshots that Howard had taken while at camp gave Pam lots of opportunities to become close friends with some of them. It would be unheard of for white kids to have black peer friends. Pam took a big leap into maturing when she made the decision to invite 12 African student nurses and three of her white school friends. We were so proud of her.

Immediately after everyone arrived I had them play a mixer game which kept them entertained for quite some time. I kept them going on games for a long time. Pam's white chums had never had an opportunity to know a black person around their age who was getting professional training. Most whites thought the blacks were less intelligent. We hoped that this gathering helped three white teenagers get another view point.

The party was a big success. The only tension or awkwardness I noticed was when it was time to leave. The white gals didn't know what to say to the black gals. Pam was her natural friendly self to both races.

Teaching Sunday School

I taught a Sunday school class of five white girls, aged 12 years old, at the Congregational church we were attending. We did a number of outside activities which interested the gals. I was trying to expose them to a world they didn't know anything about. One Saturday, when a group of nurses went to the Umnini Camp for the weekend, I took my five students and our children for the day to intermingle with the nurses and have fun at the beach.

We weren't in charge of the camp that weekend. I was pretty sure I couldn't get the girls' parents to agree to let them spend a whole weekend with Blacks. We did stay for the evening meal and evening entertainment. All in all, there were 46 of us sitting down together for the evening meal. For the evening entertainment, there were 16 different events presented—skits, singing, poems, dancing, guessing games. Even my Sunday school class got up and sang a song together.

When we were riding in our nine-passenger Combi to Umnini, I told them about the evening entertainment and they said, "We don't have to do anything do we?" I said, "Only those who want to." That was a big relief to them. I guess the other people's enthusiasm rubbed off on them, and they decided to join in and do a song as a group. Of course they started laughing and never did finish the song, but at least they tried. I had a carload of sleeping kids on our return home about 1 p.m.

One Friday night when Howard was gone overnight, I invited my Sunday school class over for supper and to stay overnight. I don't think Howard would have appreciated a bunch of giggly 12-year olds. We popped corn in the evening and played games. I turned my light out at midnight. They told me it was about 1 a.m. before they quit telling stories and jokes. The girls were up at 7:30, and

Mike helped me make waffles which they had never had before. I thought I'd never get them filled up.

After breakfast we finished making six knitted balls, about the size of a softball, for the children's ward at the hospital. We started that project about a month before when I had them over one evening. We stuffed the balls with discarded nylon hose. The girls were taught how to knit at school. After we finished making the balls about 11a.m., I took them to McCord Zulu Hospital through the children's ward for which they had made the balls. It was quite an experience for them.

They saw two children with spinal meningitis, one just a small baby. It's back was very arched with head way back towards the spine; many kwashiorkor (protein deficiency) babies; dehydrated infants getting liquid fed to them intravenously; children with bad burns; children who had fractured legs whose treatment was to have both legs suspended straight up, held up over the bed bar. Many children had tuberculosis, but were no longer contagious. I wish you could have seen the 12-years old faces—a combination of shock, horror, and sympathy. I don't think they had ever seen a mass of suffering before.

They marveled at Pam being willing to work there during the summer holidays, and she was only one year older than they were when she started working there. She was an experienced veteran by then and was able to withstand quite a bit, even death. One little child died when she was working there one day.

The knitted balls were enjoyed by the children. I took the girls home at noon and settled down to a quiet afternoon, and how quiet it did seem!

Christian Institute

I think it was in 1963 when the Christian Institute was formed. Howard and I helped get the first group together in Durban. The purpose was to get people of different denominations and different races to meet regularly and study scripture together. We wanted to breakdown denominational and racial barriers.

Rev. Beyers Naude of the Dutch Reformed Church was the instigator of the Christian Institute of South Africa. Rev. Naude was defrocked from his church for his stand. One evening he met in our house with 16 other Christian Institute members. Many of these members of many denomination and races felt the church was failing in South Africa—just like it did under Nazi rule in Germany—except for a small remnant who were courageous enough to act and speak, and even they were imprisoned and many were executed, as Bonhoeffer was.

Rev. Beyers Naude was suffering much persecution and was continually threatened for his stand against the Dutch Reformed Church, and he was classified as an enemy to the State because he stood for justice and brotherhood of man, that under God we all stand equal. Of course, this was a great threat to the Nationalists who are of the Dutch Reformed Afrikaans-speaking church. They claimed that the African was inferior, and wanted to keep them in that position, so naturally they couldn't let the Africans rise as to their individual abilities because then the Nationalists would be proven wrong.

The Nationalists passed a job restriction law which stated which jobs the Africans were allowed to hold, such as manual labor in mines, factorizing farms, domestic help, etc. They had been allowed to drive public buses only because there weren't enough whites to do it. It's a low-paying job, and there weren't enough whites willing to assume that responsibility for such a small salary. So the Government was forced to have to employ Africans. The same thing happened in the telephone service. It was quite an ordeal trying to get a long-distance operator. I usually had a book to read when I wanted to call long distance. Sometimes it would be half or three-quarters of a hour just letting the phone ring until an operator was free to answer. It was better after they employed Africans and Indians.

The Christian Institute group kept growing. After the group grew to about 12 people, we would split and form more groups. We met once a week, and then once a month, all coming together to share ideas and frustrations. As I'm writing this now in 1991, the Dutch Reformed Church admits that apartheid is sinful. Nelson Mandela, president of African National Congress, has recently been released from 25 years of imprisonment. There will be much unrest in South Africa for many, many years because of the effect of apartheid.

Banning Orders for a Very Good Friend, October 1965

We had some very sad news in October 1965. Jean Hill, one of our very good friends, was visited by the police and was put on the banned list. Banning means you cannot leave the district of your city, you cannot meet socially with people in your own home or at any meeting; you cannot write anything for publication.

Jean had been teaching Africans in her home on Saturdays, those who were having difficulty with math, Latin, or English. She'd been doing this for years without pay. She had been tutoring Pam and Dave every Saturday morning for over a year. The only thing allowed was to attend church, but if there was a fellowship hour afterwards, she was not allowed to attend that. Jean is a lay preacher in the Congregational Church, but she is no longer allowed to preach.

Banning of people who were a detriment to the State had been going on for some time. I wish I knew how many people of all races who were banned, literally hundreds. The Government often did not outlaw organizations, but they kept on banning the leaders of the organizations and soon there was no one left to lead. We think the Government really banned Jean Hill because of her keen interest and activity in "defence and aid" which is a legal defense for political prisoners and aid to families who had no source of livelihood when the breadwinner was in prison. Defence and Aid was backed by churches, not only in South Africa, but overseas as well. Jean was banned under the "Suppression

219

of Communism Act". She was no more Communist than you or I.

David's Mysterious Illness, November 1965

David had gone to a youth meeting at church on a Friday evening and came home not feeling well. His temp was 102.4 that evening. That temp wasn't acting right for the flu, so by Sunday evening I asked Dr. Magill to come and check him. His temp then was 103.8 and his spleen seemed to be enlarged somewhat, but no other definite symptoms. Dr. Magill took some blood for lab diagnosis. We had a suspicion of mononucleosis or hepatitis, but all lab tests came back negative. Then Dr. Magill took more blood on Wednesday and, by some lab indication, he had suspicions of typhoid fever. Thank goodness there was medication (Chloromycetin) for typhoid

So David started the tablets on Wednesday at 6 p.m. His temp during that night was 104.8. It took me two hours of sponging him to get his temp down to 103.8. His temp seemed to be down in morning, usually about 101 until about noon. Dr. Magill told us that in two weeks from the time he started the tablets, most all symptoms would be gone. Remember when it used to take about six weeks before they discovered the medication for typhoid, and then many people did not survive the disease? David became very weak from the disease and couldn't even hold a book to read. We got him books on tape from the Tape Aids for the Blind organization. He was so appreciative of those books on tapes that, after he got well, David began volunteering as a reader for that organization.

All of David's lab tests came back negative for typhoid, but Dr. Magill still thinks that's what it was. We found out differently on our trip to U.S.A. in June of 1966. I will tell you about that later.

A Three-Day Getaway, December 1965

After David's illness, I felt really burned out. The children seemed to be so demanding and not very considerate of me at times. It didn't seem there was hardly any time to relax, and yet I didn't feel I was accomplishing anything. Howard decided to take me away for a three-day getaway to a hotel downtown in Durban. He told the children that we expected them to take care of themselves. Ginger, 9 yrs old, was the youngest. They were to call any of our Mission colleagues if they needed to reach us.

What a wonderful time Howard and I had, having a rest from the demands from the children and work pressures! We got all our Christmas shopping done together. We went to several movies. Not having to get meals and listen to four different needs from all the kids, all at one time—well, it was a treat and just terrific getting away from it all.

The children did well taking care of themselves and getting their own meals. They were much more considerate and thoughtful of me after we returned from our getaway. They were very happy to have us back home again. I think that was a good revelation to them to realize how much they were taking us for granted and not realizing we have feelings and needs too.

Day of the Covenant

We had quite an exciting day on December 16, 1965, with the Day of the Covenant celebration. Dr. Goonam, an Indian woman doctor, whom I met at King Edwards Hospital working in the Planned Parenthood Clinic, invited our whole family to her house for the day. December 16 every year is a holiday here in celebration of the Day of the Covenant, the covenant that the Afrikaners made with God to worship Him forever if he gave them victory in the won battle with the Zulus in 1838. They did defeat the Zulus—but what a Covenant, to worship God *if* they defeated the Zulus!

So December 16th is celebrated in a number of different ways. I'm sure the Afrikaners keep it as a religious holiday and give thanks that they are still in control. The other races just consider the day as a day off work and enjoy it.

Each year on December 16th, Dr. Goonam invites her domestic staff who are African and their children. In 1965 she also invited a few Indian friends, two other white couples, and all of our family to her home for a fabulous dinner. After dinner Santa came with a huge pack on his back with a gift for everyone of us. When she called us up for our gift, we were supposed to perform with a song or recitation act. I can't remember what any of us did, except for Ginger. She recited a long poem called, "The Cat's Tea Party." Wish I had a memory like hers. We had such a fun day. Dr. Goonam said, "This is our traditional way of celebrating December 16th."

My Mom's Operation in January '66

Our thoughts were centered on our leaving for U.S.A. in June. We were already cleaning cupboards and closets to have a sale or give away things we no longer needed.

Dottie had mentioned to us in a letter in the later part of 1965 that mom had lost 16 to 18 pounds and wasn't feeling too peppy. In January she went into the hospital for tests and the doctor decided to operate. Dottie sent us a telegram right after the operation saying the doctor thought the growth he took out, which was obstructing the pancreas, may be malignant. We were making plans for my departure to be with mom. Then we received another telegram from Dottie saying the lab reports said it was benign. What a big sigh of relief for all of us.

My mom recuperated fast and got back into the swing of activities rather quickly, we thought. But she said she was being sensible and was resting when she was tired. She always believed in good nutrition and exercise to keep fit, and I guess it was paying off well in her quick recovery.

I'm writing this in 1991. My mom, 97 years old, has been in a nursing home since she was 91, but hasn't known any of us for three years. Her physical body is doing well, but her mind gave out on her. At least we had good years and memories with her for 94 yrs. I remember that she said several times when her mind was still functioning that she wished the good Lord would take her. It's so heartbreaking to visit her now because she doesn't respond to anything we say.

Dale Carnegie Course, May 1966

As time was nearing for us to return to U.S.A., I was getting anxious feelings about the possibility of being asked to speak to groups. I decided to take Dale Carnegie's "Course for Effective Speaking". The thought of taking this course frightened me, but I knew I had better do something constructive about my anxiety.

There were about 35 men and 13 women in the course I was in. It was quite an ordeal to get up and speak in front of this group each week. The spontaneous speaking was ghastly. Each meeting, not only did we have to give a prepared talk, but as we sat in our chairs after each spontaneous talk, we all shifted to the next chair over until it was our turn to talk. When you finally moved to the designated seat, you knew it was your turn next. When the speaker got through and you started to walk to the speaker's spot, you were handed a slip of paper with a word written on it that you were supposed to speak about. I did survive the course, and was very glad that I got up the courage to suffer through the misery and fear of that course. I felt much better about the possibility of being called upon to speak while we were home in U.S.A.

Packing

I can't handle the thought of packing. It's so traumatic to be so torn up and unsettled for weeks. We've never had the privilege of having movers pack for us. Anyway, I try not to think of the ordeal and just take one day at a time.

We had to pack in wooden crates because our things might have to be shipped elsewhere. We didn't know if we would get back into South Africa or not. Every little spot in the crates had to be packed tightly so nothing would rattle or shift back and forth. I thought I was getting arthritis in my fingers because they were getting painful from stuffing things in small areas. As always, one's task does get done.

We planned to have our packing done a week ahead of our leaving date so we could stay at the Swedish Mission House to rest up for our journey and also have free time for visiting. We were invited out for dinner every evening that week and Pam, 16 years old, had a delightful surprise from her school chums. A girl in her class asked Pam to go to a movie with her. Pam was to go to her house at 8 p.m. When she arrived, her friend wanted to show her something in the bedroom. When the door was opened, a huge chorus of "Surprise" was heard. Pam's whole class was there and even some boys, too. Pam said she didn't know what to say so she just let the tears fall. The surprise was a super gift to her, and she has treasured the memories of it.

CHAPTER 9. Coming Home and Going Back

Our Trip to U.S.A.

We had a well-thought out itinerary for our trip home. But as you know, sometimes well-made plans have to change. We've learned over the years to flow with the changes. It's much better than getting mad and up tight.

Our first stop was in Kitwe, Zambia. That's where the All-African Council of Churches headquarters is located. We stayed overnight there, and then went to Dar es Salaam in Tanzania for a 24-hour stop to spend some time with friends. Our next flight was canceled because of an air strike so we had to stay in Dar es Salaam for four days. The airplane company put us up at a luxurious air-conditioned hotel and paid for all our meals at the hotel. Can you believe it? We got tired of their luxurious meals and longed for a simple hamburger. We could have gone across the street to a restaurant, but that would have been at our own expense, so we ate the luxurious meals. Wish we had some of those meals now and then at the present time.

The layover in Dar es Salaam was a blessing in disguise. Mike was quite ill with a high temp when we arrived, and Dave wasn't feeling to well. We took them to a local doctor who was well acquainted with their symptoms, and he said he knew they had malaria. He didn't get them tested because we weren't going to be there long enough to get the results. He gave them both the medication for active malaria, which was an injection, and they got well very quickly. The doctor said they must have gotten it in South Africa because of the amount of time for the incubation period. South African doctors said they don't have malaria there, and they thought it was typhoid. Dave always tested negative for typhoid and was eventually diagnosed as having a Fever of Unknown Causes. Well, he must have had malaria, and every six months or so he would have a temp of unknown origin so that's what it must have been. After getting treatment to cure the malaria, neither of them has had any problems since.

Our Home for a Year in St. Joseph, Michigan

We thought that we might have to go to our Mission home in Boston for furloughed missionaries. We hated to be so far away from our extended family in Michigan, but it's pretty hard to find a completely furnished place for six people. Our sending church in St. Joseph knew of our needs, and Betty Place took on that special project. Betty was a missionary kid so she knew of the difficulty her family had in finding suitable, affordable housing while they were home on furlough.

Before we started on our trip home, we received a letter from Betty telling us she had found a downstairs furnished flat. It had two bedrooms, but had an ample heated basement that could be fixed for a bedroom for the boys. It sounded wonderful. The flat was completely furnished with a washer, dryer, vacuum cleaner, lawn mower, and even a T.V. People from the church furnished us with sheets, blankets, towels, and wash cloths. They had the basement all fixed up as a bedroom with beds for the boys by the time we got there. Can you believe that when we opened the cupboards, they and also the refrigerator were stocked with food? What a Blessed welcome homecoming! How we appreciated all their special efforts on our behalf!

Dave and Pam Budgeting Their Own Money

Dave was a senior and Pam, a junior in high school the year we were home. We knew we would be leaving Dave in college when we went back overseas. Pam also wanted to stay in U.S.A. since she would be completing the 11th grade. If she went back to South Africa, she would have had to do the 11th grade over because they required the students to do both 11th and 12th years consecutively. They are called the "matric years". No way did she relish doing the 11th grade over again.

In view of the fact that we would be leaving Dave and Pam when we went back overseas, we decided to give them each $30.00 a month to budget for all their personal needs and wants. We bought their necessary clothing, but if they wanted what we call a luxury item, they would have to budget for it. They learned a lot that year. It was a good training time for them. They learned the value of watching and waiting for sales to make their money stretch or at least to be able to buy the things they wanted.

In August, we went to our church family camp as the Missionary Resource Family. While there, we met the Briggs family with three daughters. They were all three adopted. The oldest was Pam's age. When the Briggs heard that we were looking for a family that would adopt Pam for a year while she was in her senior year, they readily asked her to be a part of their family when we went back overseas. That was wonderful to get that issue settled so quickly after we got to U.S.A. I'm sure one of my siblings would have offered her a home, but Pam wanted to stay in St. Joseph since she would be doing her 11th year there. That would give her a bit of continuity with friends.

A Special Gift by Way of the Telephone, December 8, 1971

Howard spent of a lot of time speaking in churches around U.S.A. while we were home. In early December 1966, he flew to Texas for a week of speaking engagements. That week we had the worst snowstorm in 20 years in St. Joseph. It kept us all home for four days. Schools were closed. Only the main roads were being kept open by snow removal equipment. We played a lot of games over those four days. The kids spent a part of each day trying to shovel out our long way. It was useless by the next morning. It was so full with snow again, so we decided to enjoy the beauty of our white world and were thankful for our warm house.

Howard watched the weather reports on T.V. and called us on December 8th to see how we were doing. He was basking in the warm sunshine in Texas. December 8th was our twentieth wedding anniversary. He said, "I got a gift for you." I said, "Wonderful, I can hardly wait until you get home." He said, "I can give it to you now." Now, what could he give me as a gift except his love over the phone? He said, "I've stopped smoking as a gift for you." That was a very special gift to me.

Our Mission Board had asked him to stop smoking before we went overseas, and he quit for two years. Then he started smoking again. That caused a lot of tension between us. The biggest thrust in my medical perception was preventive medicine, so I detested the thought that he could be damaging his body because of his smoking. This time he went back to smoking again after a year in a half. I was crushed and very resentful. It took me months or probably years of soul-searching to realize that the resentment I was harboring was damaging to myself and also to our relationship, so with God's help I relinquished that resentment and decided to button my lip regarding his smoking. That was a load taken off my shoulders and probably his too.

Another thing I thought through was that he should have never given that gift to me. I felt that someday he hopefully would be able to give that gift to himself. It took another 18 years before he pledged himself that gift. He went to the doctor for a physical in 1983, when we were living in Grand Rapids. The blood test and glucose tolerance tests revealed that his sugar was just above the normal. The doctor told him that if he lost 25 lbs., stopped smoking, and started exercising, he'd probably keep his sugar problem under control without medication. This was in the month of December, so the doctor said you probably should wait until after the holidays are over to start losing weight. But he didn't. We started walking everyday in the mall, even if the weather was bad. He gave up smoking and went on a diabetic exchange diet, and he did lose 25 lbs. Now that's quite a feat when giving up smoking at the same time.

He had finally given himself that gift. He hasn't smoked since then, and he's also kept his weight down. He used to joke about the fact that the only exercise he ever did was to push a pencil in his accounting job. Now he's committed to walking briskly for an hour every day. It's been a real plus for me to have him take charge of his own health maintenance.

Conference with Ginger's Teacher

Ginger was in the fifth grade the year we were home. During our first parent-teacher conference, her teacher spoke to us of his concern about Ginger. She was day-dreaming a lot and was always the last one out of the room when it was time to leave. He was also concerned that she was not doing her schoolwork according to her capabilities. We were hearing that from all her teachers in South Africa. He wanted us to make an appointment with the school's psychiatrist, which we did.

Ginger went to see him by herself, then he wanted a conference with us. The date he picked, Howard happened to be out-of-town speaking, so I ended up seeing him by myself. He told me that he didn't think we should go back to South Africa. He said she needed long-term counseling therapy. He said he thought she was schizophrenic. That really upset me. Howard was plenty upset that the psychiatrist would make a judgment on just one visit. Howard told him that there were many psychiatrists where we live in Durban, and also there was a child guidance clinic just behind his office. The psychiatrist then agreed that it would be all right to go back to South Africa, but he made us promise that we would get an appointment for her as quickly as we got back to Durban, which we did. She had counseling for six months, and we also had counseling.

The Child Guidance Clinic didn't think she was schizophrenic. Ginger was just a slow developer, and we were to help her be more independent by requiring her to make decisions. She never did get motivated to do her schoolwork up to the capacity that she was capable of and she never was into being competitive throughout all her school years. At the time I'm writing this in 1991, she has been working for nine years in a nun's nursing home in the housekeeping department and, more recently, as a supply clerk. For years she has lived on basic pay and had her own apartment. She has continued to be a responsible person, keeping all her bills paid without help from anyone. She enjoys getting together with all the family, especially the nieces and nephews. Pam and John have her over often. Ginger stays with Mark, 3 years old, while Pam and John get away for an occasional weekend.

Ginger has just recently joined a Catholic church after taking nine months of confirmation classes. The church is near to her apartment. That is nice for her since she doesn't have a car.

Time to Leave U.S.A.

The time had arrived when we would be leaving Dave and Pam to go back to South Africa. Actually Dave left us because he was spending the summer on the staff of seven different United Church of Christ summer camps for young people. He would be representing the foreign mission thrust of our church.

Our family took David to the O'Hare Airport in Chicago. We all gathered around in a circle with our arms around each other, sending him off with a prayer. This was a time of tears for us because we didn't know when we would see David again. As we stood professing our love for David and thanking God for having given us David for these past 18-1/2 years, Howard and I were deeply aware that we were making our first sacrifice since being called to foreign mission work some seven years ago.

In just a few more days, we would be parting from Pam, and this would be our second sacrifice. She was to spend the summer with the Briggs family, settling in and getting adjusted to their routines and ways before school started again in September.

All our children did well the last year in the St. Joseph schools. Mike was in the eighth grade and, along with all his school curriculum, he discovered a few other interesting subjects—a new type of clothing, long hair, and GIRLS. Since he will have to wear a uniform, cut his long hair, and go to an all-boys school in Durban, he was not overly anxious about returning to South Africa.

Getting Involved with the Catholic Movement "Cursillo"

While we were still in St. Joseph, Michigan, Buzz and Charlotte Emerson sponsored us for a Cursillo weekend retreat. This was put on by the Catholic Church to help their members "Experience Christ" in their brothers and sisters. The husbands and single men were supposed to go to the first Cursillo because of being the spiritual head in the home, and then wives and single women would go to a Cursillo weekend sometime in the future. It is a very structured weekend.

Thursday evening until Sunday afternoon, eight presentations were given by priests and seven by laypeople. We were put in a group of eight around a table with a big sheet of newsprint paper, crayons, and chalk. We were supposed to listen to the presentation. Then each table of eight was to combine efforts in drawing a picture to represent the lecture. Each table would then hold up the picture, and explain their picture to the rest of the group. There were about 40 women the time I went, and I was the only Protestant.

We both thought this would be a terrific type of retreat weekend to have in Durban, especially to try to get all the races together at one time. We bought all the literature we could find on the Cursillo Movement to take back to South Africa with us.

Soon after we got back to Durban, Howard went to see Archbishop Dennis Hurley, about getting the Cursillo started. Low and behold, they were having a meeting right

231

at that very hour, making plans to start Cursillo weekend retreats. They asked Howard if he would be a lay speaker on the very first retreat and the following retreats. It wasn't until a year later that the Cursillo retreats for women were started, and I was asked to be a lay speaker at the first retreat and all subsequent retreats.

Not only were the Cursillo retreats in South Africa good spiritual growth times, but it was a terrific opportunity to get the races together—whites, coloreds, Indians, and blacks. We all slept in big dormitory rooms and all ate at one table. This just was not done by whites in their ordinary settings. To eat off the same dishes that other races ate from was unheard of. So there was a lot of growth in experiencing others as people like themselves with similar needs, aspirations, and hopes.

For too long, the Church here in the United States has failed to practice what it preaches: the Brotherhood of Man. Only recently have the churches begun to speak out against the blasphemy of apartheid. We felt the Cursillo movement was doing a good job in helping the participants experience the Brotherhood of Man.

Pam's Return to Us, August 1968

Pam wanted to go into nurses training at Bronson Methodist Hospital in Kalamazoo, Michigan, where I had graduated from. In her senior year she took an entrance exam at Bronson Hospital, but failed the exam. She was heartbroken. She wrote and asked if she could come back to Durban to do her nursing training. We agreed, but it caused us a bit of concern that she might fall in love with a South African and marry, and maybe not go back to U.S.A. We were pleased and proud of how she managed the necessary details of travel. She said, "I had no idea it was so complicated." She stopped to visit and sightsee in London, Geneva, Accra in Ghana, and Johannesburg.

When Pam left the States, there was much race-rioting going on and it frightened her. After unpacking, she said, "It's so good to be back here where they keep blacks under control." I thought, Wow! what a lot you've got to learn, Pam. She had seen the movie "Guess Who's Coming to Dinner". Sidney Poitier wanted to marry a white girl. Pam didn't think that was right. How she matured and changed in a few years time!

Pam was readily accepted for nurses training at Entabei (at "the top of the hill" in Zulu) Hospital. This was training for only white girls. It was just two miles from our house, and she was allowed to come home for two nights a week.

Near the end of her second year, two other students and Pam wanted to get an apartment together and live off the nursing campus. We didn't like the idea very much, but we decided this should be a learning experience for Pam and the two others. This was an unfurnished apartment so they had to go to secondhand places to get furniture pots, pans, and dishes. They also had to get household insurance. Of course, she never thought about that. Then the telephone had to be hooked up. The girls had been saving money for this joint venture. Student nurses were paid so much a month while they were in training.

After a few months Pam discovered it was hard to study because the other girls had their dates over at the house, and they even stayed overnight at times. Eventually Pam moved back to the nurses' dormitory, and we were much relived. She loved her training and was doing well.

Literacy Work

Soon after we got back to Durban in 1967, I met Mrs. Dollivera. She was head of the Operation Upgrade organization which used the Laubach method of teaching reading and writing, commonly known as "Each one teach one". Mrs. Dollivera convinced me to take a correspondence course in literacy from the University of Virginia, which would equip me to be a trainer of teachers. The actual teachers of the illiterates would be persons from the various races and language groups in South Africa, who also spoke English and were trained in English. The illiterates themselves were taught by persons from their own mother tongue and culture.

Part of my literacy correspondence course was to find an illiterate person and teach him/her how to read and write. Before we left on our furlough, Pam got acquainted with the 19-year old African servant next door to us. Lydia was vivacious with an outgoing personality. She and Pam had long talks together. Lydia was so happy to see us after we got back from U.S.A. She told us she wanted so much to go to night school at the YWCA from 5:30 to 7:30 p.m., but as a servant she was much needed at that time to do the dinner dishes and help put the children to bed. She had only gone up to the second grade and then started doing domestic work in the white areas. She could speak English very well. Because of her predicament, we decided that she could work for us and live in our servants' quarters in the back. This way she could go to night school, and I would use her as my illiterate student.

Most always students are taught in their mother's tongue, but since Lydia spoke English so well, I thought I could teach her to read and write English. She learned how to read and write quickly. I drilled her on spelling and comprehension. She was promoted to fifth grade level in her night school very soon. Lydia was soon teaching a class of neighborhood servants in our garage in the evenings. She was teaching them how to read and write in Zulu, and was doing a superb job. She was a born teacher.

I enjoyed my job of training teachers and also appreciated so much having Lydia to do a lot of my household tasks. She cooked three main dishes very well, so she could even prepare meals for me when we were having company. What a boon that was for me. I spent a lot of time with the Operation Upgrade organization so her help was wonderful for me.

Buzz Bike for Mike

Mike entered tenth grade in February of 1968. We were pleased with his willingness to buckle down into the South

African school system again. He continued to be an extremely active and deeply committed member of a local Baptist church. His greatest interest was to own a "buzz bike".

Not having much opportunity to earn money, he decided to buy a two old buzz bikes from the junk yard for $30.00. He made one good buzz bike out of the two bikes. You should have seen our garage—completely littered with parts. He had no doubts about getting the parts back together again. With the addition of some new part, lots of chrome plating, six or more "final" assemblies, and much help from interested friends, he had a beautiful running 50 cc buzz bike. In South Africa, one can't drive a buzz bike until 16 years of age. You can be assured it was ready and waiting on his 16th birthday on August 4. You had to be 18 to drive a car or own a more powerful motorbike.

David's Back with Our Family, 1969

We noticed a sense of loneliness in David's letters to us. We mentioned in a letter to him that he was welcome to come back to Durban and go to University here. He called us by phone and said, "I'm coming."

Not many of his credits were transferable to the University of Natal here in Durban, but he accepted that setback pretty much in stride. Besides his studies, he was busy in various student organizations on campus, organizing talks, debates, etc., usually on political matters. He attended a work camp of University students to restore Mahatma Gandhi's home and lawn in Phoenix, less than 20 miles from Durban, to its original condition.

David also got involved with a group of young people who called themselves, "Church". They all had one thing in common. All found no satisfaction in the established churches and were bothered by the lack of action. They started collecting books, and gave about a ton of books to the poor African school near Durban. They also organized a clinic in an Indian shanty settlement. Dave was a friend of Steve Biko. Steve Biko was a medical student who was eventually imprisoned and beaten while in prison, and at one time so brutally beaten that he died from the mistreatment. There was a movie made about him called, "Cry Freedom."

It was good to have Dave back with us, and we were proud of his involvements.

Mike Leaves Us for the States, December 1969

Mike didn't think it was fair that Dave and Pam did their last year of high school in the States, and he wasn't allowed to. We just were not going to be on furlough at the right time for him to do that. He became sullen, and isolated himself in his room, only coming out for his meals.

David had been back home a couple of months, and he was Mike's roommate. Dave told us that Mike confided in him that he was thinking of committing suicide. We decided to send Mike to see a school psychologist who was a friend of ours. He told us we'd better let Mike go. He said, "Mike was pretty determined in not wanting to do the rest of his schooling in South Africa." Since Mike was the one who wanted to go, we thought he should write to whomever he thought he wanted live with and see if he could find accommodation for a year and a half. My sister Fern and family in Pennsylvania offered him a home.

Mike had been smoking for a year and a half. I said, "Either you give up smoking or stay at home." I wasn't about to have him influence his teenage cousins. He decided he would give up smoking, and I don't think he's smoked since. Mike thought we were too strict with our discipline and was glad to get away, only to find Fern and Everett had far more restrictions on their children and him than we did.

That year and a half away from us was good for him. He began to appreciate and accept us. This growing up business isn't easy.

Medical Safari

Mike had already gone to the States, so he missed out on a very interesting, overnight medical safari. Dr.

236

Merriweather, a London Congregational missionary, invited our whole family to come to Molepolole, Botswana, to go on a medical safari. He was head of a 135-bed hospital in Molepolole called, Scottish Mission Hospital. Every month he went on an overnight medical safari in the Kalahari Desert with a big lorry (truck).

We started out early one morning with overnight necessities and food and lots of medical supplies. We rode in the back of the truck sitting on our sleeping bags. As we neared a village in the desert, the local people could see the dust and hear the motor of the truck. This was a signal for anyone needing medical attention to meet at the local church. We could see people walking from every which way to the church. After most of the people had assembled, they would sit down on the ground in the shade of the church building, and Dr. Merriweather would give a short sermonette and prayers.

The people would line up to be seen by the doctor. We had set up medical supplies on a table in the church. Pam was almost finished with her second year of nurses training, so she and I did the injections when Dr. Merriweather ordered them for the patients. Obstetric examinations were done behind the altar which gave a bit of privacy. Any patients who needed more attention than Dr. Merriweather could give them were told to watch for the truck on the return trip to the hospital. They would be picked up and taken to the hospital to be treated. We stopped at, at least, four or five villages before nightfall descended on us. We built a big bonfire and ate our prepared food, and got out our cots and bedding and slept around the fire. It got very cold during the night in the desert, so we tried to keep the bonfire going.

On our way back to the hospital the next day, we stopped at each of the villages and picked up patients and family members to go with them along with chickens, goats, etc., and three big iron pots. Cooking for the patients was done outside the hospital by family members. So believe me, we had a very full truck by the time we got back to the hospital.

As we were driving between villages once, we met two Bushmen with bow and arrow out hunting food. Dr. Merriweather stopped the truck and chatted with them in their language. They were carrying a small sized tin can hung in a leather pouch. They wanted to know if anyone smoked and if someone would give them a cigarette. Howard had cigarettes with him, and he gave each of them one and they put this small tin up to their cigarette and lit them. Howard was curious what was in that tin, so they tossed it up to him. It was so hot, Howard dropped it, and those Bushmen laughed and laughed, and we did too. The tin was full of hot smoldering peat moss. They always carry this with them to start fires for cooking and warmth on their journeys for food.

We felt very privileged to have this experience of going on a medical safari in the Kalahari Desert.

CHAPTER 10. Deportation

Deported from South Africa, 1971

For a number of years the South African government had been deporting foreign church workers. On February 22, 1971, our whole family was notified that a warrant for our deportation had been issued, but was temporarily suspended pending our voluntary departure prior to the 28th of May.

We immediately went to the nurses' dormitory to inform Pam about our deportation. We didn't want her to read about it in the newspaper. She only had nine months more to complete her nurses training. Her immediate reaction was rage at us for doing this to her life. She threatened to marry her South African boyfriend that she had been dating for three months. As it happened he dropped her like a hot potato soon after he read about our deportation in the newspaper. He never called her again for a date. When she finally faced the reality of the injustice of the deportation, she again became angry.

Up to this time, Pam had been quite apolitical. She began reading books from our bookshelves on the injustices of apartheid. Pam wrote an open letter to the Minister of the Interior, and it was published in our local newspaper which I copied and will add below to these pages of memoirs.

A Young Departee's Open Letter, March 18, 1971

Sir, I, a deportee, would like to write this open letter to Mr. Gerdener (Minister of the Interior) :

Dear Mr. Gerdener,

I'm sorry but I just cannot understand your actions against our family – and may I also add – against many others who have also been served with deportation orders within the past month.

No reasons were given. Does it make you feel good to kick people out of the country without giving any reasons?

I want you to know that we as the Trumbull family are not ashamed of anything we have done in this country nor are we guilty.

I am not a boastful person, but in this case I feel I must tell you that we have done only good in this country (in the sight of God).

I have been brought up on a Christian and respectful home—knowing what is right and what is wrong. When there is injustice being done, we as Christians stand firm in what we believe.

I am not yet 21, but will be before our deportation date. My dad has told me that an appeal has never been granted. I'm not prepared to beg you for an appeal nor do I want to be the first person to be granted an appeal because I know of many more who deserve an appeal more than I do.

I suppose you know and I suppose you don't care that I am in my third year of nursing. I would be writing finals in November, if I hadn't been deported. I would like to know before I leave this country, if you would have granted me an appeal.

The assistant matron of Entabeni Hospital was willing to write to you right away but I told her not to. For the respect and love I have for my family, I will stand with them.

Mr. Gerdener, what has Ginger, my 14-year old sister done to receive such an order; what has Mike done? Do you know that he hasn't even been with us for over a year now? David, what has he done? My mom and dad, what have they done? And myself, what have I done?

The film "Z" has just come to mind. I saw parallels in that film.

At present I am trying very hard to accept this deportation order and I sincerely hope I don't leave this country with bitter feelings.

May I leave you with four virtues of life—honesty, perseverance, temperance and justice.

Yours faithfully,
Pamela Trumbull

Pam had a few weeks of leisure time before she left for the States, and I asked her if she would like to go to a weekend "Cursillo" retreat which I was helping to lead. That weekend was another step in her maturing. There were about 50 women attending from all the four races. She began seeing people as humans to respect and love. No longer was the color of the skin an issue for her.

The South African government did not give you any reasons or explanation for the deportation. What is so disturbing about the banishment of priests and Mission workers is that in most cases nobody—and least of all the people they had been working with and among—had any idea why their continued presence was undesirable or contrary to the public interest. Their only "crime" appears to be that they were foreign and that their work often involved interracial contact. We were a threat to the South African "way of life".

Howard was interrogated a number of times by the security police. These were times of great anxiety. My imagination was running over time. Would they torture him? Would they let him return home? We became very aware that our home and phone was tapped; Howard's interrogation revealed that. They had thick files on him and corrected him if he didn't answer them to their liking. We would go outside when we wanted to talk about things the security police might be interested in. We were very careful when conversing on the phone.

On February 25, just three days after our deportation orders, Howard's office was raided by six members of the Security Branch. They stayed four hours, studying documents and files. Howard was involved in giving small financial support to relations of political prisoners. Mostly to give money for wives to visit their husbands in prisons and a few rands for school uniforms for the children. The Security Branch finally left, taking a quantity of documents and files with them.

We had to find a home for our dog, Tippy. Poor Ginger, this was the second time she had to grieve for having to leave her pets. When we left U.S.A., we found a home for our dog and now again. Our second dog looked just like our first one in U.S.A. They both were named Tippy because of a white tip on the end of the tail.

Packing again! This time for sure not coming back to South Africa! We were to stop in Botswana, a country adjacent to South Africa, on our way home to see if Howard's skills could be used there.

An American Deportee Writes, June 1971

My letter was in the *Christian Leader* newspaper:

Dear Friends,

My heart is sad over leaving my many friends. I have been privileged to get beyond surface acquaintance with Africans, Indians, coloreds, and whites. I thank them all very sincerely for sharing themselves with me and enriching my life.

I have witnessed with observation and personal experience that "The Christ" with whom I'm acquainted bridges that gap and wipes away prejudice and misunderstanding between colour, race, creed, and culture. Christ in my life has helped me to accept and love those who differ from myself and, even more important, to accept and love those who disagree with me and that's a tall order. At least it is for me. "Thanks be to God who had the victory."

242

I believe that reconciliation, care, and concern between all my sisters and brothers of the human family is a necessity in order to have the will of God to win in his world – which can create a just society for all to share in.

I grieve for those in the human family who are crying out with despondency and despair. I marvel that so many have the will to go on living with such severe problems and handicaps. How can they still believe that there is a God who loves and cares for them? These people have taught me so much about Faith and Hope. I can only say, "Father forgives us and has mercy on us." We profess so glibly our love for you, but neglect so shamefully our care and concern for our world family.

I will not say "Good-bye" – because I have Faith and Hope in a different tomorrow.

Devotedly in Christ,
Mrs. Marge Trumbull

Three Months in U.S.A.

Dave and Pam left for U.S.A. the later part of March, and we got there in June. Pam had stayed with various relatives until she was to enter nurses training in August at Bronson Methodist Hospital in Kalamazoo, Michigan. Dave went to Kalamazoo, rented an apartment, and started University at Western, very soon after he returned to U.S.A.

Before we arrived in U.S.A., Pam started dating a black chap, Steve Harrison, from Dowagiac. What a difference in her attitude since 1968 when she came back to South Africa to go to nurses training there. She had just seen the movie, "Guess Who's Coming for Dinner?" Sidney Poitier played in it. He, a black, brought a white girl whom he was in love with home for dinner. Pam at that time was against interracial dating and marriage. A lot had happened to her since 1968 to change her perspectives and attitudes. We liked Steve and his family. We could perceive before we left for Botswana, Africa, that their relationship was heading toward marriage one day. We asked Steve if he could see that Pam got through her nursing training before they married, and he agreed to that request.

Pam dating a black has brought out some prejudices in my family and is causing some alienation which really grieves me. Caryl and Herman are extremely against interracal dating and marriage. They have asked us not to come to their home. I feel sorry for my mom because she is caught in the middle, trying to keep harmony with all. She had given a key to her house to Pam so that she could feel that she had a home to come to when she has a few days off from her nursing training. Mom liked Steve very much and gave her blessings to them. It is so hard thought when we had family gatherings. If we were going to be there, then Caryl and Herman won't come, so it's probably good that we left for Africa again to work in Francistown, Botswana.

When we got home in June, we were going to surprise Mike in Pennsylvania by coming to his senior high school graduation, only to find out that he had left and didn't intend to attend his graduation. As it turned out, we weren't present at any of our children's high school graduations, not that we didn't want to be though.

That summer Mike got a job in a Lutheran church camp as a head counselor team. Halfway through the summer he came down with a severe case of mononucleosis and was hospitalized. We picked him up and took him to Dave's apartment in Kalamazoo to recuperate, since we didn't have a home of our own.

On September 7th, we took Mike to settle into Shippensburg State University back in Pennsylvania. Three weeks later after we returned to Botswana, we got a letter from Mike saying he had split from the university and hoped we would understand. He said he wasn't ready to hit the books yet, and hoped he had our blessings. Naturally we would have preferred him staying in the university, but also knew we couldn't make decisions for him. We felt we had given him the best basic foundation we were capable of, and it was now up to him to make choices. If he chooses wrong, then he would just have to live with the frustrations and consequences it brings. Yes, he had our love and blessings. He said Fern and Everett had been very kind and understanding and offered to store his things for him. My siblings have been so generous and helpful to all of our family

CHAPTER 11. Botswana Beckons

Francistown, Botswana, September 1971

I think we entirely unpacked our suitcases on Sept. 14, 1971, for the first time since we had left South Africa in June. It seemed we were on the go so much from June to September that we never fully unpacked.

Our intentions were to fly to Zambia since there were no big planes from the South that went into Botswana. We had prearranged a flight on a small plane to take Howard, Ginger, and me to Francistown, Botswana. When we got to Zambia, they had no record of our reservation, and the next flight was in a week. What to do?! We really didn't want to take the train through Rhodesia to Francistown because Rhodesia had a reciprocity agreement with South Africa. While we were home in U.S.A. for those three months, Dean Ffrench Beytagh, an Anglican priest from Johannesburg, was sentenced to prison for his participation in the Aid to Dependents Fund. Howard was listed as co-conspirator. We finally decided to take our chances on the train. We were always fearful when the train attendant asked to see our passports.

We got off in Bulawayo, Zimbabwe, to see if we could leave Ginger at St. Peter's Girls Boarding School, where she was registered to attend. There was no school up to her grade yet in Botswana. This worked out well. We were able to leave her at the school, and we traveled on by train to Francistown, mighty relieved when we crossed over into the Botswana territory. Francistown reminded me of my very early childhood—dirt roads, horses pulling carts, no street lights, and small grocery shops.

247

We rented a three-bedroom prefab house—very comfy, except for one big drawback—it had a wood/ coal stove in the kitchen which heated the water in the geyser. There was a gas stove for cooking. It was the tail end of winter and the temperature was in the 80's and 90's. In the summer, it's 100–120 degrees. So you can imagine what the kitchen would be like with that wood/coal stove burning to keep us in hot water. We hoped we could have it removed and install a hand gas water heater instead, but that wasn't possible because the next renters may not be able to afford the gas heater.

Our things that we left packed in South Africa would arrive on October 28th, a little over a month after we arrived in Francistown. We borrowed a couple of beds, bedding, tables, chairs, and a few pots and dishes to get by. The hardest part was not having a refrigerator. After I got my refrigerator, shopping was a lot easier. You really couldn't plan what you would have for meals. You had to shop and see what was available. Butcher shops were open only in the morning. Milk was railed in every afternoon from Rhodesia. If you took more than you needed for that day, even if you had a frig, it would go sour I guess because it wasn't refrigerated as it was railed from Rhodesia. Frozen foods were railed from Rhodesia also and were often thawed when arriving in Francistown, so I was a bit leery of buying frozen foods too.

We soon learned to use powdered milk for drinking and cooking, and we still use powdered milk to this day. The more we were there and saw the misery and suffering of the poor, the more we were ashamed of complaining over any conditions or inconveniences. We counted our "blessings" with thanksgiving.

There was only one short distance of paved road in Francistown. Our home had a dirt road on two sides, so I was constantly battling the build up of dust in our home. Our yard had no grass—it was just too dry and the use of water was too expensive to be using on our lawns. Only the rich had lush green grass.

The mopane ("moe-pah-nee" with the emphasis on "pah") tree was indigenous to Botswana. We had a mopane tree in our front yard. It was as big as a large maple tree and had an abundance of leaves. Twice a year the mopane trees were invaded by the mopane worms (caterpillars) which were as big as a tomato worm. The worms would eat up all the leaves off the trees. If we were sitting outside on the veranda in the evening, we could hear the chewing of the mopane worm. This didn't seem to hurt the tree—leaves always grew back. The local people would gather up gunny sacks of mopane worms and put them out on screens to dry in the sun. This was a good source of protein for them. We were at a social function once and there was a bowl of dried mopane worms on the buffet table, so I tasted one. It was very bland, hardly had any taste. It would have been nice to have a dip to dip them in to give them a bit of flavor.

Language Study

In October I met a couple of Peace Corps people in town one day. Twenty-six new Peace Corps people had just recently arrived. The two I met told me that all 26 of them would be starting their month-long, intensive language training after the middle of November. I asked them if outsiders could join the group for language training. They thought so and gave me an address to write to in Gaborone. I wrote on October 21, and got my reply November 14, telling me to be at Adume Park 4 miles outside of Gaborone on Nov. 16th. This meant I had really only 24 hours to get everything in shipshape to leave because I had to leave on the 15th by train in order to be there by the 16th.

A friend took me to the train because Howard was in Gaborone at the time, so he was able to meet me when my train got into Gaborone. He was just too busy to join me in the training. Most of the people he would be dealing with spoke English, but I had no idea what I would eventually get involved in.

Howard drove me to Adume Park, which is a Boy/Girl Guides camp. We lived in very crude, mud huts with grass roofs and no lights except in the main building which had a

249

generator. Toilets were outhouses. Each hut had a bucket which we filled from one central tap to take sponge baths. I shared a hut with an energetic 70-year old Peace Corps gal who was going to teach school somewhere in Botswana. The rest of the participants were 21–24 years of age. The food was terrific. They had a wonderful African cook. The flies were much worse than in Durban. Dishwashing certainly wouldn't pass a health inspector.

Amazingly, we all stayed well. We only had three hours of language study a day to begin with. An African taught us, using no English at all. We didn't have to know what he was saying. We just had to mimic to get the feel of tone, sounds, and rhythm of the language. We were sure glad we didn't start eight hours a day. Three hours was exhausting.

We were to have two weeks of extensive group language study, then we were assigned to stay in an African village with a family who didn't speak English. I was in the village two days when I got a message that Howard had been in a car accident.

Howard's Car Accident

I was at the village with my adopted family just two days when a message was brought to me that Howard was in a car accident and was in a hospital in Francistown. I packed up and was put on the train in Gaborone, getting to Francistown (300 miles north) the next morning. I went straight to the hospital. Howard was pretty uncomfortable; however, the X-rays showed no broken bones. The X-ray machine was pretty ancient, and we did find out later that he had a broken left collar bone, sternum, and a chip off a cervical vertebra.

Howard and two others had gone to Serowe (100 miles south of Francistown) in a Datsun pick-up truck. Howard wanted to buy some thatching grass for the rondoval roof in our back yard. He wanted to use the rondoval for his office, but the roof leaked. One the way back home with a full load of thatching grass, a back tire blew and the truck overturned. The other two weren't hurt much either, just badly shocked and bruised. The truck was pretty badly damaged. The roof was in a V shape and all the windows were broken. I think the heavy load of thatching grass softened the crash.

Howard stayed only four days at the hospital. He was propped up most of the time because he was more comfortable that way. No wind-up beds in that hospital. When we thought of all the possibilities of the accident, we were so grateful that it wasn't any worse. When another fellow went back to where the accident was the next day, a lot of thatching had been stolen.

Eventually we did get the thatching to put a new roof on the rondoval, and Howard used that for his office. He had been using our screened-in front veranda and, if it would rain, his equipment and papers would get wet. I was glad to get his office off the front veranda. It seemed like we had no privacy. There were always 10 or 12 refugees waiting to see Howard. Howard was assigned by the Botswana Christian Council to be the Refugee Officer in Botswana.

Raising a Garden

At first it was quite an adjustment for me having the children all gone at once and no actual assignment to plunge into. So instead of raising children, I decided to raise a garden. It was my first experience in this venture. I finally learned what would grow and what wouldn't in this hot dry climate. I bought some cattle manure to spread in the soil and also buried my garbage in the garden area to enrich the soil. Watering was quite a chore. It was too expensive to water with a sprinkler, so each row was planted in a 2-inch trench that I would fill with water and let it soak in before refilling it.

Anyway, our garden kept us in fresh vegetables the year round. The shops would run out of fresh produce very early in the day.

I did have problems with chickens and roaming goats getting into my garden. Fortunately we had a fence all around our property. So after replanting my garden several

251

times after goats ate it, I finally was committed to closing our big gate. No more problems then.

Refugee Work

Howard found refugee work challenging, but also very frustrating. In February 1972, Mr. Van Ounwillar from the World Council of Churches came to audit the refugee accounts. The day he arrived was the day the refugees came to get their monthly money.

Howard was having problems with some of the fellows. One of the biggest problems was that some had been in Botswana as long as six years and were still receiving handouts. There was a lack of money because of the 9,000,000 refugees in Pakistan, and there just wasn't money to hand out so freely. All of the handouts had to be lowered, and some of the refugees had been warned six months before that their handouts were to be dropped at the first of the year. I guess they just didn't believe it would be so, but Howard had been firm and wouldn't give anything to the ones who had been warned six months back. Many of the others had their handouts decreased because of the lack of funds.

A few years ago, there had been plenty of money for educational scholarships, relocation, and handouts, so some of the refugees were just plain frustrated with the present hopelessness. Howard was patient with them and listened to all their grievances, but he still had to be firm with helping them to become independent. The constant year-after-year handouts were demoralizing to their personalities. It was tough in helping them change their outlooks.

The previous officer used to finally give into some of their demands, and the refugees learned they'd get what they wanted. However, Howard wasn't going to give in; besides, there weren't any funds to give. They had to learn that they would be helped for just so many months until they could either go on to some other place, perhaps for military training or further education, or find some kind of work. The problem about work in Botswana, is that they get a handout as a refugee from Howard without doing any work.

252

The local pay for work was very low—about the same as Howard's handout for a month—so naturally people would rather have a handout, but this only led to their downfall if it was kept up for very long. So Howard felt he had a real challenge to keep these fellows "men".

Consequently there was much hate floating around among the refugees towards Howard. It was a good thing that Howard had a strong character and could take being disliked so much of the time. About 40 of them staged a protest demonstration in our front yard with placards and chanting. Some of the placards said things like, "Trumbull is an autocrat. To hell with Bass Kap in refugee relief. Hunger is my bedfellow. We demand the resignation of Howard Trumbull. There's a hot seat in hell for all liars. We want our children educated. Howard Trumbull misled the Dean. It's a sin to be a refugee; Yankee go home. Howard is my shepherd, I shall not eat." The police arrested all of them and warned them about their behavior.

Also David Findly, from the President's Office in Gaborone, came to talk to them and all was calm—for a while—until payday again. There were some that were real rebel rousers and encouraged others to join them. That day they were really getting out of hand. Howard usually had them come into his office one at a time, but not that day. They wouldn't pay attention to him so he called the police. The came immediately and talked for hours with them, but still they were rude and demanding. The police finally said, "No one would get any money that day." They could come back the next day.

The next day two policemen and someone from the Security Branch were there. This time the refugees were real gentlemen. We were lucky that the police were so helpful. If it wasn't for them, I'm sure that Howard wouldn't be able to stick it out because the fellows would make it tough on us. We had police protection all night after that protest demonstration in our yard. Many of the refugees drink heavily, and David Findly didn't want to take any chances so he asked for protection for us.

Howard has been sued four times by refugees, and had to go to court. He finally got a lawyer who knew the legal machinery, so it was not quite as exhausting and insecure as the first time he was defending himself. He won all four cases.

We were glad the children weren't still with us to have had to worry about them. We weren't worried or unduly concerned about our own safety. Maybe we should have been because we eventually heard that being a Refugee Officer can be hazardous. Some had been killed. We thought everything would calm down once they got to know that Howard was fair but firm and also meant what he said. That proved to be the way it went, much more manageable.

Volunteer Work

I had thought of getting a job in the local hospital, but I found out our Mission Board did not want us to work for pay. If we did work for pay, the money was to be turned into our Board in New York, so that put a stop to my thinking about getting a job.

Ted and Muriel Stackley and their three children from Kansas were sent to Francistown by the Church World Service organization. Ted worked with the sewage problems of Botswana. Muriel and I became very good friends. We started an English class for elementary school dropouts. We used all kinds of ideas to teach English: we made up simple crossword puzzles; unscrambled jumbled sentences; spelling bees; sex education; dictation; games; songs; and, how to answer and take down messages from a telephone.

One day we had six of them over to our house to make scrapbooks for the hospital children. I served them chocolate cake and orange Kool-Aid with ice cubes. The ice cubes were the greatest interest. I don't think they had ever had any before. We also had them practice using a telephone. They called a friend of mine who gave them a message to write down. It was the first time they had ever dialed a phone or talked through a phone. It was quite an unique experience for them.

Muriel and I started an evening Bible study. About seven came regularly, only two blacks in the group. I helped supervise literacy classes that were starting. I couldn't teach because of the language barrier. So I kept track of all the classes and helped to get new classes started by local people.

I also worked one morning a week in a health clinic run by the Red Cross. All pregnant women and mothers with small children were given cooking oil and powdered milk to take home.

Social Life

Botswana had gotten its independence from Britain five years before we arrived. The Prime Minister was Siretse Khama, and he was married to a white English woman. There were no legal racial barriers in Botswana, but we didn't notice much racial mixing at social functions or in dating. We joined the Mopane Club, a community center, for $3.00 membership dues. It was a good place to meet white and black people. There was Bingo on Thursday evening, and a movie was shown on Wednesday and Sunday evenings out under the stars. Chairs were set up and the film was shown on a side of a building. No movie if it rained which was rarely because they had been having a draught for seven years. There was dancing sometimes on Saturday evening. They served steak and french fries for 30 cents. That fit our budget just fine.

We went to the movie most every evening one was shown; cost was 40 cents, cowboys or not! We needed that diversion. There was a bar in the club too, which was heavily used. I think we were the only ones drinking coke. There was another club in town, but quite expensive and only whites went to that one. There were about 600 white folks living in Francistown. Our other enjoyment was having friends in for dinner and the evening.

We attended an Anglican Church, the only English-speaking church in town. There were very few whites that came so I guess most of the other 600 whites didn't go to church at all. Eventually, we did join the other social club in

Francistown that was for whites only. We thought it would be good to meet more people.

A Job Change for Howard, April 1973

After much thought and careful consideration, Howard resigned his job as Refugee Officer as of the end of April 1973. He had lots of consultation with the Botswana Christian Council about the refugee work. The Botswana Christian Council decided to discontinue their work with refugees, mainly due to lack of cooperation of the government. They handed the refugee situation over to the government to let it handle all the problems. The Botswana Christian Council had to take all the crudeness and criticism from the refugees, so they had had enough of being the "fall guy" for the government. The Botswana Christian Council was willing to be on the Government Refugee Committee and also willing to help raise money for the handling of refugees.

Howard thought it was time to get out for himself before some of the refugees resorted to violence. He was concerned for my safety too. The Refugee Officer in Lesotho was beaten up just after Christmas, and one was killed in Ethiopia.

The Botswana Christian Council wanted Howard to stay in Botswana and coordinate its funds, which amounted to half a million dollars a year, and also to be financial advisor and consultant to medical mission institutions and Mission schools. We had to move to the capital, Gaborone. Housing was very scarce there.

The Baileys, English colleagues living in Gaborone, were leaving on a month's furlough the end of April, so we lived in their house using their furniture, etc. We stored our own things in the "Reading Room" for the refugees until we could find housing in Gaborone. This move was more inconvenient for Ginger because she had to take the train 300 more miles to Gaborone from Rhodesia. There was another girl at her school who also lived in Gaborone, and they could travel together. On her short four-day holidays,

Muriel and Ted Stackley invited her to their home in Francistown, so all worked out well. Ginger loved the Stackley family.

Spiritual Downer

While living in Durban, South Africa, we were richly blessed with spiritual food and opportunities. There we had attended an English-speaking worship service every Sunday morning, and Sunday evening we usually went to the nurses' service at the hospital next door. We were involved in a Bible study at the hospital once a week and also an ecumenical study. Howard and I both were on the planning team of the Catholic Retreat called Cursillo and helped lead the retreats. I taught 12-year old girls in Sunday school.

Then we went to live in Francistown, Botswana, where there was only one English-speaking church service and no small groups to attend. It became so apparent to us, that Christian involvement was a real need to keep the embers burning. Fortunately, I recently had read the book *Prison to Praise,* by Merlin Carothers. Carothers' theory was to give thanks and praise in all circumstances, regardless if they were dire. Those who do keep victorious and on top of the cloud because they claim God's promise, "That all works toward good for those who love the Lord." It seems pretty solid in theory, but mighty hard to do in practice. I guess that's why most of us go through so many dark nights of the soul.

Hepatitis, April 1973

Wouldn't you know, I had to go and complicate things just as we were getting our packing started for our move to Gaborone.

On April 7, a Saturday morning, I had a very low temp of 99 degrees, but by Saturday evening it was 101.8, Sunday 102, and Monday down to 100. So I thought my temp was gradually going down. I did the usual home remedies—lots of fluids and vitamin C—however, I didn't have any symptoms of sore throat, cough, cold, headache, diarrhea, aches, or pains. By Tuesday morning when my temp was

257

still 100, I though I better go to the doctor at the outpatient department of the hospital and see if they could find what was ailing me. By that afternoon when I went to the doctor, my temp was up to 103. The doctor didn't know what the cause of my temp was either. So he thought I should be admitted to the hospital to have some tests done before I took any antibiotics, which might mask the problem.

The doctor took blood for a blood count and blood culture, urine culture, and chest X rays. The first three tests had to be sent to Gaborone to a laboratory, and the results wouldn't be back for three days. After the tests were done, I was given some kind of medication to bring down the fever and then started on antibiotics. My temp gradually went down and was normal by Thursday evening, so the doctor let me go home on Friday. After I was home, I noticed my stool was somewhat grey color and my urine was dark orange, but I thought it might be due to the medication. By Sunday, I was getting jaundiced so then I knew I had hepatitis.

I didn't need to get the results back from those tests to determine my diagnosis now. I called the doctor, and he said I would have to have bed rest for about a month and not eat meat or fats. No wonder I was so uncomfortable after I took a dose of that liquid antibiotic. It was in a liquid oil base. As soon as I was no longer taking the antibiotics and didn't eat any foods with protein or fat, I remained fairly comfortable. The doctor explained the reason why I was supposed to have bed rest. He said the liver is swollen. When you walk, it bounces against bony structures of the body and could be permanently damaged.

What a horrible time to have to be in bed when I knew how much needed to be packed yet, and I was cheating some. Finally Howard decided I should go by plane to Gaborone on April 19, and stay with some friends until we could live in Baileys' home at the end of April. The doctor said I should not ride in a car on those bumpy dirt roads. I know that was the solution, but I hated to leave him with all the work to do. Ginger came home for her three-week holiday from school (before I left), so she helped a lot.

On May 5, Howard started having a temperature. I kept him in bed and, because I had suspicions it might be hepatitis, I didn't give him any food with fat or protein. In about a week he was jaundiced. Fortunately, he never did experience the extreme burning discomfort I did because he didn't eat any protein or fat. But one thing I was worried about was whether he would stay in bed or not. So I decided to prolong my bed rest and stay down with him. We rather enjoyed our confinement. Friends brought us books and magazines to read and we listened to the radio a lot. No T.V. yet in Botswana. Fortunately, the Baileys' servant wanted to stay on and work for us so she did all the laundry, cleaning, and grocery shopping. I got up long enough to fix our meals. A month passed all too quickly, and it was time for Howard to get working at his new job.

Pam's Wedding—April 21, 1973

Lots of plans and decisions were discussed through letters from Pam to us. At one time Pam and Steve planned to be married in Dowagiac and have the reception at the V.F.W. hall, but Pam wanted Larry Stanton, a minister friend of all of our family, to marry them. He lived in St. Joseph and was the minister of our Congregational Church when we were home on furlough. The Stantons had been missionaries at one time and knew the heartache of leaving grown children back in the U.S.A., so they were mom and dad to our kids while we were in Botswana. Then Betty Place, in St. Joseph, wrote to me and said she wanted to give a wedding shower for Pam and wanted a list of my friends in St. Joe to invite to the shower. Pam and Steve's final decision was to be married by Larry Stanton in the Congregational Church in St. Joseph where we worshipped before becoming missionaries. The Women's Fellowship wanted to take care of the wedding reception in the fellowship hall as a gift to Pam and Steve.

Pam asked me if I could design and write up her wedding invitations. Well, that was quite a task for me who was not very creative, but I tackled it with determination and finally came up with what I thought was a satisfactory idea.

Dick Sales drew the cover of the invitation for me. He drew an African rondoval with a thatched roof and a boy and girl hand in hand walking down the path away from the rondoval. On the cover it said, "We Will Walk Together." The invitation inside read:

Howard and Marge Trumbull of Botswana Africa regret that we will not be able to be present at our daughters wedding. But we would be pleased if you could share their joy when

Pamela Beth Trumbull

and

Steven Charles Harrison

declare their love for one another
by uniting together in marriage
on April 21, 1973 at 2 p.m. in the

First Congregational Church,
2001 Niles Ave.,
St. Joseph, Michigan.

You are invited to the reception
in the Church Hall after the wedding ceremony.

We told Pam there wasn't any place in Botswana where I could get any fancy printing done so the invitations were mimeographed on a Roneo machine. Pam and I decided it would be much more financially practical to send the invitations from the States. I put a 1c Botswana stamp on each envelope, and Pam put the proper American postage beside the 1c Botswana stamp when she sent them out.

Howard and I were sad that we couldn't be present at their wedding, but we did send a short note to be read by Larry Stanton at their wedding. We sent it to Larry and told him not to tell them that he was going to read it. We wanted it to be a surprise for Pam and Steve. We got a letter from Larry a couple weeks after the wedding, and he said everything went so beautifully, but said also he about blew it all when he got choked reading our letter. He said it was the highlight of the service. This is the letter I wrote:

Dear Pam and Steve,

You know how we yearn to be with you today and share in this joyous occasion. This even had interwoven meaning for two families whom you have brought together, and we rejoice in our new-found friendships.

And to you, who have come to share their wedding vows, we are grateful because we as parents and Pam and Steve know that no human life has any meaning whatsoever, unless it is related to other human lives. Pam and Steve know that their loving relationship cannot have meaning in themselves apart from friends and people with whom they relate. So Pam and Steve have invited you to share their wedding vows because essentially they cannot live together as man and wife and as two people who care for each other unless they have a community of people who care for them.

Pam and Steve, we pray and will continue to pray that you will have sufficient wisdom and understanding to be able to meet and transcend any and all difficulties which may arise as you live together throughout the coming years. We pray that in and through each other you may find the diversity of your eternal personalities and that the unity which binds you will be enriched and deepened by your individual personalities.

We challenge you both, Steve and Pam, to keep open and searching for God's way in your lives as individuals and in your relationship together.

We love you dearly and are with you in spirit,

Mom and Dad

Pam and Steve honeymooned in Trinidad and Tobago in the West Indies.

Ginger, 17 Years Old, Leaves Us for the U.S.A., August 1973

When Howard and I were down in bed with hepatitis, we had lots of time to think and do some planning for the near future. At that time Ginger was in her first year of Matric (eleventh grade) at St. Peter's Boarding School in Bulawayo. She started at St. Peter's in her "0" level (tenth grade). At the year exams, she failed two subjects—English and biology. She was allowed to start the Matric year, but would have to take the English and biology exam in mid year and if she failed again, she would have to take them over and also take that Matric year over.

Apparently she wasn't motivated enough to put effort into extra studying. When she was home for a week in the spring, she didn't do any studying. We were concerned about using the Board's money for an extra year of expensive boarding school. We also thought she should have one year of high school in U.S.A. to reculturate herself and to get caught up on whatever college entrance subjects she still needed to take. She still didn't know about what she wanted for her future, possibly nursing. They had good guidance counselors in U.S.A. schools and, no doubt, they could help her with other ideas.

She did pass her biology exam but failed English exam. That was a tell-tale sign for us to see how she would feel about doing her senior year of school in U.S.A. We felt she wasn't too keen about the idea at first. She did like the boarding school experience. We told her to think it over and to let us know in a month when she would be home again from school. In the meantime we wrote to several of our relatives to see about the possibility of taking Ginger for the coming school year. Betty and Al Trumbull wrote back immediately and said they would like to take her. They planned to go camping and boating over Labor Day weekend. They thought Ginger would like that idea.

When Ginger came home in June, she seemed a bit more used to the idea of returning to U.S.A., and when she found out she would be living with Betty and Al and family, that put some excitement in her eyes. So we started making plans for her departure. She went back to school until mid August.

With heavy hearts and tears in our eyes, we sent our last born, Ginger, off to U.S.A. on Aug. 14th. Ted Braun from our New York office agreed to meet her at the Kennedy Airport and help her transfer to the La Guardia Airport, at 6 a.m. too! We were so grateful to him for his sacrificial deed.

I had quite a time trying to get her things sent to U.S.A. We couldn't send a trunk because there was no strapping agency in Botswana, so I decided to pack everything in two heavy-duty cardboard boxes and sent them parcel post. Each box was to contain only 22 pounds. They both arrived to Ginger in six weeks time and intact—wonder of wonders.

Ginger wrote that she was taking political issues, American history, English, gym, typing, and driver's ed. On her first test in English she got an "A" and for political issues, a "C". That must have given her encouragement since she had failed all of her exams at St. Peter's Boarding School before leaving for U.S.A. Ginger attended school from 8:00 – 12:30 and got a job at Burger King from 3:00 – 8:00 p.m., so she was a busy gal. Besides, she started taking piano lessons and also kept up with her studying at school. We were proud of her.

Mike Visits Us, November 1973

Our Church Board offered transportation fees for our children to visit us once, if they are in University studying.

Mike had been a counselor at a Lutheran church camp the summer of 1972, and he became very fond of the Lutheran pastor and his family who led the camp sessions during the summer. They offered to have him live with them in Marquette, Michigan, if he wanted to go to university in Marquette. Mike had left the university in Shippensburg, Pennsylvania after only three weeks.

263

He moved to Benton Harbor, Michigan, to work in a plastics factory, and I guess that experience woke him up to the fact that he'd better go into University and get an education. So when Pastor West offered him a home and a chance to go to University he decided to accept his offer. There were five children in the family, and Mike enjoyed the relationships and bonding with the family. He loved the family bull sessions they all had at the dinner table. That year was a good growing time for Mike. It's wonderful how God intertwines our lives with others and just at the right time.

It was after his one year at Northern Michigan University in Marquette that he decided to travel the next school year. He left U.S.A. in late September, and traveled through Europe and Africa before coming to us on November 26th. While he was in Spain, he had all his traveling gear stolen while he was sleeping in a youth hostel one night. He said if he had to do it over again, he would pick just a few places and spend enough time at each place to get to know the people, customs, and culture.

Mike said he had written four or five letters to us which never got to us, telling us of his arrival time. To confuse the situation further, we had moved to another house so he didn't have our new phone number. He called the Baileys in whose house we lived in for eight months. We had given him that phone number. The Baileys called us, and Mike was finally reunited with us. He looked pretty forlorn. He was sick. He thought he had eaten some bad food the day before. He was o.k. in a few days and appreciated getting his energy back.

Botswana was having a gasoline shortage, so we didn't think we could justify driving Mike around Botswana. We let our friends and colleagues know that Mike wanted to visit different areas and to let us know if they were planning a trip. He did get up to Maun (600 miles north of us). It was a shame it had to be over Christmas, but he had to take the offer when it came up. He left with Albert and Florence Lock on December 14th and went to Serowe. He stayed a couple of days, and then hitched a ride to Francistown to stay with Allan and Katherine Willcocks until December 28th. Then the Locks picked him up again and went up to Maun. He was fortunate to also be taken to "Mareme Game Park" for three days while he was up in Maun.

He came back to us on January 1. He said it seemed strange to be having Christmas with English folks. Their customs and food are different. We had Christmas dinner at the Baileys, English colleagues. Let me tell you the food that was served.

We had four different kinds of meat—turkey, pork roast, fillet roast, and sausages—mashed potatoes and roasted potatoes, carrots, Brussels sprouts, Christmas pudding with brandy sauce, and Christmas fruit cake. Party crackers were besides each plate which contained a paper hat and some small toy like a whistle. That would be more like what we would use on New Year's Eve. We all looked a bit silly eating Christmas dinner with our fancy hats on. Mike said he had a good time, but had had enough of English folks. I knew what he meant.

It was quite an adjustment to come back to Botswana where we had no American colleagues. We got along great with the Baileys but some of our other English colleagues were a bit preppy—too prim and proper for us. But it was good for us. We learned to be more accepting of other people's ways and customs.

Mike left for the U.S.A. January 28, 1974, and went to St. Joseph to stay with Larry and Connie Stanton. Connie got Mike a job in a daycare center for $2.00 an hour. He wasn't able to save much money so he wrote to our Board and asked if he could get a two-month advance on his college course, which they agreed to. So Mike entered the spring term at Thomas Jefferson College in Grand Rapids, Michigan. He planned to work again at Pine Lake Camp in Wisconsin for the summer where he was promoted to assistant program director. Thomas Jefferson College allowed him 1 credit for his summer experience. Thomas Jefferson was freer in its approach to method of education.

265

Mike got a Masters degree in clinical humanistic psychology from Merrill Palmer Institute, Wayne State University.

CHAPTER 12. Never Too Old to Learn

Midwife Training, March 1974 to April 1975

I started my training March 4, 1974. There were 25 of us taking the training. I was the only white. The rest of the students were 29 years younger than I was, but they treated me as an equal and I was grateful for that. Each day we had a lecture from 7:30–8:30. The rest of the time we were assigned to the wards in the hospital. Our hours were 7:30–4:30, or split shift, 7:30–1:00 and 4:30–7:30; also, two-month shifts were 7:30 p.m. to 7:30 a.m. with no time off. That's when I got in most of my deliveries.

Most of the students were used to the hospital because they did their general training there. So when we were assigned to the wards, there was no orientation, and believe me! I was plenty confused for a couple of weeks. But I just watched the others carefully and snooped around to find out where supplies were kept. It was such a handicap not knowing the language well enough to converse in it and, of course, the other nurses talked together in Setswana, so I missed out on a lot. All our classes were taught in English, and we used Margaret Miles' textbook.

I also had to learn how to make do and to improvise. Often there wasn't enough equipment, like having only one razor to shave the pelvic area. So if two patients came in at once in the same stage of labor almost at the point of delivery, one got shaved with the razor and the other one with no razor (just the blade). I didn't find that easy. I was used to adequate and enough equipment so that they can be kept sterile between patients. I worried about the cross-infection that must have been taking place there, but that's the way it was in a developing country where the budget wasn't adequate to do the job properly. The patients only paid a small fee, and the government foots the rest of the expenses. We did the best we could and tried to keep things as sterile as possible.

At this time, Howard was asked to change jobs and work for the Church's institutions to help them sort out financial problems, so from March to June he worked in Moeding, 40 miles away at a high school. He stayed there Monday through Friday because of the gas shortage, inadequate travel expenses, and bad dirt roads. I was very glad I was as busy as he was, otherwise I would have been so lonesome and bored. I rode a bike to and from the hospital. It only took me six minutes.

We ran prenatal clinics Tuesday and Thursday mornings. The patient's weight was recorded, urine tested, B/P taken, and uterus palpated to determine the number of weeks pregnant and position of baby, and we listened to fetus heart tones. I got pretty accurate at determining the number of weeks pregnant by feeling the size of the uterus. Many of the patients couldn't remember their date of their last menstrual period. I was surprised at the number of pre-eclamptic patients there were in Botswana. One out of four women were pre-eclamptic for their first baby and for subsequent births, it was one out of 10. It was probably due to lack of protein in their diets. Also, there were a lot of Caesarian operations. They thought it might be due to the heavy loads young girls carry on their heads which could have altered their pelvic structure.

We had to observe ten births before we could deliver one ourselves. On April 17, only one and half months after I started my training, I delivered my first baby. It was the patient's first baby, and I had to do an episiotomy and sew her up afterwards. What a job, especially since I really had had no experience! We really weren't taught with hands-on experience. We just watched other nurses when they sutured tears and episiotomies. So I got on with it the best I could. The biggest problem was keeping the field visible. Either tissue or blood got in the way. We didn't have any retractors to use. We just had to hold the vaginal area open with our fingers. I got pretty good at suturing by the time my year was up. Of course we tried very hard not to have any tears or episiotomies, but once in a while it happened.

When I did my two months of night duty, 7:30 p.m. to 7:30 a.m., I thought I would get some free time to maybe write a letter or do some studying. Actually, I usually only got one 30-minute break and that was only long enough to have a cup of coffee. At 11:30 we were brought coffee and tea and bread with nothing on it, just plain, and then at 4:00 a.m. we were brought coffee and tea but nothing else. Some of the other students told me that they lost weight on night duty. I could easily see why that was so. We usually managed about five hours of sleep during the day because of classes from 8:00 to 9:00 and 3:30 to 4:30. We also had to take time to eat. I held up all right but I did skip a couple of afternoon classes occasionally to catch up on some needed sleep. Saturday and Sunday were nice because of no classes, so I was able to get some extra sleep on those days.

We had a month of district work during our training. If there were no problems, moms and their babies stayed in the hospital two or three days, and they were followed up on in their homes for ten days. Three of us nurses would go in the hospital car to their homes and check on mom and baby. We did a lot of health teaching. It was very interesting going into the different style of African homes. Some were pathetic. You could see the sky through the roof in some homes. Some had only one blanket, no furniture, and nothing for the baby to wear. It made my heart ache. The biggest drawback to district work the month I was assigned was the heat and terrible bumpy roads and dust. It was 100 degrees in the shade that month. I was filthy and exhausted by the end of the day.

We also had three months of public health education. I could see why this course was of such value. A lot of the graduates were sent to clinics way out in the bush, and they needed a wide scope of training. We learned about culture and some of the drawbacks of some of the beliefs, environment and how it affects health, communication—

269

verbal and nonverbal, all about indigenous communicable diseases—how to diagnose and treat, the necessity of immunization campaigns, nutrition, and family planning. We even learned how to insert uterine loops. Two months was spent in learning the theory, and the last month was practical training.

We were sent to different clinics to stay for a month. Five of us students were sent to Serowe (250 miles north of Gaborone). Two of the nurses found accommodation in the village and three of us stayed in the nurses' home at the hospital. We were lucky to each have our own room. The room was nicely equipped with a bed, vanity, bedside stand, chair, and wardrobe. We ate our meals (typical African diet) in the nurses' dining room. Breakfast was mealie meal porridge, bread (no butter or any other spread), and tea or coffee. Noon meal was a piece of meat, potato, rice or soup. The only vegetable we had for the whole meal was cooked cabbage. Supper was the same as breakfast. I finally bought a jar of peanut butter. Dry bread isn't so nice, and I thought I needed more protein. Fortunately, oranges were in season so I bought oranges for a bit of vitamin C. One Saturday I went with two African nurses into the shopping areas. As a stranger, you'd never know it was a shopping area. The shops are scattered, not all in one block like most shopping areas.

Three days a week we stayed at the hospital and worked in the antenatal clinic, postnatal clinic, and T.B. clinic. Also we did home visits in the village, promoting proper toilets and talking to mothers about family planning. The rest of the time we were assigned to the Lady Khama Clinic, working in the child welfare clinic, malnutrition clinic, and family planning clinic. The Lady Khama Clinic was a 20-minute walk. I really felt that I was in a rural setting—cows, goats, donkeys, and chickens to greet me no matter where I walked. I think I did quite well being plunked entirely in the local culture. I wish I could have had a better command of the Setswana language. It was so frustrating not to be able to communicate adequately.

Serowe is a village of about 20,000 people. Most all of the local people live in mud rondovals with thatched roofs. A lot of the women make homemade beer for sale, their only source of income. At least three-fourths of the women are not married, but still have three or four children.

After the month was over, it was good to get back to Gaborone and to Howard. It was a special boon to discover how very much we missed each other. We wrote to each other every day. This was the longest period that we had ever been separated from each other. It was good for us to have that separation because it made us realize how very deep our love was for each other. Somehow we never gave it much thought when we were constantly together. So we found a new appreciation for each other and a love that never stops growing and expanding as the years go by. We were so grateful for God's grace, mercy, and forgiveness which was a binding force in our marriage.

The long-awaited exterior exam results finally came. I passed with merit. I was so thrilled. My disciplined study efforts really paid off, but it sure wasn't easy at the time. I began to understand how hard the South African (English school) system was, and I had far more empathy for our children's S.A. school years.

Our weekly exams were all essay type, and sometimes there were only three questions which we had to do in an hour and a half. It seemed invariable. I always left some important detail out and, of course, I was marked down— also for misspelled words!! I tried to write so fast so I would finish the exam, and usually didn't have time to reread and correct mistakes. But I learned a lot having to study so much and that's what I was interested in—learning and retaining the important aspects of obstetrics. We had to be prepared to answer everything from our thick Margaret Miles *Obstetrics Book* from cover to cover and couldn't leave out one detail.

We had a very nice graduation ceremony. Bishop Murphy (Catholic) gave the address. We were served tea and goodies after the ceremony.

271

Pilot License for Howard

While I was taking my midwife course, Howard thought and debated with himself for three months whether he should take flying lessons and get a pilot's license. Even before we were married, he was interested in getting a pilot's license. He had started to take flying lessons and then had to stop because of going into the Army Air Force. Then marriage, kids, and work had to take priority.

A number of people came into his life recently and gave him the urge to want to get his pilot's license. He loved the flying lessons, and we thought of the long-range possibility of his new skill. Many times the Mission needed and hired a plane and pilot to take them to meetings. It was very hard on cars to travel the dirt roads and also, not knowing if you could cross the riverbed, when you came to a river. There weren't any bridges. As it turned out, Howard's new skill was valuable to the Mission. It was cheaper to charter a plane than drive, but only if you didn't have to hire a pilot. So Howard piloted many people back and forth to meetings.

One time when I was doing my public health and clinic work in Serowe, he had a forced landing. He was flying back to Gaborone from Maun (600 miles north of Gaborone) with three passengers. The weather got bad and the clouds were so low that they lost their way, so he decided to land in a field. Serowe was only 25 or 30 miles away. All went well; Howard bought the plane down in the field all right. It was a bit bumpy, but the plane stayed right side up. They paid a man with a tractor and then a lorry (truck) came to take them to Serowe. It took them five hours to go 30 miles because the roads were so bad. They were brought to the hospital where I was staying. What a surprise for me to see them.

Dick Sales, one of the passengers on the plane said, "What some husbands won't do to see their wives!" We were mighty thankful we could joke about it, knowing what a tragedy it might have been. They eventually were taken to the train to go back to Gaborone (250 miles south). An experienced pilot flew the plane out of the field and back to Gaborone.

I only went up once with Howard. One weekend we flew up to Maun (600 miles north). Howard had to work on the books at the maternity center. I took my nurse's uniform and worked in the maternity center while we were there. I delivered two babies and fed the premature babies every three hours. Both moms had to have episiotomies. Pat taught me a new technique of suturing which was faster and looked neater. Pat had the maternity clinic well-organized and equipped. It was much better than the hospital in Gaborone where I had my midwife training.

Pat Hollenly, the missionary there, sometimes put in 100 hours a week because of the lack of trained help. I went on a call with Pat into the bush about 10:30 at night. We had to go ten miles, but we had only five miles of road and then had to go cross-country with help of a guide who was in the car with us. The foliage was up to the headlights. Anyways, all went well, and we were able to get the mom back to the hospital for delivery.

Actually, I didn't do well flying in a small plane. I got motion sickness so I wasn't very eager to fly with Howard again.

Our Next Assignment ??

For over a year our future assignment had been unknown. It all seemed so complicated and uncertain, but still we didn't fret much. God usually had it all planned out long before he lets us in on the details. The government had taken over our Christian institutions so Howard had been assigned as financial officer to our Book Center next term because it was losing money. He thought the Church should sell it and rent the buildings. This would take them farther ahead financially. Besides, it wasn't strictly a religious Book Center anymore. It only had a small section of religious books so Howard definitely didn't want to go back to work there.

We even toyed with the idea of coming back to work for the government of Botswana with Howard as hospital administrator and me as a nurse in the hospital. We had heard that there was a lot of unemployment in U.S.A., and Howard's age being 55 was not a plus for finding employment.

In the meantime Pam had written to us about talking to a Don Potter who lived in Dowagiac. He said he had a relative working in Liberia who went into the mission field the same time we did. He mentioned that their names were Paul and Betty Getty. Pam said it sounded familiar. We were in missionary training with them back in 1961, but had lost track of them. Pam had sent us their address so I sent them off two of our past Christmas letters, and we started writing back and forth. I mentioned about our uncertain future and that we may come back to Botswana and work for the government. They wrote right back and said they had been looking for a hospital administrator and were always short of nurses. Would we consider stopping in Liberia on our way home and see what we thought about working there? They were Methodists, which would fit fine with our backgrounds. So plans began to shape up for our future.

Once more we lived in a mess for over a month as we decided what personal things to pack for shipment. We had to organize another big household sale like we did when we left U.S.A. in 1961. We had an auction then, but there was no such thing here so we had to sell it all on our own. If we did finally decide to work in Liberia, there was a furnished home so we wouldn't have to start all over like we did when we came to South Africa in 1961. We left Botswana for U.S.A. with a stopover in Liberia on May 15, 1975.

Our week stopover Liberia seemed very short. We were picked up at the airport in Monrovia, the capital of Liberia, and were driven inland to a village called Ganta. There the Methodist Mission had built a hospital and leprosy settlement. Dr. Paul Getty was terribly overworked, being the manager, financial officer, and doctor not only of the general hospital but also the leprosy hospital and settlement.

Betty, his wife, said she would not come back for another term unless they had more help. It looked very much like this would be our next assignment. We could see the need, and we had the skills they needed.

We went to the early morning devotions in the Chapel led by a local native Christian. After the devotions we asked Dr. Getty what language he was speaking. Dr. Getty looked surprised and said, "English," then we looked surprised. We hadn't understood a thing he said. Liberia has an unusual historical link to the United States. Liberia was established in 1874 by freed American black slaves who returned to Africa. Their descendants had governed the country until 1980.

As it turned out, we didn't go to Liberia and maybe it was just as well. After 1980, Liberia was chaotic. The Ganta Mission is no longer functioning. The hospital will need a lot of rebuilding when it's safe for missionaries to return to Liberia.

CHAPTER 13. Meanwhile, Back in the States

What Was Happening to Dave, Pam, Mike and Ginger?

In August of 1974, Dave was still in University in Kalamazoo, getting a Masters degree in African studies with a particular emphasis in the socio-anthropological aspects of the religious movements in Southern Africa. By December of that year, he thought his African studies seemed rather constraining so he switched to comparative religion, mythology and self-discovery. To help his financial situation, he was house-sitting five different times for a few months each time he moved. He lived in very nice homes, and sometimes had the use of a car that the couple had left.

Pam and Steve rented a small house on Lowell Street, just kitty-corner across the street from Steve's folks. That turned out to be a mistake, as it was too close to his folks for Pam. They lived there for about a year and a half. They both worked the afternoon/evening shift; Steve, in the police force from 4:00 to midnight and Pam, 3:00–11:00 at the hospital. She drove to work and Steve rode his bike, then Pam picked him up after work. They put a bike rack on their car for Steve's bike. Eventually they moved to Pine Tree Apartments across town. In January 1975, they vacationed in the Virgin Islands, not to far from where they had their honeymoon in the spring of 1973.

After Mike's vacation with us in Botswana in January 1974, he got an advance on his college funding from our Board and entered Thomas Jefferson College, part of Grand Valley State University in Grand Rapids, Michigan. He was interested in community living and found a home to rent in Jennison. Actually, we hadn't heard from Mike in almost a year. And then a tape arrived from him, but a few days

277

before that, some papers arrived that had to be filled in for financial assistance. Nary a personal note about himself.

I happened to be away for a month for my district work in midwife training in Serowe. I'm glad I wasn't receiving those papers with no personal note because that would have been discouraging and disappointing, wondering if he thought we were robots without any feelings or value. I suppose this is a world-wide dilemma. Mothers invest so much of their time, energy, emotions, and talents in bringing up the children, and it's a real psychological blow when they leave the nest. An added distress is when there's no communication. Fortunately for myself and for our children, I was determined not to depend on my children or my husband for my well-being or fulfillment.

On the tape Mike described every room in the house. Then he came to the downstairs bedroom, and he said, "Judy and I share this bedroom." So that was our introduction to Judy in his life. That was quite a bombshell for us. We had been hearing and reading about young folks just living together without being married. That was foreign concept when we were married. Mike received a teaching degree from Thomas Jefferson College.

Ginger lived with Al and Betty Trumbull in Columbus, Ohio during her senior year of high school. After graduation in June 1974, Pam and Steve offered to have her live with them in Dowagiac. Ginger took an eight-week nurse aide course and liked it. She went to the Watervliet Hospital in a carpool for her practical hospital training. She got a job at the Dowagiac Hospital, and was given a three-month probation period before being hired as a regular employee.

Pam wrote to us and said that it was very hard having Ginger live with them in their tiny house. Their bedroom didn't have a door—only a heavy curtain in the doorway. Pam was worried about how difficult it was becoming in their married life, having no privacy. Pam was also upset about Ginger's immaturity and not taking any initiative in doing necessary work around the house. She was also being careless about leaving lights and T.V. on when she left the house and no one was there. Pam finally told her she would have to find some place else to live.

Ginger found a room to rent with kitchen privileges with a black family who had two children. The location was on North Front Street. She had to pay $15.00 a week. She walked to the hospital to start work at 3:00 p.m. and got a ride home at 11:00 p.m. At the end of the three-month probation period, she was let go. I guess she was daydreaming a lot and also too interested in watching the T.V. in patients' rooms. Needless to say that gave us quite a bit concern. She did have about $600 in her savings which would see her through for awhile. Howard and I talked and prayed about it and came to realize that this might help her mature by discovering what it means to be an adult and have to cope with meeting her own expenses.

I had written to Muriel Stackley about Ginger's situation, never dreaming that Muriel would write to Ginger and invite her to their home in Kansas for a visit. Of course Ginger was thrilled and went to Kansas about March 1, 1975. Muriel wrote to us saying that Ginger responded quite well to life within the family. She loved having younger siblings to relate to, to shepherd a bit and to speak with. Ginger and Theron (10 years) played four-hour Monopoly games. She played cards with Javan (8), read a lot to 4-year old Tamm, and worked at jigsaw puzzles with Mother Stackley, Ted's mom who lived with them. This little vacation turned into permanancy. We wrote to Ginger that she would have to find some kind of job to help pay the Stackleys for her keep. She did find a job, cleaning and making beds at a motel.

Back to U.S.A., Ohio First, Summer 1975

While we were home we rented a 4-cylinder Chevy hatchback from Lou Lyman's car agency in Ohio. Lou had visited us in South Africa and said he would rent us a car whenever we were on furlough in the States.

We first went to Kansas to visit the Stackleys and make some decisions about Ginger's future. They all attended the

New Creation Fellowship Church. New Creation Fellowship was one of the many "Christian Community Living" churches that were springing up all around the U.S.A. We had read about them while still in Botswana and had planned to visit a number of them while we were in U.S.A. We thought that kind of lifestyle—living in large Christian households might be right for the future and a possibility for us at retirement. It was agreed amongst all of us that Ginger would remain with the Stackleys, while we spent some time visiting some Christian extended-family living fellowships.

We visited Reba Place in Evanston, Illinois, and also Plow Creek in that state and New Hope in Elkhart, Indiana, which were mainly Mennonite backgrounds, then Messiah (Anglican) in Detroit, and the last one we visited was Christ's Community (Christian Reformed) in Grand Rapids, Michigan.

Christ's Community had a ministry to young people who needed nurturing and guidance. We asked them if we could bring Ginger to live with one of the households. And also if we could live there until our future assignment was decided upon. We wanted to experience that kind of living for the possibility for our retirement years. They agreed to both requests. So we went back to Kansas and picked up Ginger, and the three of us lived in the Joose household. Wayne Joose was the assistant pastor of Christ's Community. There were about 12 different households. This was about mid June 1975. We thought we would know about our future by the end of September.

Some of the members of the household worked outside the household. Their salaries contributed to the expenses of the household. The rest of us worked in the household— cooking, canning, laundry, and cleaning. A lot of counseling took place in the household because of the ministry to young people. Mealtime was what I liked the best. All 20 of us sat around the big dining room. We had only one conversation at a time that we listened to, and then another person would share about how the day went. So it was a peaceful mealtime, and we appreciated getting to know the people in the household by personal sharing.

Our Decision of Mid-October 1975

Living in this Christian community extended family was very appealing to me. It felt like we were in tune with early Christianity as portrayed in the Bible chapters of Acts. It was good to live in a household where we were committed to live in harmony and love and work out our disagreements in a peaceful way, and to not feel that one was a loser and one the winner. That only caused a lot of resentment.

Our Board in New York had worked out a satisfactory arrangement about loaning us to work for the Methodist Mission Board in Liberia. We had taken all our necessary shots for returning overseas. Then a decision had to be made. I wanted very much to stay in U.S.A. and remain in Christ's Community, especially since all our children were in U.S.A. It was very hard for me to think of not seeing them for such a long time. I also wanted to work on our marriage relationship that needed help and guidance in some areas. Christ's Community leadership had counseling sessions for married couples. Howard really wanted to go back overseas, but he too enjoyed living in this warm extended-family household and he did listen to my needs. So we decided together to stay here in U.S.A. Howard called the New York Board to explain to them and I wrote a long letter to Paul and Betty Getty in Liberia telling them we weren't coming. That was a hard letter to write, knowing the need there. So our 15 years of overseas mission work ended.

Another Move in June 1976

After about 12 months of living in Christ's Community, Howard became distrustful and critical of the leadership. One evening we heard John Perkins (black) speak. He was the leader of Voice of Calvary Mission in Jackson, Mississippi. He was the author of two books. The Voice of Calvary Mission was involved in evangelism and helping young black people develop leadership skills. Howard was impressed with his talk and chatted with John and his wife.

He found out they had been looking for someone skilled in business and finance to help them with their bookkeeping and financial records. Howard appeared very interested, and John's wife said," You are an answer to our intense prayers." I was devastated and didn't want to leave. I cried one whole day. I just couldn't stop the tears and that's not like me. I rarely cry.

We left for Mississippi in June. Voice of Calvary had groups of young people come there to do volunteer work in Jackson. We were housed in a big home where a group of eight girls lived while they did their volunteer work. We were in charge of that household. During the day, Howard worked in their office on the finances. I worked in the kitchen and helped to do the cooking for 50 to 70 people. Believe me, that was hot work. Mississippi was hot in the summer, and we didn't have air-conditioning. I learned how to cook in large quantities, and I enjoyed the people. Since Howard worked in the administration, he became aware of the misuse of funds and after six months, we moved again.

Living with Pam, Steve and Sara

Pam and Steve offered to let us use their basement which had a bed in it, while we looked for job opportunities. Howard sent out 300 resumes, but no luck. Apparently his age of 50+ was a big deterrent. I got a job right away at the local nursing home, full-time, working 3:00 to 11:00 p.m. We stayed with Pam, Steve and Sara for three months, and then we decided we should really look for a furnished apartment in town (Dowagiac). We didn't want to outstay our welcome and, at this time, Howard was still trying to find a job.

We decided to take the Grand Rapids paper. After three months of living in the apartment, he found a job in Grand Rapids at the Area Agency on Aging in the finance department. I stayed on in Dowagiac for a month to give the nursing home adequate time to find a replacement for me.

Grand Rapids, Michigan, 1977–1985

We rented one side of a duplex and bought furnishings. It was beginning to feel like we were putting down roots again. I wondered how I could use my midwife training without having a U.S.A. degree, so we went to Springfield, Ohio, to investigate its three-month refresher program which offered a U.S.A. degree for foreign-trained midwives. They told me I would have to work in an obstetric department for a year to get acclimated to U.S.A. culture and standards before I could take the three-month refresher course.

I found a job at the Salvation Army Hospital for unwed mothers on the 11:00 p.m. to 7:00 a.m. shift. After a year of working, I found out that the Springfield refresher course was no longer in progress. In fact, the only U.S.A. refresher course was in Philadelphia, Pennsylvania. I took a plane to Philadelphia to be interviewed for one of three available training slots. I wasn't chosen. I think a lot had to do with my age. The other applicants were young and had many working years ahead of them.

Midwifery Once More, This Time Back in the States

Back in Grand Rapids, I heard about a meeting of Home Birth Midwives, which I attended. Most of them were trained on the job and did not have R.N. degrees. Homebirths were in the pioneering stage again in the U.S.A. Many people of my generation were born at home, but it became fashionable to have your birth in a hospital. Along came technology, and many women were unhappy with their experiences in the hospital. They couldn't even have their spouses in with them in the delivery room. Homebirths became available for women who wanted a more humane and natural experience. Many couples had hospital insurance, but choose homebirth to be able to have the labor and birth the way they wanted it.

Some of the pregnant women in Christ's Community began to ask me if I would be with them for a homebirth. Jan Harkless, an R.N. who was at the meeting of homebirth midwives, decided to team up with me and we started a

283

home-birthing business. At the time I was still working 11:00 p.m. to 7:00 a.m. at the Salvation Army Hospital, and that worked out real well. I would be the only one on duty at night and when the unwed mothers who lived in a dormitory connected to the hospital thought they were in labor, they would come over to the hospital and I would check them to see if they were in labor and then had to decide when to call the doctor to come for the delivery. Doctors didn't want to be called too early and be disturbed from their sleep.

I was wishing that at least one of the mothers would go faster than expected so I could deliver the baby, but it never happened. I always got the doctor there on time. When my home mothers would go into labor during the night, they would call me at the hospital and I would determine about where they were in their labor. We would keep in touch about every hour, and then I would call Jan Harkless when I thought someone should be there. I never missed a homebirth while I was working at the Salvation Army Hospital. Eventually the Salvation Army decided to close, as their services with unwed mothers were not needed very much because it wasn't such a stigma for a girl to get pregnant without being married.

While living in Christ's Community, an outreach of the Christian Reformed Church in Grand Rapids, I saw a notice in a co-op food store that said all those interested in midwifery should contact a certain phone number. When I called the number, Jan Harkless answered. She also was a Registered Nurse. Together we designed a course to teach laywomen how to do "home births" safely. We had a doctor willing to back us up if we had any problems. During seven years of home deliveries, I did around 250 home births.

One of our students was named Yolanda. She came to visit me a month ago in early April 2008. Yolanda is still doing home births in the Grand Rapids, Michigan, area.

Goshen, Indiana, 1989–2004

We moved to Goshen, Indiana, in 1989. We had heard from other people talking about what wonderful facilities they had for retirees. They had four levels of health care when it came time for when we might need the care. We thought we could keep our children from worrying about us, and designated our daughter, Pam, our "Legal Health Representative." More about that later; first, what we did while in Goshen.

Camp Nurse Summers, 1992 and 1993

Howard and I attended a two-day senior citizen program at Camp Fredenswald near Cassopolis, Michigan, in the fall of 1991. Camp Fredenswald was started by minorities in 1951, and many people have enjoyed fellowship, fun, and inspirational encounters over the years. The camp can accommodate up to 220 people. Programs are scheduled all during the year. The chef is superb and plans very nutritious meals.

At the time we attended a Senior program in 1991, Howard mentioned to the director that I was an R.N. He talked to me before we left the retreat about volunteering as a camp nurse during the summer. So I did one week of camp nursing in 1992 and one week in 1993. Actually they need nurses for six weeks in the summer, so other nurses also agreed to volunteer their time.

During the week I was there both years, there were 90 third and fourth graders and 40 high school age. Fortunately I did not have any real emergency problems. There were cuts and bruises, sprained ankles, water in the ear, rashes, spider and insect bites, bee and wasp stings, and upset tummies. Some of the tummy problems were a virus and some were just plain homesickness which caused the tummy upset. The kids have a wonderful time at camp. It is a really great experience for them. Many come back year after year.

There were at least 350 volunteers working at least one day at Camp Fredenswald last year. We also help in the kitchen a few weekends during the year. Howard went with me for the week in 1992 and helped in the maintenance department painting swings. That kind of work is not something he enjoys doing, so although he dragged me to

Camp Fredenswald in 1993, he stayed home and fended for himself.

Elderhostel Program

Elderhostel is an educational adventure for older adults looking for something different. It makes these later years a time of new beginnings, opportunities, and challenges.

Elderhostel programs were started in 1975. It has grown since the early years form a few hundred hostels on a handful of New England college campuses into an international network of 1,800 participating institutions. In 1992 almost 250,000 people enrolled in Elderhostel programs. Elderhostel encourages diversity and welcomes people of all races, creeds, and religions. Participants have to be 60 years of age or older to be eligible.

The programs are a week long from Sunday afternoon until Saturday after breakfast. Accommodation is usually the college dorms with two to a room and the bathrooms down the hall. As participants are getting older, they are asking for better accommodations, so now the Elderhostel programs are commonly held in motels where we have private baths. Meals are eaten in the college cafeteria. Three academic courses meet for one and a half hours each weekday; they're scheduled so that you can make take all three each day. Usually there are other curricular activities in the afternoon after the last class ends at 3 p.m. and also in the evening. The courses are not for credit. There is no homework or preparatory work or grades.

You do not need any specific prior educational background. All you need is an inquiring mind. You find yourself in class with all kinds of people, from those who never finished high school to those with a number of impressive degrees. A common interest in the subject matter is what brings you together.

We started attending Elderhostel's programs in 1987 and, by June 1999, we have attended 23 Elderhostel programs. We both enjoy them so much. It is the only type of vacation we take except, of course, visiting our family. So you see we are trying to keep our brain cells exercised and active, plus at the same time enjoy every minute of it.

Religions Cooperating for Peace, September 1993

Howard, our son Dave, and I attended the Parliament of the World's Religions in Chicago at the Palmer House, a Hilton hotel, August 28 through September 4, 1993. There were over 170 international co-sponsors signed up to support this Parliament. We were surprised when we checked in to get our nametags and materials for the week that over 7,000 people had registered. It was thought that perhaps 3,500 persons would register.

Dave and his family live in Chicago, so we commuted to the Palmer House by car each day. We had about four hours of sleep each night. I was amazed how well I held up with dozing throughout the lectures. I am sure it was due to the high level of energy surging from the constant flow of spiritual content. The most frustrating and time-consuming job was choosing which lectures, seminars, and workshops to go to each day. We wished we could have been in ten different places for those slotted lectures. We had over 600 choices to choose from for the 36 periods during the week.

Many of us able-bodied people used the stairs to get to our scheduled lectures that could have been anywhere from the first to the seventh floors. Stair-climbing, elevator rides, and standing in line for the Plenary Lessons were times to have good conversations with a variety of people from many traditions and nationalities. We all wore large tags hung around our necks with elastic strings. The tag had our name, city, state and also religious affiliation (optional). I think I was the only one from a Mennonite church. There were tight security controls and no one was allowed into the Plenary Lessons, lectures, seminars or workshops without the visible nametags hung around your neck.

The Plenary Lessons became quite a challenge. Of course everyone would have liked to have been in the main auditorium, but that was impossible. They did have a large overflow room where the program could be seen on a big television screen. To assure ourselves of good seats in the main auditorium, we would line up outside the main door from one to one and a half hours ahead of the scheduled session. It was so interesting talking with such a variety of people so the time went fast. The doors opened 20 minutes before the session and about ten people were allowed in at a time. There were many volunteers inside the auditorium to check to see if everyone had their nametags on.

Now let me tell you a little about the history of this event. The first gathering was called the World Parliament of Religions (WPOR), and was held in 1893 in Chicago during the Columbian Exposition. This Parliament was the first formal, public meeting of representatives from the major religions in the history of the world. It has been called a watershed event in American religious history. It marked the beginning of interfaith dialogue in the USA.

The 1893 WPOR left both a legacy of interfaith dialogue and an unfinished agenda for greater cooperation and understanding. L.G. Nicholls, formally moderator of the General Assembly of the Presbyterian Church, wrote to the 1893 Parliament:

> I trust that your largest hopes concerning the Parliament may be fully realized. I am not surprised that narrow-minded people in our own church ever should oppose it. There are some good bigots who imagine that God will not cease working until he has made all people Presbyterians,

And Bishop B.W. Arnett, of the African Methodist Episcopal Church, wrote, "The great battle of the future will not be the Fatherhood of God, nor that we need a redeemer or a model man between God and man, but to acknowledge the Brotherhood of man practically."

In 1988 a group of people of different faiths began meeting to plan a Century of the Parliament in 1993. The centenary of the WPOR offered a unique opportunity for the community of religions to come together in a spirit of harmony and friendship. While commemorating the original Parliament of 1893, it was to build on its foundation an atmosphere of peace and unity, truth and clarity, and to establish interfaith understanding and cooperation at the local and international levels. Leaders of the world's major religions committed themselves to a spiritual quest for peace, sexual equality, and respect for all faiths. The Dalai Lama, the exiled Tibetan Buddhist leader, said at a news conference, "All religious carry the same message—compassion, forgiveness, love—and each philosophy, each tradition has a powerful mechanism to do well."

Presentations and workshops during the week addressed critical world issues, seeking fresh approaches to problems of vital concern—poverty, racism, and ecology, human rights, justice, and world space.

Dr. Paulos Margregarious, Metropolitan of Delhi, the Orthodox Syrian Church of the East and President for Asia, World Council of Churches said,

> What is before us is a rich deep, penetrating understanding of each other's religions. Not a common religion which puts everything together into one pot; we do not want a religious ethic that unites all religions. What we want is a Global concourse of all religions—a flowing together, a running together, of all religions; active dynamics without losing their identity, but in relating to each other, understanding each other with mutual respect, and moving towards specific goals.

The Global Ethic, which organizers hope will be one of the main legacies of the Parliament, attempts to sat minimal ethical standards to which all faiths and individuals can be held accountable. The statements of ethics condemn environmental abuses, calls disarmament the commandment of the times, and deplores sexual exploration and sexual discrimination as one of the worst forms of human degradation. The Global Ethics Committee stated, "We commit ourselves to a culture of non-violence, justice, and peace. We shall not oppress, injure, torture or kill other human beings, forsaking violence as a means for settling differences."

The 1993 Parliament of the World's Religions extended an extraordinary dialogue which occurred 100 years ago. The time was right for this gathering. It evidences with a growing awareness of the limitations of our technological and political ingenuity. It responds to a growing confidence in the power of spiritual understanding and the desire for wisdom because we face enormous challenges, we will ask ourselves challenging questions. These are intended to engage us all despite our difference. For example:

1. What is the place in our faith tradition of new revelations, wisdoms or understanding concerning human participation in our common future on Earth?

2. What may the wisdom of our faith tradition teach us about hatred and violence against those who differ in faith, culture, race or gender?

3. What do we or our faith traditions offer as an alternative vision for living peacefully and sustainable together with others and with the Earth?

All these questions are not only for the international community, but also for our own U.S.A. We are fast becoming a pluralistic religious society. That was a stimulating and mind-expanding week.

Howard's Second Heart Bypass, August 17, 1995

About a year and a half ago, Howard started to have a slight angina only when he did his daily hour walk. It subsided if he slowed down. We went to a cardiologist, and he had Howard take a Thallium Stress Test. That turned out pretty good, so the cardiologist suggested he medicate three times a day. When that didn't do much good, Howard went off that and started putting on a 2 mg nitro patch when he got up. That worked really well, except he got a daily headache.

So he reduced the nitro patch to 1 mg each day, and that gave no problems and also conquered his angina.

In about July 1995, Howard started having a bit of angina even when wearing the nitro patch. The cardiologist decided he wanted to do a heart catheterization which was scheduled for August 16. It showed all the bypasses clogging up again. Howard stayed overnight at the hospital and was scheduled for the surgery the next morning at 7:30.

I was able to get back to the hospital before he was taken to surgery. The surgeon and cardiologist both warned us there may be more complications for the second bypass. While I was sitting in the surgery waiting room, in walked Mike about 11 a.m. I had no idea he would be with us. Pam came early afternoon. Howard finally opened his eyes about 8 p.m., our last visit before going back to our apartment in Goshen. He could not talk because he still had the endotrachea in his throat. They did not take it out because he was still bleeding some and, if it did not stop, they would have to take him back to surgery. The bleeding did not stop, and he went back to surgery at about 2:30 a.m. That was the first complication.

Three days later, his heart was in atrial fibrillation so a cardioversion procedure was done. That put his heart in regular rhythm for 18 hours, and we were rejoicing. Then when his heart went into atrial fibrillation again, another cardioversion was the second complication. This time it did not help. So it was decided to use medication and hope it would eventually go into the right rhythm.

A few days later, I noticed his stools were black and tarry. He had a bleeding stress ulcer. He had an endoscopic procedure which showed both a gastric and a duodenal ulcer, the third complication. He was put on a new drug called Prilosec. The bleeding stopped, but all in all he had to have 12 units of blood. I stayed overnight in his room one night when his hemoglobin went down to 6. The usual stay for bypass surgery is five to six days. Howard went home on the 12th day. His heart still was in atrial fibrillation so   his progress at home was very, very slow. It seemed like he slept all day and night. I knew something wasn't right, but what?

I took him to the clinic where I do volunteer work to check his hemoglobin, and it was 10. We finally called the cardiologist. He looked up the Prilosec medication in the *PDR* book and read that 1% have trouble with extreme tiredness and sleep. The printed-out side effects were headache, constipation, cough, dizziness, rash. I guess they do not print the side effect of just 1% of people taking a medication. The cardiologist took him off that medication, and he did a lot better. Oh! Another thing that was discovered through a blood test in the hospital was a *H. pylori* infection which accompanies most people who have ulcers, so he had to take two weeks of medications for that: tetracycline, Flagyl, and Pepto-Bismol.

Because of this slow recuperation, he could not start the rehabilitation program for a month. That first Monday we went to the rehab program, we were so glad to see on the monitor that his heart was in the right rhythm. He went to the rehab program three times a week for a month. Each time we noticed progress and regaining strength.

Another situation he had to put up with was a black pressure area under his right heel. That happened while he was on the surgery cart. That was very sore and took almost two months to go away. The surgeon and cardiologist sure knew what they were talking about when they said there would be more complications with the second bypass.

Our cardiologist was really advocating that all his patients read Dr. Dean Ornish's book called *Reversing Heart Disease*. We had already read it, so we started on a very low-fat vegetarian diet, hoping that this would help his vessels from clogging up again. The cardiologist also put him on Pravachol. He wants his cholesterol below 200 and his L.D.L. below 100. In October, before going on Pravachol, his cholesterol was 228 and L.D.L. 156. Two months later, the cholesterol was 194 and L.D.L. 131, the L.D.L. still too high. We'll have to call the cardiologist and see if he needs to change the medication. The Cardiac Rehab Program is starting a low-fat vegetarian support group and a time for sharing recipes. One good outcome of his surgery was that he lost 25 pounds and being on a low-fat vegetarian diet he is keeping off those pounds.

New Classes to Teach

I taught bridge for three months in the summers of 1994–97 with new students each summer. We had a friend here in Manor IV that wanted to teach bridge, but with all her medical problems and being 88, she did not feel up to it. She said. "Why don't you do it?" I've played bridge for a long time, but wasn't very good at it. But then I thought why not? I'll know more than my students.

I taught two tables of beginners over at the Senior Center on Wednesday afternoons. I suggested they get the book, *The Fun Way to Successful Bridge,* by Harry Lampert. It's written in cartoons which gives a visual way to remember bidding and responses. I was pleased and amazed at their progress. My oldest student was 87, and she is still playing every Thursday afternoon in the Senior Center. She is 91 now and playing well. I coordinate eight tables of bridge every Thursday. Teaching bridge was very good for me. I'm playing much better bridge now. I have confidence and am more aggressive with taking risks in bidding. They say teaching is a great way of learning the subject. I can verify that fact.

Started in a Group of Tap Dancers, June 1996

I've always liked any kind of dancing. My dancing days were over soon after Howard and I got married. He always said it felt like he had two left feet and didn't like dancing very much. In June of 1996, I joined the dance class at the Elkhart YMCA on Tuesday mornings 9 a.m. to noon. You have to be 60 years or older to be a part of the group. The oldest member is 82 years old. There are 22 members in the class.

When I started, I was given lessons every Tuesday for three months on basic tap steps and a lot of different techniques. I started performing with the group at various functions in February 1997. Our basic dance costume is a black bodysuit, black leotards, and black shorts. Then we bought brighter outfits with different colored, sparkly leotards, and sometimes shirts and hats. We know about 30 different dances with all kinds of music and keep learning new ones regularly. We perform anywhere and anytime we are asked by different organizations, like nursing homes, mall openings, schools, senior pageants, Moose lodges, senior center, Elks Club, fairs, Amish Acres, and churches. We perform on the average of three times a month. We call ourselves the Rockerettes—we would rather rock on our own feet than in rocking chairs. It's great fun and good exercise.

Cataract Surgery, Early 1998 at Age 75

My cataract surgery was done on my right eye on January 7, 1998, and on my left one February 10, 1998. How fortunate we are these days to have such good technology and no stitching. What a difference from a number of years ago when you had to lay flat for five days with sand bags beside you head so you wouldn't turn your head. I went home an hour after surgery with no restrictions. I had to put a couple different drops in the eye for three weeks.

What a change in my eyesight! The colors were different in nature and clothes. The eyesight was so gradual in deterioration that I didn't realize all the changes taking place. And it's wonderful to read the road signs far enough away to get in the right lane if you need to turn.

Gall Bladder Surgery for Howard, March 1998

Our speculation was that Howard would have the laparoscopic surgery (four little holes) and would be in the hospital just over night. The doctor had warned us that 10% of patients have the old-fashioned surgery and, wouldn't you know, Howard was one of those 10% people. He awoke to three tubes in his belly, a nose gastric tube, and IVs. The doctor discovered a severe narrowing in his bile duct near where it empties in the small intestine, so he had to do some extensive work there to relieve the narrowing. Normal gall bladder surgery hospital stays are four to five days, but Howard's was extended to ten days.

He didn't have anything to eat or drink for five days. When he was released, he had a T-tube remaining in the bile duct to the exterior abdomen. That was in his bile duct for seven weeks. Howard had pain for the entire time, often having to take Darvocet. When the T-tube was removed, he didn't have anymore pain. What a relief! He soon gained his strength and was back to walking an hour every day.

My First Surgery, March 1999

About four months before my surgery, I was feeling always very tired. Was old age creeping up on me? I finally want to see Dr. Mathis, a cardiologist. He ordered a number of cardiac tests and learned that I had an aortic value leak. The doctor put me on some medications, and I did feel better for a while. My B/P kept going higher and higher.

For three years before my surgery, my B/P was fairly consistent. The systolic number was anywhere from 130–160 and my diastolic number was 50–60. These were most often 100 beats between the systolic and diastolic number. I had recently read that this could be true when you had an aortic value leak and the cardiologist confirmed that was true. I was not anxious or particularly concerned about my forthcoming surgery. In fact, I slept well the night before it. The surgery went well. The day after surgery, my B/P really dropped low. There was much concern that I may have a blood clot in the lung, so I was taken to a room where I had a few tests. I had an echocardiogram with the doctor going into a vein in my groin to pass the catheter up into my lung for several tests, but all was negative. What a relief!

Five days after surgery, I had a cardioversion because my heart was in atrial fibrillation. After that procedure, my heart went right into the right rhythm. The next day I had a pacemaker put in. Then I went home, much to Howard's protests. I was home for four days, not doing very well. Back into the hospital I went because of atrial fibrillation again. My heart went into the right rhythm after I was in the hospital for a few hours. The doctor had thought he was going to have to do another cardio-vert procedure. I was pleased I didn't have to go through that again. I went home in a couple of days.

My hemoglobin (Hbg) was 8.3. That was the reason why I was exhausted and short of breath on any exertion. The doctor said blood transfusions aren't given so much anymore because of possible problems. I was to take an iron pill daily and eat plenty of red meat. My Hbg was up to 10 in a month and a half; at two and a half months, it was 11, within normal range for a woman.

I was way behind in being able to do much walking, according to the walking schedule I was sent home with. I guess with my setbacks and low Hbg, it would take me a longer time to increase my walking. One of my friends had the operation a few years ago and she said it took almost a year before she felt like her normal self. So I'll just have to be patient. I was 108 pounds when I had my surgery, and went down to 98 pounds. I'm eating high calorie foods, but I'm not doing well in gaining my weight back. Just like my friend, I finally was feeling more like my normal self after a year since my surgery.

Taken to ER of Goshen Hospital, January 11, 2004

I fainted in the dining room at Greencroft while we lived in Goshen, Indiana. Someone called the EMS, and they took me to the ER. After doing a number of tests and blood tests, it was discovered I had low sodium. I was on a Lasix mediation to control my blood pressure. The Lasix caused my sodium to be low, so I had to go off Lasix and use other meds to control my blood pressure. My low sodium soon returned to normal.

Our Move to Kalamazoo

Howard and I were living in Goshen, Indiana, at a large retirement center which had four levels of health care. We thought we would make it easier on our four children as we aged and needed health care. They wouldn't have to worry about us as we would be well taken care of.

Actually our daughter, Pam, was designated our "Legal Health Care Representative." She lived in Kalamazoo, Michigan. It took her about one and a half hours to drive to Goshen to visit us. Pam convinced us to move to Kalamazoo so she could look after us as we kept getting older. So, after almost 15 years in Goshen, we moved in July 2004 to live in a big senior apartment building just four blocks from Pam's house. We love it that she drops in to see us quite often, almost every day.

Discovering I Had Uterine Cancer

On November 17, 2006, I had a Pap smear, and there was blood in the vagina. So my doctor sent me to get an ultrasound of the uterus. The results told me to get a hysteroscopy and D&C of the uterus on March 20, 2007. I was sent to Dr. Bakri, OBGYN oncologist. A complete C.T. scan was done from neck down to the pubic area. No metastases were noted, so I just had to get a hysterectomy. The uterus, fallopian tubes, and ovaries were removed. I was thankful I didn't need any chemotherapy or radiation too. Dr. Bakri did my surgery on June 11, 2007.

Fluid appeared in pleural space in bottom of right lung. A thoracentesis was done on July 3, 2007, when 950 cc of fluid was taken out. After my uterine surgery, I was so out of breath whenever I would try to walk it kept me from getting my strength back. After that thoracentesis, my lung had more room to expand so I wasn't so out of breath after that procedure and I began to get my strength back from uterine surgery.

Friday, September 15, 2007

I went to the hospital because of breathing difficulties. I've had C.O.P.D (chronic obstructed pulmonary disease) for many years, but this time on September 15, my breathing was much worse. Howard took me to Bronson Hospital Emergency clinic. After much testing, a stenosis (a narrowing of the value opening) of the bovine aortic value

297

put in 1999 was revealed which would keep getting worse. The doctor sent me home on hospice care. I said, "But isn't that when the prognosis is just six months to live?" The doctor predicted I had about 18 months to live, and he said they would never remove me from hospice care because my condition would continue to get worse.

As of December 4, I will soon have to be on oxygen. My pulse was 88, and that's usually when you have to start needing oxygen. I'm still doing okay without the O2, but I will probably be needing it soon.

March 2008

Now we are getting ready to face moving to Woodside, an assisted living facility, on Thursday, March 27, 2008, because of medical problems. Woodside is part of the Friendship Village complex, and it too is not very far from our daughter, Pam, who will be able to visit us regularly.

~

INDEX

~